THE CRUSADE FOR FORGOTTEN SOULS

The Crusade for Forgotten Souls

Reforming Minnesota's Mental Institutions

1946–1954

Susan Bartlett Foote

 University of Minnesota Press
Minneapolis / London

Portions of this book were previously published in Susan Bartlett Foote, "Finding Engla Schey: A Catalyst for Mental Hospital Reform in Minnesota," *Minnesota History* 64, no. 6 (Summer 2015): 248–61.

Published by the University of Minnesota Press
111 Third Avenue South, Suite 290
Minneapolis, MN 55401-2520
http://www.upress.umn.edu

Printed in the United States of America on acid-free paper

The University of Minnesota is an equal-opportunity educator and employer.

23 22 21 20 19 18   10 9 8 7 6 5 4 3 2 1

Library of Congress Cataloging-in-Publication Data
Foote, Susan Bartlett, author.
The crusade for forgotten souls : reforming Minnesota's mental institutions,
    1946–1954 / Susan Bartlett Foote.
Minneapolis, MN : University of Minnesota Press, [2018] | Includes bibliographical references
    and index. |
Identifiers: LCCN 2017055867 (print) | ISBN 978-1-5179-0364-0 (pb)
Subjects: | MESH: Commitment of Mentally Ill–history | Mentally Ill Persons–history |
    Psychiatric Nursing–history | Hospitals, Psychiatric–organization & administration |
    History, 20th Century | Minnesota
Classification: LCC RC445.M58 (print) | NLM WM 11 AM6 | DDC 362.2/109776–dc23
LC record available at https://lccn.loc.gov/2017055867

To the memory of Arthur Foote
1911–1999

CONTENTS

Historian Jill Lepore has concluded, "History is what is written and can be found; what isn't saved is lost, sunken and rotted, eaten by the earth."[1] Historians rely on what is written and can be found. By a stroke of luck, the story told in *The Crusade for Forgotten Souls* found me. It fell on my head, literally, while I was cleaning out my son's closet in 2013. As I reached up to a high shelf, a large bag stuffed with papers tumbled down. Picking up the contents, I discovered personal papers of his grandfather Arthur Foote, my former father-in-law, given to my son after his grandfather's death in 1999. The bag included speeches typed on an old manual typewriter with handwritten edits, unpublished reports, graphic photographs of mental hospital conditions, and a large scrapbook filled with yellowed newspaper clippings from the 1940s. Here it was, what Foote had saved, in his grandson's closet.

It seemed to me, a retired professor of health policy and long-ago history major, that there might be the makings of a story, though I didn't yet anticipate its scope. Very little had been written about the reform of Minnesota's mental institutions. Governor Luther Youngdahl's biography did include a short description of his role. One fact, in particular, caught my attention: "It all started with Engla Schey, an attendant in one of the hospitals."[2] Who was this Engla Schey, not mentioned in any of the Foote materials, with the given name that I learned meant "angel" in Norwegian? The scanty public records were enough to intrigue but not explain. Through another stroke of luck, I located a great-grandniece, descended from Engla's sister, who had boxes of Engla's letters, journals, and autobiographical stories that brought the surreal world of mental institutions, and Engla's role in reforming them, to life. This was a historian's dream.

Armed with these extraordinary primary sources, I began a persistent search for missing pieces of the puzzle. Many of the key actors were ordinary people, not public figures, which presented challenges to unearthing their motives and contributions. The odyssey included county historical society records (Anoka, Olmsted, Ottertail, Marshall, and Ramsey), Harvard's Andover-Harvard Theological Library, and church papers in St. Paul and Minneapolis, Minnesota, and Stockton and Sacramento, California. I traveled across Minnesota, visiting sites of the mental hospitals and a school for the "imbeciles and feeble-minded," as it was called at the time. I explored towns, cemeteries, and churches. The Minnesota Historical Society's library became my second home as I pored over old newspapers, mental hospital records, church records, and personal papers. The Historical Society also houses the State Archives, which provided access to legislative records, and official and personal papers of public officials.

The resulting story involves the confluence of many fields—history of mental health treatment, the politics and culture of Minnesota, and the role of Unitarian churches in shaping social change. It is now seventy years since the Minnesota Unitarians took on the cause of mental health, and sixty-five years since Governor Youngdahl left the state and mental health reform behind. Why, then, write about this effort and why read about it now? After all, the massive mental hospitals are gone; some, like the enormous Fergus Falls Hospital, left a vacant hulk, others were torn down or put to other uses. Time has marched along, and now there are new treatments, new approaches, and new challenges. Didn't the state apologize in 2010 for the mistreatment in its institutions? Don't all the dead now have headstones?[3]

While it is always the reader's prerogative to decide the value of any historical account, I hope the story of the Crusade for Forgotten Souls will resonate. These intrepid reformers crossed partisan, ethnic, gender, and class barriers. They shared a passion to make the world a better place and left an important legacy behind.

When Foote's papers fell on my head, I had no idea what lay before me, both in the research and the writing of this book. Along the way, I discovered a deeper motive than to produce a final product, as important as that has been. It is a motive that kept me focused and moving forward. Writer and publisher James Atlas expressed it best when he said, "I wrote to answer questions I had—the motive of all art, whatever the ostensible subject. There were things I urgently needed to know."[4]

■ ■ ■

I'd like to acknowledge the many people who helped me in my quest for what I needed to know to tell this story.

Thanks to family members of important reformers: Drs. John and Ruth Schey, Roxanne Butzer, Sarah and Carl Steefel, Ethan Foote, Frances Foote Stehman, Dan McKay, Wendy Jerome, Wanda Davies, and Margaret Rarig. Deep appreciation to Rob and Janne Eller-Isaacs and members of Unity Church, especially the Archives Committee, and Gretchen Clemence of the First Unitarian Society of Minneapolis.

For firsthand information on mental hospitals and tours of the facilities: Shirley Lynch and Mabel Huss (Anoka State Hospital); Lew Linde (Hastings State Hospital); Dr. Trude Tice, Jim Secord, and Teresa Roberts (Rochester State Hospital); Bill and Ginny Adams and anonymous former staff (Fergus Falls). Loiell and Mary Dyrud, State Senator Leroy and Carol Stumpf, Judge John Tunheim, Marilyn Soren, and Karen Humphrey opened up the world of Norwegian immigrants in northern Minnesota. Thanks to Judge Donovan Frank for his knowledge of commitment law, and Todd Mahon, then executive director of the Anoka County Historical Society and his staff, who assembled and organized extensive materials on the State Hospital that they generously made available to me.

I'm grateful to Anne Kaplan at the Minnesota Historical Society for her editorial assistance on my 2015 article in *Minnesota History*. Andy Steiner, a health reporter for MinnPost, took an early interest in this topic as well. I am also thankful for the enthusiasm and helpful attention of Kristian Tvedten, my editor at the University of Minnesota Press. I send kudos to the literate women of my book club for their moral support.

Special thanks to Geri Joseph, who made history through her prize-winning reporting on conditions in the hospitals, and who shared memories of her involvement with the reform and the reformers, and to the late Minnesota historian Hyman Berman, who was generous with his time and knowledge about Minnesota politics. Thanks to the wit and wisdom of Norman Sherman, who was a young political operative in Minneapolis during the 1940s. I appreciate Colleen Wieck of Minnesota Governor's Council on Developmental Disabilities and Sue Abderholden, National Alliance on Mental Illness (NAMI) Minnesota, who shared their knowledge of today's challenges for the mentally ill and intellectually disabled.

I'm exceedingly grateful to Carol Stumpf for her ability to dig out facts and for sharing the joys of discovery with me. Billie Young and Sheila Cooper helpfully read and commented on early drafts. Finally, thanks to my husband, David Durenberger, who shared his knowledge of and love for Minnesota, and who served as my driver, enthusiastic companion, and occasional trespasser, as we looked for clues across the state from Marshall County in the north to Olmsted in the south. He was a patient reader and listener, and a most generous provider of moral support when I needed it most.

INTRODUCTION

On Halloween night in 1949, Minnesota's governor Luther Youngdahl stood before an enormous pile of straitjackets, leather straps, and other restraints used on patients in Anoka State Hospital. He lit the torch and the fire roared. The iconic photograph of the scene captured his gleeful expression, as the flames climbed higher than the broad shoulders of the athletic governor.

The bonfire was a symbolic act that signaled not just the end of the use of restraints in all seven of Minnesota's mental hospitals, but a new era in mental health care. In 1948 the Republican Youngdahl had pushed for reforms, dubbing his effort "The Crusade for Forgotten Souls." In the 1949 session, the Minnesota legislature passed his comprehensive bill mandating significant improvements in funding, conditions, and staffing. He appointed Dr. Ralph Rossen, an acclaimed psychiatrist and superintendent at Hastings State Hospital, to head the new office of the commissioner of mental health. The Halloween bonfire was Youngdahl's way of saying the work of implementation had begun. His goal was to move Minnesota's mental institutions from among the worst in the nation to a model for the future.

Youngdahl's crusade brought him national attention. The Menninger Clinic in Kansas, the leading psychiatric practice in the country, celebrated his success. The National Governors Association held him up as a role model. Youngdahl was so popular in Minnesota that Senator Hubert Humphrey, concerned for his own reelection in 1954, persuaded President Harry Truman to appoint the Republican Youngdahl to the federal bench in Washington, D.C., in 1951. By 1953, C. Elmer Anderson, Youngdahl's weak successor, could not stop tight-fisted conservatives in the legislature from dismantling key provisions. The reformers only achieved the first step of their vision.

There was little to suggest that mental health would be a political issue when Youngdahl first ran for governor in 1946. At that time, nearly eleven thousand inmates languished in Minnesota's mental hospitals, including many senile elderly, nonconformists, and the impoverished, along with those we would call mentally ill today. They were isolated from the world, inadequately clothed and fed, restrained and untreated, out of sight and out of mind. Another thirty-five hundred children and adults, labeled "mentally deficient," were housed in the State School for Feeble-Minded at Faribault and the State Colony for Epileptics in Cambridge. Those who died without relatives were buried in graves marked with numbers, not names. Shame silenced individual "inmates" and their families; shame silenced underpaid employees who hesitated to admit they worked in the "bughouses" with the "lunatics." Cynical public officials withheld the facts. The public didn't know or didn't seem to care.

How had conditions in Minnesota institutions become so deplor-

Staff and patients watch as Governor Luther Youngdahl burns straitjackets, leather straps, and other devices used to restrain patients at Anoka State Hospital, October 31, 1949. Photograph by the *St. Paul Dispatch/Pioneer Press.* Courtesy of the Minnesota Historical Society.

able? Minnesota, like many other states, had once demonstrated a commitment to resources for the mentally ill with optimism about the benefits of institutional treatment. In the early days of the nation, there was no developed social welfare system and little concern or empathy for destitute or troubled individuals. Towns managed their own, and the mentally ill were often found in jails, workhouses, and poorhouses. As populations grew, it became clear that local governments were ill equipped and often unwilling to finance and oversee efforts to manage those in need.[1]

Society's views on mental illness began to change by the mid-nineteenth century. First, Enlightenment values and scientific currents encouraged rational and humane solutions to a myriad of social problems. In the area of mental illness, the Quakers in England and the United States were among the first to advocate treatment, not just custody, of the insane. Second, the care and treatment of the insane began to be seen as the responsibility of state government.[2]

Dorothea Dix, the persistent moral crusader, alerted the public and politicians to the suffering and needs of the mentally ill in the 1840s and 1850s. Dix was part of the awakening view of the perfectibility of human beings through social action, especially among the New England Unitarians of whom she was a part.[3] She exposed the extraordinary cruelty toward the mentally ill in prisons, poorhouses, and private "madhouses" in Massachusetts. She carried her crusade to many states, investigating, testifying, and publicizing problems and lobbying governments to build and expand state facilities.[4]

The Civil War disrupted reform efforts in mental health, as the nation's attention was diverted to the conflict. After the war, however, there was a public building boom of institutions for the insane. By 1880 there were 140 public and private mental hospitals in the United States that cared for nearly forty-one thousand patients. Sociologist Gerald Grob called the effort "a graphic demonstration of the moral and financial commitment of Americans to the mentally ill."[5] Other experts were less sanguine. Historian David Rothman viewed these "protected environments" as primarily mechanisms of social control.[6]

By 1858 mental hospital construction nationally was in full swing. The new state of Minnesota followed the trends. Statehood brought a surge of population growth; there were 250,000 residents by 1865. Many of these new residents faced significant challenges, including eking out a living in a new land and coping with dislocation, poverty, homesickness, and despair. There was no statewide authority, funds, or inclination to help those with mental challenges. As other states had done in earlier times, Minnesota counties tried to make ad hoc arrangements for those in need of care without adequate resources or expertise to do so.[7]

In response to the problem, the state established the Minnesota Hospital for the Insane in St. Peter in 1866. It was the forty-second public facility in the United States. Over the next several decades, Minnesota constructed two additional hospitals—Rochester in 1879 and Fergus Falls in 1899—but could never keep pace with demand.[8] These first three institutions reflected a national period of optimism in the institutional capacity to "cure." With little scientific knowledge, mental imbalance during this time was associated with such "disorders" as immorality, intemperance, poverty, excessive study, epilepsy, or religious excitement.[9]

Minnesota also opened the State School for Feeble-Minded at Faribault in 1879, and the State Colony for Epileptics in 1925. Parents had few options for developmentally disabled children, and soon Faribault became overcrowded as well.

Experts thought asylum architecture and location played a positive role in cures. Dr. Thomas Kirkbride, a Pennsylvania psychiatrist, believed the design of institutions could influence behavior in socially desirable ways. The hospitals at both Fergus Falls and Rochester followed the "Kirkbride" model—they were large, light-filled buildings intentionally located outside nearby towns or cities, wholly self-sufficient with their own farming and food production, power stations, and medical care. The goal was to separate patients from bad influences through highly structured and controlled environments that were isolated from society. At that time treatment for mental disorders also included opium, morphine, tonics, laxatives, baths, and bloodletting.[10]

Disillusionment grew, however, about the ability of these institutions to accomplish the cures they touted, even as the demand for space in them continued apace. Given the overcrowding at the existing institutions, Minnesota built "asylums" for patients who were deemed "incurable." These patients were to be transferred from receiving hospitals, which admitted new patients. At the asylums, which operated at a lower cost, they would receive only custodial care.[11]

Anoka State Asylum opened in 1900, followed by the Hastings State Asylum in 1901.[12] The asylum at Willmar, originally conceived for inebriates, began taking "hopeless" cases in 1912. The state asylums were considered the end of the line for those in need of care. They were designed on a cottage plan consisting of smaller buildings grouped together, often connected by tunnels, and were a popular alternative to the Kirkbride model from 1900 to 1920. Asylums were considered more homelike, and allowed patients to be easily grouped by behavior or condition. An added advantage was that it was cheaper to build smaller facilities and to expand them one building at a time to meet patient demand.[13]

In 1937 the state legislature dropped the label "asylum" in favor of "hospital," arguing that "it is a proper thing to do and is in keeping with the modern treatment of nervous and mental patients. . . . The term 'asylum' . . . has come to have an unpleasant meaning in the minds of the people."[14] The name change appears to have had no effect on the conditions under which patients had to live. As the 1940 US Public Health Service (USPHS) survey made clear, "Change did not produce appropriations sufficient to create as good standards as in . . . the other . . . institutions" (44).

Nor did the state rigorously adhere to the "transfer only" policy for the asylums, so that the patient population, in general, did not deviate substantially from those in the receiving hospitals. Patients were categorized by behavior, not diagnosis, and the hospitals had a range of individuals in all patient categories, including "disturbed or assaultive," old and feeble, able-bodied with liberties, and "run of the mill." Essentially, the asylums became dumping grounds for chronic cases to save the state money by providing only bare minimum custodial "care."[15]

The 1940 USPHS survey applied minimum standards, developed by the American Psychiatric Association in 1926, by which to measure a state's mental hospital program. Minnesota fell below standards on the key measures of per capita spending and staffing ratios. The USPHS found deficiencies in the buildings, including unsanitary kitchens, poor heat and ventilation, and lack of adequate clothing, food, and supplies. Minnesota institutions were cited for inadequate recreational and occupational programs, lack of social workers, and general neglect of patients. The data also showed that the three asylums in the system—Anoka, Hastings, and Willmar—operated at significantly lower cost than the already deficient state hospitals, with fewer staff per capita at all levels, and less money for food and other provisions (150). The surveyors reported, "The people of Minnesota come predominantly from frugal stock and the policy of the state has been to keep its expenditures low" (3).

With regard to the use of restraints, however, the data told a different story. The USPHS survey bluntly called Minnesota's use of restraints "deplorable." The survey found: "The apparatus in use are jackets, wristlets and belts, canvas muffs, leather muffs, anklets, and sheets wrapped around the bed. Some of these type of apparatus ought to be placed in the hospital museum—and nowhere else" (150–51).[16] It continued:

> Mechanical restraint is used in every institution and in a variety of forms. There is a system of control and regulation by physicians perhaps not very strictly exercised. The use of restraint appears not to be limited to the most urgent conditions and is carried to an inexcusable extent in some places. (83)

Noting that Michigan and Illinois had abolished mechanical restraints, the USPHS conclusion was that "it should be possible for Minnesota to stop the obtrusive use of these measures" (44).

Superintendents justified restraint use as an appropriate response to overcrowding, understaffing, and inadequate security. The surveyors measured significant differences in the numbers of patients in restraint from hospital to hospital in Minnesota. Hastings only had five people in restraint on the day measured, while Rochester had seventy-three, and Anoka sixty (44, 67). Rochester had a bigger budget and better staffing. Why such substantial variation? The difference between Hastings and Anoka, both asylums with similar staffing and architecture, was also stark. Anoka consistently had the highest levels of restraint use in Minnesota, with many patients kept for days or weeks in physical restraints or locked away in isolation rooms.[17]

Restraint use was not inevitable. It was not ordained by low staffing ratios or low budgets. The use of restraints was a choice based on the culture of the institution, set by the superintendent at the top. Hastings had low restraint use because its superintendent, Dr. Ralph Rossen, believed restraints made patients more difficult, not less so. Indeed, the survey noted, "At Hastings, where a lay attitude toward such matters had prevailed unrestrictedly for years, a vigorous campaign has reduced restraint most commendably" (45). Dr. Rossen was the youngest superintendent in the system. His stance on restraints challenged the prevailing norms in Minnesota.

In 1938 Governor Harold Stassen, the new young Republican reformer, campaigned on a platform to clean up corruption in government. He replaced the Board of Control, which had overseen the mental institutions among others, after concluding the board members were ill equipped and politically motivated. He reorganized the Department of Social Security into three divisions—Social Welfare, Employment and Security, and Public Institutions (DPI). The directors of these divisions would serve four-year terms, would not engage in partisan politics, and would be "selected on the basis of ability and experience in their respective fields of service without regard to political affiliations."[18] The Mental Health Unit in the DPI had oversight of the mental hospitals and the State School at Faribault.

The political changes of 1938, while important, did not reverse the results of years of frugality and mismanagement. William Erickson, former superintendent at St. Peter State Hospital, noted that the Depression and World War II "drew money and attention away from the problems of institutionalized patients for half a century."[19]

In May 1946 the popular magazine *Life* ran an exposé of the nation's mental hospitals, calling the abject conditions and human suffering a shame and disgrace.[20] Minnesota, like most other states, remained in denial. The *St. Paul Pioneer Press* opined, "Such conditions may exist in other parts of the country. But it should give the people of Minnesota great pride that there are no snake pits in Minnesota."[21] During Youngdahl's first campaign for governor in 1946, the Republican Party, in collaboration with public officials, suppressed disclosure of dismal conditions at the school for "feeble-minded" children in Faribault. In Youngdahl's first two-year term (1947–49), his signature issues did not include mental health.

Minnesota Unitarians, however, grew concerned about the national reports of shameful conditions in mental hospitals. In the fall of 1946, the Minnesota Unitarian Conference, a handful of churches with less than two thousand parishioners statewide, agreed to learn more about conditions in Minnesota. In the fall of 1947, they went public with their findings. After a dramatic confrontation, they showed the governor a political pathway to reform.

Youngdahl provided the political leadership. Through his Christian faith and humanitarian instincts, he believed deeply in the worth of all God's children, even the least among them. He passionately embraced the plight of the mentally ill and the developmentally disabled, called "mentally retarded" at the time. He appointed like-minded administrators and activated an advisory council of prominent psychiatrists to advise him.

Political leadership was a necessary but not sufficient condition. Youngdahl made common cause with the Unitarians, overcoming objections of his inner circle to his association with these "atheists." They became his strongest backers and were the principled advocates who laid the legislative groundwork for the rights of patients to receive care in a modern mental health system. The Unitarians also helped build the county-based citizens groups who successfully pressured reluctant legislators to pass the reform package.

Three important leaders emerged from the Unitarian ranks, each cut from very different cloth, with widely divergent backgrounds, shaped by their own unique experiences, and playing critical roles in the effort.

Engla Schey, the catalyst, was the daughter of poor Norwegian immigrant farmers in northern Minnesota; she worked as an attendant at a state hospital. Appalled at the conditions, she began a one-woman effort to "spread the gospel of mental health reform" in Minnesota. Schey's frank disclosures persuaded the Unitarians to push for mental health reform. Her passionate concern for patients and her experience as an attendant ensured that patients and the often scorned low-level personnel had a voice.

Reverend Arthur Foote was the modest visionary who led the Unitarian effort. New England born and bred, he was the minister at Unity Unitarian Church in St. Paul. As chair of the MUC Committee on Mental Hospitals, he fostered the group on its "arduous climb" from protest to constructive political engagement.[22] The Unitarians became the trusted voice in the crusade because of Foote's firm commitment to fact-based advocacy by independent laypersons who represented the public interest, not their self-interest.

Genevieve Steefel, a well-connected political activist, was all intellect and impatient energy. Steefel was the secretary of the MUC Committee on Mental Hospitals, of which Foote was chair. She not only kept the notes, she also wove the facts into detailed and effective reports and gathered experts together to strengthen reformers' arguments or to refute unsupported statements from the opposition. Foote was the public face of the group. Steefel was the substance and discipline behind it.

Geri Hoffner, an intrepid young *Minneapolis Tribune* reporter, represents a third important force in the crusade. In the spring of 1949, "Minnesota Bedlam" ran in the *Tribune*. Hoffner's blockbuster eleven-part series awakened readers to the truth about life inside the state's mental institutions. The series galvanized the public, was the impetus behind the successful citizens campaign, and remains to this day a model of honest and courageous investigative journalism.

The Crusade for Forgotten Souls left a legacy for all Americans, not just for Minnesota. The Crusaders shined light on the reprehensible conditions in institutions for the mentally ill and mentally disabled. They fought for a better way: a mental health system with patient welfare at the core, grounded in science, not superstition, free from stigma, and aimed at education, prevention, and cure. They took the first and critically important leap forward.

Much has changed in the intervening seventy years. Witness the development of new drugs, important advances in scientific understanding of the brain, and the movement out of custodial hospitals to community alternatives. The federal government has poured billions of dollars into research, prevention, education, community services, and access to care, so the states no longer must go it alone.

All of the states in the country continue to provide mental health services. There have been road maps drawn, legal and legislative victories, money appropriated, and new programs begun. More work remains, however. The National Alliance for Mental Illness issues periodic report cards evaluating the progress of the states. In 2006 the average grade was a D. Subsequent years have seen only modest improvements, although Minnesota, New York, and Virginia have the strongest commitment to improving mental health legislation. Minnesota's governor Mark Dayton appointed a task force in 2016, and the report sets forth aspirations of what remains to be done.[23] Many states still receive failing grades.[24] Threats to past achievements in mental health access continue and are especially acute as the Affordable Care Act faces calls for repeal and replacement.

But, even in Minnesota, recent front-page headlines cause one to ask, what year is it anyway? A small recent sample: "In Jail, in Limbo, Untreated: Minnesota's Unraveling Mental Health System"; "Families Demand St. Peter Reforms: Beating Death of Patient at Mental Hospital Triggers a Call for Outside Oversight"; and "Psych Bed Shortage Jams ERs."[25] Anoka Regional Treatment Center, the site of the former state hospital, now is under federal oversight owing to decades of neglect, putting patients at risk, using restraints, and providing generic and inadequate treatment plans.[26] Gaps in the state's mental health safety net have led to patients cleared for release languishing in high-cost state hospital beds because there is no place for them to transition back to society.[27]

The vision of the Crusade for Forgotten Souls, which calls for the fundamental right of every patient to care and treatment in a comprehensive mental health system, has not yet been achieved. While periodic progress has been made in Minnesota and elsewhere, now more than ever we need the ingredients found in the crusade so many years ago: sustained political leadership at state and national levels, widespread public support, advocates devoted to the public interest, and a respected press with courageous reporters freely committed to telling the truth.

The Crusade for Forgotten Souls reminds us of a better way, and the goal of this book is to ensure that its lessons will not be forgotten.

ONE

Voices of Forgotten Souls

Come again. It's just like somebody from heaven coming into
hell to see me.

■ *Mrs. C, patient at Rochester State Hospital, to Engla Schey*

On a cold blustery night in the fall of 1947, Engla Schey retired to her room in the staff dormitories on the grounds of Rochester
State Hospital, a mental institution in southeastern Minnesota. This
was not so much home as a place to put her feet up at the end of grueling
shifts as an attendant, the lowest "caste," as she often said, in the institutional hierarchy.

Engla, which means "angel" in Norwegian, was in her early fifties, of
slight build, weighing only one hundred and three pounds and standing just five feet two. A hank of graying hair was perennially escaping
the restraining effort of bobby pins and falling into her pale blue eyes.
She had a limp due to a bout of polio she suffered as a child in far northern Marshall County, Minnesota, where she was born and grew up. She
endured migraine headaches and insomnia caused by the pressures of
her job.

Ignored by the doctors and disdained by the nurses, attendants
routinely cleaned, fed, and managed large wards. The job was considered custodial, but attendants also provided the primary social
contact with patients in the wards. Many patients spent their hours
in idleness, often tied up with leather straps or in straitjackets (which
were commonly referred to as camisoles). Those who were able worked
long hours out of doors in the barns and fields, or labored in food service, cleaning, laundry, sewing, blacksmith shops, and even caring for
other patients.[1]

Who were the unfortunate Minnesotans who found themselves shut
away in these places, and why were they there?

Engla Schey, the intrepid, dedicated fighter for mental hospital reform, 1940s. Courtesy of Roxanne Butzer.

The causes of mental illness were poorly understood. As sociologist Gerald Grob noted, "The absence of accurate data and a psychiatric classification nosology based largely on symptoms rather than etiology renders it virtually impossible to describe the hundreds of thousands of mental hospital residents with any degree of precision."[2] However flawed the statistics, Minnesota's institutional population, like those in other states, fell into three broad categories.[3]

First, roughly half of those institutionalized suffered from what we would consider mental illness today, with diagnoses of schizophrenia, manic depression, or various psychoses. The prevalent treatments, such as cold packs, hydrotherapy, and restraints, were ineffective. By the midforties, some Minnesota hospitals were experimenting with electroshock therapy and lobotomies. These treatments were used to subdue or punish disruptive patients as much as to "cure" them.[4] Most were considered incurable or chronic, and many remained in the institutions for twenty years or more. Lifelong stays were not uncommon.[5]

A portion of this group included those suffering from tertiary syphilis. In its advanced stages, syphilis caused massive damage to the central nervous system. These patients developed extreme behavioral symptoms as they deteriorated to their inevitable death.[6] In the pre-penicillin era, doctors induced malarial fever or insulin comas that were believed to "burn out" the disease. These treatments were dangerous and largely ineffective.[7]

Senile elderly patients comprised almost 40 percent of the admissions, and 15 percent of the total hospital population in Minnesota.[8] Desperate families who couldn't care for their elderly relatives at home had few alternatives. Private rest homes were costly and inadequate. One probate judge described a private facility as an "old makeshift, smelly, fire-trap of a so-called rest home or old folks home."[9] Families with limited resources had to resort to the state's mental hospitals, where patients whose infirmities were typical of old age were treated as "insane" wards of the state. Neglected and disoriented upon arrival at one of these institutions, most of the senile cases died within six months of admission.[10]

The rest, close to 30 percent, were classified as "others" and included people with transient difficulties associated with grief or economic distress, along with social deviants, moral misfits, nonconformists, and those whose families found them undesirable or inconvenient. For these patients, the state hospital bore a greater resemblance to the old poorhouses where destitute people were sent as a means of social control, not for treatment.[11]

The institutions sorted patients according to categories based on their behavior, not their diagnosis. Violent or uncooperative patients occupied "assaultive" or "disturbed" wards, the senile were "bed" patients, and able-bodied, cooperative patients resided in "self-government" wards. Most did not enter the institutions voluntarily. In 1947, 83 percent of patients in Minnesota were involuntarily committed.[12] Once someone, usually a spouse or other family member, petitioned the court for commitment, a sheriff brought the patient in for a trial that often included jail time until a hearing was scheduled. After a formal commitment proceeding, individuals were at the mercy of the institution and of the guardian appointed to act on their behalf. If a patient was "restored to sanity," he or she could not be "paroled" from the hospital without the guardian's permission.[13]

Families of mentally deficient or epileptic children also had no options in the community. Desperate parents often reluctantly surrendered their children to Faribault or Cambridge, consigning their youngsters to overcrowded and understaffed wards where they were neglected, restrained, and sometimes abused.[14] Once children were formally committed, they were wards of the state, and parents lost the right to remove them from the institution if they wished to take them home.

Engla had chosen to spend her life among these forgotten people. She brought a rare sense of empathy and compassion to all the patients, listening to their stories and comforting them in their trials. To her, they were not categories or diagnoses; they were people, and sometimes also friends. They were individuals with names; they were not just numbers that could be found on the markers of those who had been buried in the cemeteries on hospital grounds.

Engla also aspired to be a writer, and, no matter how exhausted, she tried to write in her journal every day. Her journals offer a rare opportunity to learn their names and listen to the voices of these forgotten ones.

Many of the patients were delusional and often violent.

Liz

I had a migraine headache. My good friend Mrs. Z who is also an attendant here, brought me some black coffee and said: "what set you off on the ward last night?" I said: "I guess it was Liz again." Liz is considered the most assaultive patient in the institution for a week or two at regular intervals. I had been previously warned that she might blow her top tonight. When I asked her to go to bed she stared me down and said she was going to sit up all night. I had always thought it was a mistake to call extra help, rip her clothes off and force her into a camisole and strap her into a bed like some steer restrained for branding. I now had a chance to prove my theory false or true.

I went to the office and removed my glasses and came back to her.

"What did you take your glasses off for? Are you afraid of me? Am I getting sick again? I haven't ever hurt you have I?" she asked me. "If I did, I didn't mean to. I'm quite sure I'll never hurt you. You have always been so friendly to me." "Will you be ready to go to bed in half an hour?" I asked. "If you say so, I will," she replied. In half an hour I came back wearing my glasses. I pulled her snug fitting turtleneck slipover sweater over her head, took her brassiere, girdle, shoes and stockings off and put a state muslin nightgown on. She did not want to go to the toilet but I finally got her there. She lingered on the stool half an hour and I had to push her to bed. She said "goodnight" and called me by name.

I thought of the many previous times when she was "going into her spell" how she had been pounced on, hit, scolded, and tied down like an animal. She hated most of the nurses. Tomorrow she would surely be tied down for another week or two. Maybe I would be asked to help and she would begin to hate me too. "So you got a migraine headache to escape it," Mrs. Z laughed. "Not consciously, these things are too painful for me to develop deliberately," I said.

Patient R

At noon I fed R. She was strapped to her bed like some frightened animal. I put the tray on a table and sat on the bed by her head facing her feet because I didn't want to see her wild tortured eyes. I tried to think about something else as I shoved the large tablespoon in and out of her mouth—Finally she said, "Are you mad at me too, or is it all right to talk to you?" "You know you can always talk to me," I said.

"I know you have always been kind to me; but I don't know what I did just before I was tied down. I know I screamed and hollered. I wouldn't have done it if I could have helped it. I just couldn't keep from it. I know everybody gets scared when I scream. . . . Then I get all mixed up and scared and begin to fight and I really don't know what I'm doing. But I never do anything on purpose because I am mean. I simply can't help what I do."

Patient W

Patient W was screaming. She said her husband didn't love her anymore. She had married him when she was 17 years old. They had a beautiful home and a fishing boat. He hadn't come to see her at all during the 18 months she had been "locked up." The poor woman didn't know that her nervous system was loused up with syphilis and unless the fever treatment could burn those devils out of her brain she would be locked up forever.

Judging from what she told me about her husband I suspected he wouldn't wait for her. If the hospital did succeed in getting her recovered from syphilis and she went home to find that her husband had another woman she would probably go crazy all over again for some other reason.

"My husband don't love me anymore," she kept howling over and over again. "My husband is beautiful. He got big blue eyes and new teeth. He got a fishing yacht. We used to go fishing every Sunday. . . . Gee we'd have fun." Her pretty face would light up with a smile at times. Sometimes when she talked about the chicken and apple pie she'd prepare for supper she would seem almost normal. "I always fixed what my husband liked," she said. And then she'd writhe as if in agony and howl, "but I'll never cook for him again. He has another woman. He never comes to see me. He took me here and left me. He doesn't love me anymore. I'm going to kill myself. I love that man so much I can't live without him."

Mrs. W was reared to be a nice girl. She married her first beau. Her parents gave her a lovely church wedding. For years this ugly bug had been irritating her brain, until one day she went crazy. Her husband took her to the mental hospital and left her there. What a price this woman had to pay for her love.

Engla also worked with the elderly senile patients. Due to their condition, it was difficult to build personal relationships with most of them. A letter from Mrs. Valerie Boe, a distraught daughter, to the governor in 1947 illustrates the challenges facing families with few resources and aging loved ones.

Mrs. J. Sepold

My mother Mrs. J. Sepold, who is 83 years of age, was admitted (to Rochester State Hospital) on February 15th, 1947, as a senile case. It was only after our Rest Homes here in Minneapolis refused to have her that I was forced to commit her to Rochester State Hospital. I say "forced", because I work every day and could not give her the proper care.

On January 4th of this year she fell and badly fractured her ankle. General Hospital set her ankle and she remained there for about ten days after which she was transferred to a Rest Home because they could no longer accommodate her at the hospital due to the over-crowded condition. This Home wasn't the best by far—so through the help of the Old Age Assistance Office we found two Homes which would have been suitable, but both in turn refused to have her when they found she was quite a care.

On February 14th, she was to have had an X-ray and taken at General Hospital and she was to leave for Rochester on the 15th. Again on account of the shortage of beds at the Hospital they were unable to have her.

The morning of the 15th she was taken to Rochester only after I was assured her ankle would be looked after immediately on her arrival there.

I was told a waiting period of three weeks was required before visitors could be admitted; so March 8th being the first opportunity, I went to see her and found her in a most pitiable condition.

She still had on her heavy cast, almost up to her hip. That would have been alright had her condition required it—but her ankle had not as much as been looked at. Her foot was just blue and badly swollen. The doctor informed me he didn't even know she had a fracture!!!

Because she was walking barefoot, getting around the best she could, she had glass or splinters in her other foot. . . . Don't they look after those poor people there??????? I know there is a shortage of help—but it seems to me someone there has fallen down on their job, oh so badly. Her night garment was in tatters. Do they think that kind of care will help to encourage or benefit a patient? Do they think that because a patient is there that no one loves or care for that person? I could not help but think that when I saw my mother. I don't know how I'll do it or how I'll manage, but I'm taking her out of that place as quickly as possible.[15]

Many of the patients were elderly and suffering from senility. Engla recorded the dismal conditions senile patients endured in a letter to a leading psychiatrist:

When I came back from my vacation I found twenty-one senile women tied like dogs in a kennel on benches in two small bedrooms. The night nurse . . . was weeping. The charge nurse said to me, "There is nothing you can do about it, Miss Nelson likes it this way and I like it. That is all that is necessary."[16]

On another occasion, she expressed frustration at the lack of staff to care and watch over them:

I came down to breakfast at 6 am. A nurse was terribly excited because a patient had died during the night and the attendant in charge of this ward of 97 senile old ladies did not know what hour she died. I said "Don't let that bother you, I worked in an institution in this state where frail senile old ladies were found dead incarcerated in camisoles. Besides 97 senile old ladies are too many even for a nurse to take care of at night let alone an untrained attendant," I said.

Many of the patients had no apparent mental illnesses, but had been sent away by family members for personal, not medical reasons.

Lucille
Lucille's parents had committed her because they were ashamed of her out-of-wedlock pregnancy:

Back in the ward this evening was hectic. One of the old warhorses was running the show. Patient Lucille was in the ward for a prefrontal lobotomy, incarcerated in a camisole, weeping and pacing around—The first time I had seen her on our ward she was pregnant. She was beautiful, intelligent and comparatively calm. She marveled that the patients didn't show the intolerant attitude toward her that normal people show towards unmarried pregnant women. "Mental hospitals would be the best place for unmarried women to live out their pregnancy period," she volunteered.

One night she talked to me. "I was working hard," she said, "at a job I hated. Ammunition factory—boring routine, but there was always the evening to look forward to—I was engaged—we were to be married. I knew this terrible job would soon end. And I would have my own home. Then I began hearing that my boyfriend was stepping out on me. I checked up and found that it was true. I wanted to wait with sexual relations until we were married. He got it on the side—One night I stepped out, got drunk—got pregnant. It wouldn't have happened if I had been sober. And I wouldn't have got drunk if I hadn't been mad from grief."

I was on the ward when her baby came. She went through it like a buck. And was so proud of her baby. I was on night duty that night. She was lying in one room and he in another. Then one day she was told her breasts were to be dried up. She knew what she had feared all along was going to happen. The welfare agency would take her child. She would never see it again.

"They can't do this to me," she howled—"It's my baby. I'm its mother. I gave birth to it. They can't tear it from me like they can take a calf from a cow. I won't get over it like a cow. They will drive me mad.'"

Then she was transferred to another ward. She became hostile. She was restrained for months. Now they were giving her a prefrontal lobotomy. "Look what they put me through. Sure I was cooperative when I was pregnant. And when the baby was here. But I ceased being cooperative after that. They weren't fair with me. I'm not crazy. I couldn't stand that ward. No normal person could. All I needed was a fair chance. Keep my baby and get out of here."

I'm for giving her that chance—I believe she can make it on her own. And supposing she didn't? Why not give her a chance? But there is no agency in Minnesota to help her out. Her relatives apparently can't cope with her. It is nobody's business to help her out. She will probably stay until she is driven completely mad unless somebody does something soon.

Some of the patients admitted themselves after traumatic experiences left them temporarily unable to cope.

Dr. L

Engla described Dr. L, who had been uprooted from his dental practice during the war:

Dr. L said: "Hard to become reestablished after. There was no money—closed our office to come down. After losing $1500. Surprised at so many people staying here who apparently are normal, staying year after year. Some working with the efficiency of normal people and others just standing or sitting around or lying in bed. Many received no treatment—just lopped around."

He had noticed the lack of adequate reading material. A basket of books on the ward for the able bodied people to come up and choose from—not much effort to help the bed patients. "Its terrible just locked up—not knowing why or for how long—many of these people just needed a rest, a change. When they got rested up and restored to normalcy, they couldn't get out. It seems horrible. I didn't know such things could be. The public has no idea how it is."

He showed me a letter from his 17 year-old daughter proudly. "She doesn't seem to mind I'm here,'" he hastened to explain. "Maybe all I needed was a rest. I'm not sure about the need of these shock treatments—It seems to make me forget. Do something to my memory. Perhaps it was just a rest I needed or a change—Maybe fishing on the North Shore would have been just as good as shock treatment."

Min

Min was one of the patients who had been taken advantage of in her grief and locked away:

Then there was Min. Her parents and husband were dead. She had a guardian. She had been happily married to the same man for 30 years—no children. Few social contacts, "just us two—that seemed all that was necessary. Married young—no business training—never worked. He handled everything. Then almost overnight I was left a widow. The grief was too much."

She was a tremendous problem on the assaultive ward. Her guardian readily ok'ed a prefrontal lobotomy. She was assaultive and used obscene language for a week or so after her surgery, but then she became normal. No delusions, no hallucinations. The superintendent told her she was now ready to go home. Her guardian came to see her. He could not believe his own eyes at the change. He seemed disappointed in a way. . . . She was disturbed again that night. He had sold her lake cottage without consulting her. The one she and her husband had spent so many pleasant seasons in. It was a cozy heated place and she thought she would rent the city house and live in the lake cottage the year around. He admitted reluctantly that he had sold some of her personal effects that meant so much to her sentimentally. For weeks and weeks and months, she waited for the guardian to come, but finally she began to despair. She was entirely at the mercy of her guardian. She will probably be driven mad again and be institutionalized forever. I'm quite sure with a reasonable chance she could make it out in the world again. It seems doubtful that her guardian will give her that chance without coercion and it's nobody's business to get these people out of the hospital.

Engla despaired at the rampant racism directed at nonwhite patients.

Mrs. C

Mrs. C—colored lady was on one of the patient self-government wards. She was the only colored lady there and she seemed so lonely. When I went up there every week to give her "The Spokesman" (colored newspaper) after I had finished it, I always found her sitting alone off in the corner of the ward. She always chatted with me pleasantly and was profuse in her appreciation of the newspaper. She always seemed clear minded, well informed, and intelligent.

One day I was told she was on C3 (the most assaultive ward). A nurse volunteered that there had been some trouble between a white and colored patient. The supervisor couldn't get heads nor tails to it and it was obvious one or the other had to be disciplined, so she took the colored patient on the assaultive ward. I found her (Mrs. C) weeping, but she quickly dried her tears, thanked me for the newspaper, patted my shoulder and said, "You always bring me cheer." I found her there again a week later. There was terrible noise and obscene language and two huge attendants walking around spouting threats, trying to maintain order. I found her crouched in a corner near the dining room shivering with fear and humiliation.

She was glad to see me. She spoke to me about the discrimination she had suffered from both patients and employees because of her color. . . . When I left she said, "Come again. It's just like somebody from heaven coming into hell to see me."

I asked the charge nurse why she was on the ward. The charge nurse didn't know and it wasn't any of her business. The supervisor brought her down and that was that. She was mild mannered, polite, clear minded, not a case for the ward. "It's just another case of race prejudice," I retorted. She said, "They had to take someone off the ward. I guess some of the white women here don't like colored folks. We get most of them here. They really don't belong on the worst ward. If they were white they could keep them on better wards."

The Nephew

A visitor told Engla the story of the fate of his young nephew. She reported their conversation:

"There was nothing much wrong with him. He and his brother couldn't get along on the farm and the brother don't want him back on the farm."

"Maybe he shouldn't go back to that farm if his brother is running it," I said.

"But where else can he go the law says someone must be responsible for him. For a year and the superintendent says he can go—he alright—he don't need to stay here anymore. He has no place to go except home. The brother who runs the farm won't have him home, he's afraid of him. The parent has to listen to any son who can run the farm. The guy is only 30 and has been alright for months. I'm his uncle and I can't stand around and let him stay here for the rest of his life. Unless a relative does something, they just stay forever. Its terrible the laws they have in this country."

Sewing Room Women

Engla knew many of the patients did not belong in a mental institution, but were aware of the stigma they would face if they returned to their homes:

A woman about sixty, who had been committed when she began to "act queer" during menopause took charge of the cutting. She had long since been restored to sanity in the medical sense of the term. She said she could never go out into the world and meet her friends again after having been a patient in a mental hospital. She could never get a job. Nobody would trust her. She wouldn't be able to stand people always looking on her with suspicion. Furthermore she didn't want to be a burden on her relatives. She was a good seamstress and felt she could more than work for her expenses if she stayed on in the mental hospital.

I looked at patient Jesse, who operated a power machine at terrific speed eight hours a day, making expertly tailored men's pants and shirts. She became unbalanced because she couldn't get a job during the Depression and didn't want to go on relief. She had been medically sane for many years. She would rather remain in the mental hospital than sponge on her children. The mental hospital should have put her on the payroll. There is a perfect example of slave labor in a Christian country, I said to myself.

Engla did not work at Faribault, though she was aware of the conditions for the developmentally disabled. Here is a firsthand account from a nameless resident at Faribault whose letter to Governor Youngdahl survives:

Dear Sir:

Will drop a few lines let you know I here nineteen long years and that's too long for anyone that can make their own living. I just wont stay here any longer on account of these people being so mean. They hit them with coat hangers and broomhandles and keys. I must ask you to do me a favor please see if I can get a chance out soon. . . . Theres know reason I should be here for Just because I was poor but I am poorer now since I am under the state and we don't even get any sugar or coffee here now that's not right we have to do all the hard work and these employers set in their chair all day long. I sure deserve a chance for I never done anything wrong or never ran away and the food here is not fit to eat . . . they eat all our butter and they don't expect us to buy anything good for only forty cents I earn that a dirty shame. I have allways been good and will not stay here I would like to get work at a farm I am capable to hold my Job and am strong and health they hit them so they get black and blue marks all over. . . . I have never seen or heard of such mean and crazy people they sure are cruel here.[17]

■ ■ ■

Engla lived among Liz, Min, Mrs. C. and many others during her years as an attendant in Minnesota's mental hospitals. Despite the dismal conditions—the loneliness and isolation of dormitory life, the low pay and the exhausting work, the indifference of superintendents and professional staff—Engla labored on. She knew these patients as individuals. She could not condone their mistreatment and suffering. She could not put them out of sight and out of mind.

Why did this daughter of Norwegian immigrants choose to work in a mental hospital system with so few rewards and so many challenges? How did she become a crusader for change? Why did she make common cause with Minnesota Unitarians, a small sect of less than two thousand people statewide? How did the mild-mannered Unitarian minister Arthur Foote and the driven activist Genevieve Steefel, who harbored her own personal brush with mental institutions, persuade Governor Luther Youngdahl, a Swedish Lutheran Republican, to take up the cause of mental health reform? How did these citizens build a statewide movement for reform, give voice to the voiceless, overcome the stigma, and successfully design the blueprint for a modern mental health system? What legacy have they left for us?

TWO

Finding Engla Schey

I have never been able to acquiesce about things I did
not agree.

■ *Engla Schey*

A visitor to the Schey place in Marshall County, Minnesota,
finds vast flat plains that sweep toward the horizon as far as the eye can
see. Low ridges or moraines, formed thousands of years ago as a glacier
moved across the land, punctuate the prairie landscape. Native spruce
trees dominate the ridges, giving rise to its name—Spruce Valley.[1] This
is the land of long harsh winters and backbreaking efforts to tame and
till the rocky soil in the spring, summer, and fall. Eight miles from the
nearest town of Newfolden, the lazy Middle River, a branch of the Red
River, courses through fields.[2] No original buildings remain. All that is
left is the stand of oaks, spruce, and willows that once shaded the home
where Engla Schey was born in 1895 and spent her youth.

Scandinavian pioneer life is often told as a heroic narrative, with
courageous men and reluctant but dedicated wives carrying their traditional values with them to build a new life.[3] This mythological view
of struggle and success can obscure the lives of real people. Minnesota historian Rudolph Vecoli has cautioned: "Many were defeated
and crushed by the harsh conditions they encountered in America.
Industrial accidents, unemployment, exploitation, alcoholism, famil-
ial abuse, crime and vice were facts of immigrant life. . . . This is said
not to denigrate our immigrant ancestors, but to remind us that they
too were human beings with all the weaknesses and foibles to which
human flesh is heir."[4]

The Scheys certainly faced their share of challenges. Engla's father,
Anders, was born in 1865 in the town of Naustdal, a municipality in
Sogn og Fjordane in western Norway. The picturesque community

borders a blue-green fjord, with farms on the shores of its placid waters. Snow-capped mountains with high granite walls enclose the valley on both sides. The beauty of the place, however, was no match for the enormous difficulties of raising a large family on the land. The Schey family (*schey* means "flat place for grazing") had thirteen children. Anders was the last child. After his birth, his mother, Johanna, was unable to care for him. The infant's poverty-stricken father, Ole, sent him to the neighboring village of Lokebo to be raised by Ole's childless sister Olina and her husband, Henrik. Anders called the couple "Faste," a Norwegian colloquialism for father's sister, and "Fasteman," respectively.

Nine of Ole Schey's children are believed to have emigrated during the late nineteenth century. In 1869, when young Anders was only four years old, two of his older brothers, twenty-six-year-old Henrik (Henry) with his wife, Ingebord, and twenty-year-old Thoral (Tom), left Norway and joined thousands of Norwegians in Minnesota.[5] Like most of the Scandinavian immigrants, they knew farming and their dream was to own land. When the federal government released eight million acres in northwest Minnesota for settlement, the Schey brothers were part of the land rush that followed.[6] They settled in Marshall County, five miles east of Argyle in the fertile Red River Valley.

Anders began his journey to America at age eighteen in 1883. He headed north to be near his brothers and worked as a laborer until he could afford to homestead.[7] Because all of the desirable Red River Valley land had been claimed, Anders settled for a rockier, less fertile parcel thirty miles east in Spruce Valley. Within a few years, Anders staked his claim, built a cabin, and began to work the land. He became active in town life, serving as the Spruce Valley township assessor for four years in the 1890s.[8]

Once he had established a farm and built a homestead, Anders sent for others—Faste and Fasteman, his surrogate parents who had raised him in Norway, and his intended bride, Helene. Though unrelated, they all took the name of their Norwegian village of Lokebo when they arrived.[9]

Faste and Fasteman came in 1891 and settled into Anders's original log cabin. He built a larger place across the road for his future family. As Engla described later, "In return for raising Dad, he sent for them after he became established on a farm in this country and they lived out their days with us." Fasteman acquired his 160-acre claim nearby, but the elderly couple remained in the little log house near Anders.

Anders sent for Helene in 1887.[10] She insisted on a winter departure from Norway, against her mother's wishes. Without time for the preparation of a traditional wedding trunk, Helene's mother gave her daughter her own trunk for the journey. Helene was just twenty-one years old when she arrived in America. She and Anders did not marry until 1894 or 1895, when he was established on his farm. Like many other young Norwegian and Swedish girls, Helene spent the intervening years in domestic service before moving to Spruce Valley. Though the labor was hard and the hours long, conditions and wages were better in America.[11] Engla later wrote, "Mother had worked in a well-to-do American home and had learned Yankee ways."

By 1895 the young Schey family household consisted of husband and wife, Anders (age twenty-nine) and Helene (twenty-seven), living with Faste (seventy-one) and Fasteman (sixty-two) Lokebo. Four children soon arrived. Engla, "the angel," named after her maternal grandmother, was born in November 1895. Three siblings followed—Josie in 1897, Ole in 1900, and Helen in 1907.

Anders had arrived in Minnesota on the cusp of an immigration boom. The population of Marshall County grew to 992 in 1890 and expanded to 15,698 by 1900, peaking in 1920 at 19,443.[12] Newfolden, adjacent to Spruce Valley, was the center of town life. Norwegians were the dominant group although there were also large numbers of Swedes and later Finns. The town became a bustling place with schools, churches, and businesses.[13]

Within this little community, Engla was sandy-haired, blue-eyed, and wore wire rim glasses. Not a beauty like her sister, not sweet tempered like her brother, she was bright, intense, and passionate. Her world revolved around helping in the house and on the farm, attending a one-room school, church-related activities, and trips to town—all common experiences for children on the frontier. Engla later wrote essays about her childhood and early life, five of which survive and provide a window into her thoughts and feelings.

A constellation of three adults—her parents and Faste—shaped Engla's view of the world and her place within it. She adored her father and was always underfoot. He helped her with schoolwork and coached her for debates and spelling bees. Anders referred to her as "Daddy's girl" and liked to hear the neighbors say, "She's a chip off the old block. Her Dad all over again."

When Engla was nine or ten, she contracted polio and stayed out of school for a year. Her father was distraught. She recalled a neighbor saying to him, "Now I know there ain't nothin' you won't do for Engla. I 'member how you said you would give your whole 440 acre farm to anyone that could make Engla walk again, when the doctor said she never would." Engla did walk again but had a residual limp that made her self-conscious and unable to run in the schoolyard as she had before.

As a child, Engla also spent many hours with Faste. Her touching words describing this loving woman convey her depth of affection. Faste was a source of love and fun:

> Faste was seldom too busy to stop anything she was doing to comfort or advise us when we ran to her with our childish problems. Although she was so crippled with rheumatism that it was difficult

Spruce Valley homestead, 1897. From left, Henrik ("Fasteman") and Olina ("Faste"), two-year-old Engla (in stripes), Anders, and Helene, holding baby Josie. The name Faste was colloquial for "father's sister." Anders was raised by his aunt Olina and uncle Henrik in Norway. Engla wrote that he brought them to America to "live out their days with us." Courtesy of Ruth and John Schey.

for her to walk, she often leaned both hands heavily on her cane and asked my sister, brother and me to "dance" as she called it around her to the tune of Norwegian songs that she had taught us. . . .

Faste came from peasant stock in Norway. She managed to learn to read although she never attended school and she could only write her name; but she never once in my hearing complained about her lack of opportunities. She always seemed to be busy with spinning, knitting, mending or doing her housework. She used to bake some delicious Norwegian pastry, which she shared generously with my other sister, brother and me. It apparently was a Norwegian custom to treat overnight guests with breakfast in bed. One night when her husband was away I slept with her. (Dad had put a heavy rope in the ceiling that she could use to turn herself within bed). But this morning she got up while I was still asleep and when she finally woke me she brought a tray with those fat, delicious [treats] of hers and coffee for me to have in bed.

Engla's relationship with her mother, however, was full of tension and conflict that haunted her throughout her life: "Mother was a perfectionist and seemed to be forever working. We had to learn to crochet, tat, and do fancy work which didn't seem to make any sense to me. 'Don't let me ever catch you girls sitting around with idle hands,' mother used to say."

Engla often sought refuge in her father's world, and Anders was an understanding and supportive force. Sister Josie reminisced:

> "It was a good thing that dad rescued you from housework and let you do the things you enjoyed doing on the farm." Engla responded, "Yes, Dad told me I don't want any lazy kids around this place, if you can't help your mother, I'll hire someone to help her and you can run that self dumping hayrake and a mower as good as any man. I was jubilant and I'm sure mother was too."

Her parents' fundamental rift over religion was very troubling for Engla, as well as for the family and its interactions with the community. For most immigrant Scandinavian settlers, the Lutheran church was the center of community life. John Tunheim, a descendant of Newfolden pastor Samuel Tunheim, wrote, "The church was essential as inspiration for the homesteaders as they struggled to eke out an existence."[14] Lutheranism, the state religion of Norway, faced many new challenges in America. Without the structure of a state church, as there had been in Norway, individual churches, in different synods or "free" of any control, evolved.[15] Despite these differences, most still adhered to strict standards of behavior.

In the 1880s and 1990s, Newfolden had six different churches, many meeting in private homes, for a population of several hundred souls.[16] The Scheys attended the Newfolden Mission Society, formally organized in 1906.[17] The rules for Christian behavior were clear and strictly enforced. Engla recalled, "Dancing, drinking, card playing and 'such works of the devil' were forbidden to us when I lived in the community." Her mother, Helene, was devoted to this pietistic and stern Lutheranism. Anders, however, was known as a "freethinker." As Engla recalled, "Mother said, 'you are just a sinful pitiful human. You cannot comprehend the mind of God.' But, Dad said, 'Always keep an enquiring mind.'"

In contrast to the worldview of her mother and the community, Anders defied many of its restrictions. Even within the small community of Spruce Valley, Anders found ways to open the mind of his young daughter:

> I had a father who . . . did not hold any Jew responsible for the cruci-
> fixion of the Jew Jesus, except those Jews who actually participated
> in the crime. Furthermore, we entertained all the Jewish peddlers
> who came into our community to sell goods overnight because
> most of the religious fanatics wouldn't entertain people of the race
> that crucified Jesus. They sent them to us. I always looked forward
> to these occasions. Mother would fry eggs in butter instead of bacon
> grease. The entire family, including the farm hands would sit around
> the table and the peddler would tell us marvelous stories from other
> lands. Although Dad would never charge these men for board for
> themselves and the horses, they would usually leave a present for me
> and mother.

Engla's father was even willing to break the proscriptions on alcohol, despite the fact that the Mission Society was the home of the Christian Temperance Union. Every year for Easter and Christmas Anders gave Faste and Fasteman a large bottle of whiskey. When Uncle Tom visited from Argyle, they would partake of the whiskey in the log cabin across the road. No doubt Helene was enraged by consumption of alcohol, a terrible breach of the community's religious tenets, under her own roof. Like other local children her age, Engla trembled before the images of a burning hell and a wrathful God. She remembered her mother opening the door of the oven, pointing to the roaring inferno, and comparing it to the fires of hell. Her mother insisted that Anders deserved just such a fiery fate. Engla recalled her mother burning her husband's mail and magazines because they were sinful and she didn't want them in the house.

Even Faste was not guaranteed a place in heaven according to Helene and others in the community. Faste and Fasteman were pious folk, but their religious practices fell short of the community's prevailing religious norms:

> The only time Faste hesitated to be disturbed was at their daily after supper devotions. Fasteman, whose eyes were failing, had brought a large print Bible and two hymn books with him from Norway. Every evening while still seated at the supper table, Fasteman read a chapter from the Bible, then they would sing a couple of hymns, after which they would repeat the Lord's Prayer in unison. If any of us children came in during devotion, we seated ourselves quietly and with folded hands and listened reverently to the ritual. . . . Many of the professing Christians were concerned because she had never publicly testified to being either saved or sanctified and many thoroughly believed that this was essential to entrance to heaven and those who were not saved would burn in hell "throughout everlasting eternity."

Engla, who loved her father and her Faste deeply, was unable to accept the community's judgments about them. She later commented, "Lutheran churches in my little village. This was the only social life I was permitted those days and it was bad for sensitive children like me."

Engla's young life was not without friendship and joy. She began her schooling in District 47 in Spruce Valley. The school was organized in 1903, when she was seven years old, and was located only a short distance from the Schey farm.[18] She had very fond memories of her days in the one-room schoolhouse. On a trip back to her hometown in the late 1950s, she wanted to revisit it:

> It may sound silly but I think that one room schoolhouse is the most wonderful building I have ever seen. It has been pulling me back for years . . . those wonderful people, who were so helpful and rushed to lift me up, when after a year in bed with polio, I came back to school with an iron brace on my leg.

While peering in the window of the schoolhouse over forty years later, Engla, her sister Josie, and their friend David remembered happy days with homemade bats and swings, and books in short supply. David recalled:

> "You started being a crusader quite early. You remember once without warning when you had finished your prescribed 'I love America' speech, you said you were glad you were Norwegian. You would hate to think that your ancestors stole the land from the Indians or used Negroes as slaves.
>
> "They clapped more for that than any other part of the program," my sister said. "Wonder what the Yankee teacher thought, but after all that applause from the audience, what could she say."

When Engla was only thirteen, a series of tragedies struck the Schey family and life forever changed. The first tragedy was Faste's death.

Schey family portrait, taken in Thief River Falls, circa 1913. From left, mother, Helene (seated), Josie, Helen, Ole, Engla, and father, Anders. Courtesy of Ruth and John Schey.

Faste had begun to fail after the death of her husband in 1908, and she died the following year. Events surrounding Faste's death profoundly affected Engla:

> Finally one morning Faste did not get out of bed, as she had every morning before since I had known her. When on the third day she was still in bed and refused to eat, I heard mother tell Mrs. Anderson to come and pray for her. "I think her time has come," I heard mother say. There was no one to wipe the sweet drops from her damp body or try to spoon cold water into her fever-wracked mouth as Faste had done for her husband. Even our maid was on the knees with mother and two other prayer women circling the bed and begging God to "save her undying soul." At that time I was so disturbed about the prospect of this selfless woman spending her endless eternity in a Lake of Fire that I just stood there motionless and did not even think about administering to her much needed comfort. . . .
>
> Fortunately for Faste she died on her third day in bed. At the village store where they also handled funeral supplies, I picked out a large picture of Angels fluttering down to gather someone up in their arms and carry them to heaven. The store manager who knew Faste said this would be very appropriate for no one that he knew deserved heaven any more than Faste. On the seven mile ride home with the casket in the slay; I speculated a lot about her meeting with her husband and I thought she would be one of the first ones I would look for when I arrived at the pearly gates. I did not say much to dad, seated by my side and urging the farm team to move more quickly for dad had never since I knew him been sure of the existence of "streets of gold" and he did not believe that a loving God would burn people forever and ever. After thinking it over, I wasn't so sure myself. . . .
>
> The picture I had thought so appropriate at the General store was labeled sacrilegious by some of the Christians after they were informed that Faste had gone to her grave without confessing God as her savior. I saw the picture taken down and heard a voice say, "We have no proof that this good woman went to heaven." The thought of Faste burning in hell forever and ever so unnerved me that I started to scream, "Faste is not dead. Faste is not dead." My father, who was labeled a freethinker by now took me into a bedroom and held me there until we saw the slays beginning to move out toward the graveyard. He let me know then that he did not believe in a literal hell and that comforted me. Dad said, "You will have to accept the fact that

Faste is dead." On dad's advice I went to my room and wrote in my diary, When I saw Faste whose fingers had always been so quick to wipe away my tears, lie there with her arms folded in silent unconcern, then I knew that Faste was dead.

In 1911, two years after the death of Faste, the Schey family faced a second life-altering change when Anders sold the farm. Owning land was the dream of immigrants like the Scheys. Land provided a home, a livelihood, and standing in the community. Anders had acquired a sizable amount of acreage. In addition to his homestead tract of 160 acres, he had taken out a mortgage in 1902 and later purchased an additional 120 acres in 1906. When Fasteman died two years later, Anders inherited his 160 acres as well. But in June 1911, Anders sold all 440 acres for $8,000, less $1,000 to pay off a private debt and an additional amount for delinquent property taxes. The family then moved to a house in town.

It is not clear what led to the sale of the farm. Engla's writing provides no clue. In her essay "The Auction," she described the sale of implements and livestock and her grief over the loss of her favorite horse, Jim, but did not mention why the sale occurred. The regional economy was strong in the decade leading up to World War I. Was Anders personally overextended and unable to pay the mortgage on the land? Did he run short on energy and ambition? Did his reputation as a freethinker or even a nonbeliever in a disapproving community cause despondency or despair? He had no alternative employment plan, and after the sale, worked as a laborer on the land of others—a major fall in status and security.

Then, a third blow hit. Anders's brother Tom died in February 1912. Tragedy had stalked this branch of the family for years and Tom's death was devastating. The families were close. Tom and Anna had four children. The two older boys, Stephen and Oliver, were much older than Anders's children, but their daughters, Emma and Jennie, were Engla's dear cousins and lifelong friends.[19]

Stephen served in the Spanish-American War, and died of consumption in 1902 at age twenty-two. His death unhinged his mother, Anna, who became severely depressed. The family struggled to care for her, and she spent a year in Fergus Falls State Hospital in 1907–8.[20] She was discharged as "recovered," but tragedy struck again. Her remaining son, Oliver, died of pneumonia in 1910 at age twenty-one, followed by the death of her husband, Tom, two years later.[21]

After the deaths of all the men in the family, Anna's two daughters took responsibility for their ill mother. They sold the farm, lived briefly in St. Cloud, then moved to Minneapolis, where Emma took a teaching position and Jennie trained to be a nurse. Anna's mental health continued to deteriorate as the daughters struggled to keep their mother at home. After stints in private rest homes, Emma moved her mother to Rochester State Hospital in 1918.[22] Her admission records indicate that her condition was serious:

> Patient realizes that her condition is not normal and that it does not hurt her to go without food. Says it is impossible for her to eat. Says that she has heard people say she has committed an unpardonable sin but does not know what this could be. Has heard the voice of God talking to her but does not know what he said; does not remember saying that she was to save the world or that her sons were still living; thinks if she only can cry it would "lighten" her chest.[23]

The sisters tried once to bring their mother home. The record indicates that Anna was "paroled" for a brief seventeen days in 1920, but was returned to Rochester State Hospital and spent the rest of her life there. She died of acute bronchitis in February 1926.

In three short years, the Schey family suffered many losses. A few months after her Uncle Tom's death, Engla graduated from eighth grade in the spring of 1912 at age sixteen.[24] She was an excellent student. "I was considered one of the bright ones. It was predicted that I would amount to something." Her future was uncertain. There was no public high school in the area at that time, and Anders wanted more for his promising daughter. At considerable sacrifice, Engla went on to Oak Grove Lutheran Ladies Seminary in Fargo, North Dakota, one hundred and twenty miles from home. Oak Grove was a "Christian high school for girls of Norwegian heritage living in rural areas" that had been founded just six years earlier.[25] Engla did not mention her time at Oak Grove in any of her writings. What did this sixteen-year-old girl, so burdened with emotional scars, feel living so far from home? All we know is that she completed one year of study there in 1913, doing well in all her courses.[26]

Moorhead, Minnesota, is across the Red River from Fargo. Engla enrolled in Moorhead Normal School the following fall. The school had been founded in 1888 with the mission to train elementary school teachers and had recently expanded to include training for high school teachers as demand for high school training grew in rural communities.[27] Attending normal school would have been a significant opportunity for a young girl from Spruce Valley, a chance to become a teacher and to leave her challenging home life and find a place for herself in the larger world.

Engla struggled at Moorhead during her two years there.[28] The school's goal was to imbue Yankee refinement in the young ladies. The president of the school and much of the faculty were New Englanders. "As in many mid-western communities a hundred years ago, people of New England birth were deferred to. They conveyed the impression that they were bringing education and culture into a newly settled land."[29] The young ladies lived in dormitories that were intended to reflect "Christian homes where every effort may be put forth to maintain the amenities of life, which prevail in homes of refinement and good cheer." Even the Young Women's Christian Association had a decidedly elite tone, encouraging work "such as friendly visiting at institutions and homes, sewing and calisthenics for children, teaching English to foreigners, and services along other lines to people whose lives are different from their own."[30]

Engla surely chafed at the elitism of the school. She did not aspire to the world of gracious living. She had a fighting spirit—and other plans. Engla left Moorhead in the summer of 1915, and on August 25, entered the Salvation Army's School for Officers' Training in Chicago.[31] She was nineteen years old.

In the early years of the twentieth century, the Salvation Army was a highly visible and attractive organization for Scandinavians in Minnesota.[32] In fact, there were so many in the Scandinavian units that they were separately administered from the rest of the organization. In a time of limited opportunities for women, the SA welcomed women of Northern European descent as essential to serving poor women and their families, and further provided them a sense of community and a spiritual environment.[33]

Given her rejection of the wrathful and vengeful God of her mother's pietistic Lutheranism, it might seem incongruous that Engla would join and ultimately devote fourteen years to a religious organization committed to saving souls for Jesus. Engla was not without a spiritual side, and it was likely the organization's nonjudgmental spiritualism and social welfare mission that appealed to her. As Edward McKinley described in his history of the Salvation Army:

The help offered was typically immediate and practical; a day-work employment service . . . small sums to purchase kerosene, coal, or food; a warm cup of coffee, soup, and a place to sleep, simple kindly family counseling . . . directing especially desperate persons to Salvation Army institutions better equipped to provide long-term attention. Its services were delivered with energetic good will and, unlike some Christian organizations that insisted on distinguishing the deserving and the undeserving poor, were available to all.[34]

Engla threw herself into her new mission. The training school offered courses in academics, music, and the doctrines and discipline of the Salvation Army. While there, Engla learned bookkeeping and how to play the violin and organ. Aside from a brief assignment in Minneapolis as an emergency relief worker, her first placements were primarily in small communities in the Upper Midwest.[35] Salvation Army activities were integral to life in small towns. An entry from the local paper in Appleton, Wisconsin, reported, "Captain Schey in charge of Sunday school, praise service, Young People's meeting, and a Salvation meeting."[36]

But Engla was anxious to work with people in greatest need. In 1921, the *Appleton Post-Crescent* reported that Captain Schey "expects to be transferred to a larger city where she will work in the slums, an occupation in which she has had much experience."[37] Her new assignments included several years at the St. Paul Rescue Home that provided housing and hospital care for unwed mothers and their children, four years at the settlement house in the slums of Milwaukee, and eighteen months in the settlement house on Chicago's impoverished South Side.[38]

Engla had a deep respect for the Salvation Army throughout her life. She later reflected:

Those people have zeal for Humanity. After all these years the public still has unbounded confidence in them. They can get almost anything they go after. They have competent advisory boards composed of leading business and professionals to advise them. They not only advise but take care of the property deals. . . . Maybe, after all, the humble shall inherit the earth. They really get things done. I worked with them for a while. There was none of the common alibis that there was no money or adequate personnel. Every Army member was a soldier to help when necessary outside of his own working time. If an institution ran short of food, we just went out to some large

The Schey cousins, 1920s. Clockwise from bottom: Engla, in her Salvation Army uniform, cousins Jennie and Emma, and sister Josie. Jennie and Emma were Engla's lifelong friends. Courtesy of Roxanne Butzer.

grocery place and stated the facts and came home with food. I would get into the station wagon with some disabled old man to help lift the stuff. I would drive the truck from place to place, make my speech and the shaking man would help haul it into the truck.

While Engla toiled in the service of others, life was difficult for the Schey family back in Newfolden. Anders had once operated a large farm, participated in town affairs, and supported his extended family. Now he was reduced to working as a farm laborer on the land of others. Worse still, he continued to be branded as a dangerous freethinker, not trusted by his wife or by those for whom he worked. Engla recounted a telling conversation:

> "I wonder what happened to that free thinker who followed the harvest?" the daughter asked. "You really enjoyed him, didn't you Dad?"
>
> "We always bunked together, he and I, when we went threshing together," the father smiled. "He was a student at the University of Minnesota. They didn't trust free thinkers in the barn. Afraid people who didn't believe in God might set fire to it, so they had us sleep in the house where they could watch us. But then some of the women got to listening to our conversation outside our bedroom door. One day a woman exclaimed, "I don't want such men in the house, I don't think they believe in our Lord." We slept in a straw stack then.

To make matters worse, the rural economy was in a deep slump. During World War I, the demand for food rose, farmers increased output, and land prices soared. In 1918, however, when the war ended, food exports fell by more than 50 percent, and demand at home also dropped while production remained high. Farm income plummeted precipitously and the rural areas suffered bank failures, defaults on loans, and "acute agricultural distress."[39] Times were hard, and particularly challenging for a farm laborer who was now in his early sixties.

The children were all leaving home. Engla had been the first to go. The remaining three Schey siblings all left the community by the early 1920s. There was no farm to hold them and life at home was unhappy. Josie graduated from the District 47 school in 1914. She married William Hoppe of Wisconsin after he returned from service in World War I. By 1923 they lived in Appleton, Wisconsin, with their two children.

Ole was one of four students in the first graduating class of the new high school in Newfolden in 1918. He attended the University of

Minnesota and received a BS degree. He returned north to teach, then became a superintendent in rural school districts. When the Depression came, he returned to the university and paid his own way while completing an MA in mathematics in 1935.[40]

The youngest Schey daughter, Helen, had met Swede Oscar Yngve, a graduate of Gustavus Adolphus College, when he was superintendent of Newfolden schools in 1920 and she was a student. They were married after Helen graduated from the district school. Following several stints in rural school districts, they settled in Minneapolis in the 1930s, where Yngve taught at Roosevelt High School and Helen worked as a sales clerk at Dayton's department store. They had no children. Left alone, Helene and Anders stayed in their home in Newfolden and took in boarders to make ends meet.

On October 30, 1926, Anders made a fateful decision. He had struggled with loneliness and harbored a deep sadness for years. Perhaps the funeral of Anna, his brother Tom's widow after nine years at Rochester State Hospital, on a bitterly cold February day in Argyle, intensified his condition. On a chilly autumn morning of that year, without telling anyone, he boarded a train alone. He took the Soo Line from Newfolden to Thief River Falls and transferred to the Great Northern Railway, traveling 120 miles to Fergus Falls. Watching the fields, trees, and rivers pass, he experienced fear, dread, and perhaps relief.

At Fergus Falls, Anders trudged from the railroad spur that ran to his destination. The imposing stone structure loomed before him, the largest building in Minnesota, nearly a third of a mile long. A fortress, a jail, or a refuge from the world he could no longer manage. He glanced up at the stone tower, ascended the steps under the grand portico, and crossed into the vast main lobby and through the glass enclosure to the reception area. His footsteps echoed on the tiled floor. On that day, Anders checked himself in to the Fergus Falls State Hospital for the Insane. As Engla later wrote, "He wanted to work out his own salvation among strangers."

In this period, the hospital was severely overcrowded with a population of 1,611 patients and a capacity of only 1,000.[41] Anders was assigned to a ward based on his medical condition and mental state. Although he did not want his family to know, the hospital contacted them. Ole, who was superintendent of schools in Lake Bronson, Minnesota, at the time, traveled over two hundred miles south to Fergus Falls to deal with his father's surprise decision. Anders had been voluntarily admitted to the hospital and refused to go home.[42]

After nine months, Anders was considered "improved," and he was discharged on July 27, 1927. The return home was painful and short lived. Helene equated his mental issues with the work of the devil, a condition she felt Anders deserved. He continued to be depressed and subsequent hospital records noted that he was suicidal.

When it became clear that Anders could not thrive at home with Helene, Engla made the long, and certainly anguishing, train trip from Chicago, where she was serving in the Salvation Army's South Side Settlement House, to Newfolden. She accompanied her father back to Fergus Falls State Hospital. Engla grieved to see her father in his hopeless state, choosing to abandon family and home for a mental institution. On July 7, 1928, Anders signed his application for voluntary admission and Engla was the witness to his intention.[43] He was sixty-three

Fergus Falls State Hospital, circa 1928. The building, based on the Kirkbride plan, was the third hospital for the insane in Minnesota. It opened in 1890 and was completed in 1912. The building was more than one-third of a mile long and housed nearly two thousand patients by 1930. Courtesy of the Minnesota Historical Society.

years old. Three years later, he was formally committed, a process that made him an official ward of the state. When he experienced bouts of depression, he stayed in bed. When he was able, he worked. Anders was assigned to the congregant dining room where patients prepared, served, and cleaned up three meals a day for nearly two thousand people.

Anders never returned home. He died at Fergus Falls twenty-seven years later in 1955. Helene and Anders never divorced, but they led separate lives. In Newfolden, Helene worked as a housekeeper and rented rooms to lodgers. In 1935 she left home and moved in with her daughter Helen and her husband in Minneapolis. She did not return to Newfolden, though she remained close to her pastor there, Reverend Myhrer. He and his wife visited her in Minneapolis and, at her request, he presided at her funeral service in March 1957.

A little more than a year after bringing her father back to the Fergus Falls State Hospital, Engla resigned her commission in the Salvation Army after fourteen years of service. She moved in the 1930s to accept a job as a social worker with the St. Louis Provident Association in St. Louis, Missouri. Provident was founded in 1860 by a group of local businessmen to address the social and economic needs of the city. In the 1930s, the company administered relief for the Works Progress Administration (WPA) and provided jobs to the unemployed as part of Franklin Roosevelt's New Deal.[44]

During her years in St. Louis, Engla once again demonstrated her compassion for the most unfortunate people and her drive to fight for them against all odds. The country was in the grips of the Great Depression, and Provident's management reflected the hard-core racism of the South at the time. Both clients and social workers were scrupulously segregated. Engla was assigned a white caseload. Apparently she had made comments that called into question her white heritage. She joked about her "roaming Viking ancestors," saying, "Who knows where they went and how many different bloods they might have picked up in their wanderings?" She was reprimanded, nearly terminated, for making light of racial identity. Willing to give her one more chance, management assigned her to the "communist load," which included activists working amidst poor African Americans. When asked, "Can you be just as unprejudiced and fair to communists as you are to Negroes?," she responded, "I wouldn't discriminate against a person because of his political or religious belief anymore than I would because of his color."

Engla described her communist load as a group of unemployed, impoverished "Negroes that were led by a blonde Norwegian self-admitted Communist, who peacefully protested the inequitable handouts." The relief system allotted African American babies only one-third as much relief as white babies. The leader was adept at organizing marches against inequity and securing press coverage documenting the manner in which they were violently dispersed. Engla befriended this unemployed organizer, found him a job as a labor organizer, and helped get equity in the treatment of blacks and whites. During her days in St. Louis, Engla continued her fight for the underdog, the impoverished, and the dispossessed.

Engla's father was often on her mind, however. She was living over seven hundred miles from her beloved dad. During this period, Engla paid a rare visit to her father at Fergus Falls State Hospital. The visit was a turning point in her life. In a compelling story titled "No One Cares for Doggie," she recounted the upsetting but ultimately pivotal visit.[45] She observed the crowded conditions and the neglect and indifference of the staff. When she learned that her father rarely spoke to anyone at the hospital, she begged him to tell her why:

> The father turned around to face the daughter and said, "I want to tell you a story and then I think you will understand why I don't bother to talk with the attendants and doctors. There was a dog once that could talk but he didn't want to. They just wanted to hear him talk to amuse themselves and he didn't care to oblige them. They called to him. 'Doggie talk.' They patted him on the head and said to him 'nice doggie please talk.' Finally a kind lady who really cared said to him, 'Doggie, why don't you talk? We know you can talk. Then why don't you talk?' And then because this lady really cared he told her, 'Because nobody cares about doggie anyway.'"

Engla tried to rekindle the strong bonds that the two had shared when she was a little girl, but without success:

> "Don't you remember Dad how you always said that we understood each other and that I'd always be your own little girl so long as we both lived." Then after a long pause the daughter said, "Listen Dad I'm still that same girl."
>
> "No you're not that same girl. You're an old woman now, much too old for your years. The years and anxieties of the world have

stooped your shoulders and furrowed you face. You look like an old woman now."

"How old Dad?" asked the shocked daughter.

"I know how many years you are—in years you're not old—you've lived too intensely—you've felt too much. That's what makes you so old. No, you'll never be my little girl any more. There's too many years between us."

"The years can't change things between us Dad. We still understand each other," wept the daughter. "Dad, don't you remember," pleaded the daughter, "Daddy's girl you used to say." . . . Do you mean to say all that has changed?" she said, wiping the tears from her eyes.

"I don't want to remember it. I want to forget the past," he sighed. "All my life I have been so alone," he said. He pleaded with her to go away and get a rest "but don't go around the family: you won't find peace and rest there any more than I would. Go away somewhere by yourself." . . .

At the hotel room that night she tried to piece together her father's tragic life and cursed fate that it should have dealt thus with such a wonderful man.

The next day, when he saw his daughter, that old familiar disturbed look came over his face—he turned his face to the wall as if he wanted to shut out some tragic scene. It was obvious that he had made a new place and life for himself and he didn't want anyone around to remind him of his old life.

Devastated, she began to despair. Then, she had an epiphany:

Quick as a flash it came to her what she must do—she would go forth and do all she could to improve conditions in mental hospitals as speedily as possible. That was the best way to help father.

Her mind went back again to that quotation she used to answer the roll call with in grammar school:

Do something worth living for
Do something worth dying for
Do something to show there's
A mind, heart and soul within you.

Almost accidentally she had stumbled on a cause to work for that was bigger than herself, her father, and her entire family, and it made her happy.

Engla had lost her father. But she had found her calling. She was soon to bring her crusading spirit and commitment to the patients in the asylums of Minnesota. In the 1940 census, the census taker listed Engla Schey among the "hired" individuals, along with the hundreds of "inmates," as part of the "household" known as "Anoka State Hospital (insane asylum)."

THREE

Engla Crashes the Gates

You will not like it here.
> ■ *Dr. Walter P. Gardner, superintendent, Anoka State Hospital*

Keys jangling, the nurse in a starched white uniform marched up the stone steps and unlocked the door to Cottage Three, one of ten imposing brick-and-stone buildings set in a semicircle on the asylum grounds in Anoka. Engla followed, carrying all her worldly belongings in two suitcases. She stepped into the building where she would live and work. It was a dark depressing gray; no color anywhere. The first floor was designed to include reception and recreation rooms but, due to overcrowding, now housed a doctor's quarters and space for female staff. She trudged up the open stairway to the second floor, the stale air tinged with odors of urine and disinfectant. She saw women in camisoles strapped to wooden benches, their hair shaved off, wearing similar baggy denim dresses. They drooled and ranted and raged. There were feces on the floor. Metal beds were lined up, nearly touching each other.[1]

The nurse led the way up a narrower staircase to Engla's third-floor quarters—one cramped room with a slanted ceiling, a bed, desk, and dresser. She would share the small bathroom at the end of the hall with all the other attendants. "This is it," said the nurse curtly and disappeared down the stairs. Engla stood at the dormered window, which was too small to allow much light or to catch the breezes that blew off the Rum River in the distance. She could hear the cries and moans of the patients below, a sound that would hum in her ears all day and haunt her dreams at night. She put down her suitcases, sat on the metal bed, and swept her graying hair out of her eyes. She was forty-three years old. This dingy attic room was now home.

It hadn't been easy to land this position—Attendant 1—the lowest rung on the institutional ladder. She had resigned her social work position in St. Louis and temporarily moved into the home of her sister Helen and her husband, Oscar Yngve, a small stucco bungalow in south Minneapolis. Her mother lived there too. Helene had grown stout and perennially dressed in a duster, elastic stockings, and a ruffled apron. She clung to her strict religious views, spoke only Norwegian, and forbade any mention of her husband, Anders. Engla had never gotten along with her mother, and no doubt she had been anxious to find a position and get settled on her own.

After several rejections, Engla "finally crashed the gates," as she put it, at Anoka State Hospital in 1939.[2] She had not been encouraged during the job interview with Superintendent Dr. Walter P. Gardner and Esther Nelson, the supervisor of nurses. Dr. Gardner, small in stature, with a receding hairline, glasses, and a thin mustache, sat behind his desk, hands folded, and listened silently to Engla as she described her social work background and her desire to help unfortunates. He sighed with the air of a passive and defeated man. His only response: "You will not like it here."[3]

Nelson stood straight beside the desk. She was tall and thin, with tight dark curls under her crisp white cap. She was so stiff it seemed as if she had been starched along with her immaculate uniform. Nelson prided herself on running a tight ship. She had credentials, and she commanded respect from the underlings. She also had her favorites, and she knew Engla would not be one of them. She peered over her wire-rimmed glasses, showed her long teeth in an expression somewhere between a smirk and a smile, and said, "It would be quite a let down after social work."[4]

There were no social workers at Anoka. The only opening was the entry-level attendant, a custodial position that required only an eighth-grade education and domestic skills. Engla, clearly overqualified, was disappointed but remained optimistic about advancement in the future. Attendants worked a forty-eight-hour week, often in split shifts, with one day off. The hospital required unmarried female attendants to live on the premises. The pay was forty-five dollars a month from which a small amount was deducted for room and board.[5] Engla began on probation for the first month.

Now, here she was. She would work among and for people like her father—those who were locked away, called inmates, and carrying the shameful label "insane." For a moment her resolve wavered, then her determination kicked in. Okay, she thought, let's get at it. She was shocked at what she saw. Her humanitarian instincts were immediately on full alert:

> I refused to put a patient in camisole right off the bat and I took a patient who had crouched like a dog on a leash, tied in a six stool toilet, out on a porch and I objected to camisole patients having all of their supper, including dessert and liquid served in a tin bowl and scooped into them like slopping the hogs, so I got off to a bad start.[6]

Engla learned quickly that the institution had a strict hierarchy, a "caste system" as she later called it. The superintendent was at the top, followed by "the professionals"—doctors and nurses, with attendants at rock bottom. Attendants did not defy authority; they were expected to obey. The "higher-ups" set the tone. At Anoka, the institutional culture was one of coercion and control.

Superintendent Gardner's management style was passive. He had psychiatric training but provided no patient care. There was only one full-time physician on staff for the 1,440 patients. Dr. Rogers, an elderly man with severe Parkinson's disease, came to Anoka when he could no longer sustain a private practice. He treated patients' medical needs, not their psychological ones. Rogers had accepted the culture of control. As Engla wrote in her journal, Rogers advised:

> There are two ways to handle these patients—1. Reason and persuasion or 2. Fear. The first method takes insight into mental illness and training. Very few nurses and attendants . . . have training in psychiatry so they must handle them the only way they know how—They must make them do as they say through fear and punishment. . . . That's' why it is necessary to have God and the devil, so we can have someone to scare people with and make them behave themselves.

Gardner ceded substantial authority to Nursing Supervisor Nelson. She ran the show while embodying a cold, detached bureaucratic attitude. She cautioned Engla, "The state is an impersonal thing. It can get along without me or you or anybody. I can do just exactly as they want me to do it. If they tell me to put every patient in the institution in camisole I will do it. If they tell me to take them out I will do that. I just work here."

After her first three weeks, Engla was called into the superintendent's office. Dr. Gardner confided in a quiet voice, "I am told you can't catch on to this job. I know it isn't for lack of intelligence that you can't catch on. Why can't you catch on?" Engla explained her concerns about the system. Maybe he admired her spark of compassion, something he may have lost in his own long years of asylum work. Dr. Gardner responded, "That's what I thought. I'll use my own judgment and put you on the payroll."[7]

Engla survived probation. She resolved to learn more about mental illness and to develop skills to interact positively with patients. She intended to work her way up so that she could influence the culture, even if only for one ward, show her value by example, and make life better for patients.

The campus included a main building for administration, with two wings for male patients. The sexes were strictly segregated. Male attendants handled the men. Women filled the cottages. The cottages were constructed in a circular pattern around an open courtyard. Eight

Anoka State Hospital staff, July 1940. Front row, left of center, Dr. Walter P. Gardner, superintendent. Front row, second from far left, Esther Nelson, supervisor of nurses. Attendants were not pictured among the professional staff in this photograph. Courtesy of the Anoka County Historical Society.

hours a day, six days a week, Engla fed, dressed, cleaned, and managed large wards of women.

The cottages were extensively overcrowded. Their original capacity was seventy, but they each held over one hundred patients in the 1940s.[8] Space intended for recreation or dayrooms became quarters for staff and the doctor. The federal surveyors noted: "It is distressing to find women's disturbed wards in which there are barely enough seats, in which useful activity is at a minimum and in which extra beds must be set up at night in order to give all the patients a place to sleep."[9] Cottage Ten served as a hospital ward for patients with medical problems. The building had no elevator, so patients had to be carried from their beds downstairs to the treatment facilities and operating room.[10]

Staffing became increasingly inadequate during this period, with many younger employees called to serve in the military, or leaving to

Anoca State Hospital July 1940   GRB

[handwritten: → Partial ww-22]

take positions in war industries. The hospitals paid low wages, and working conditions were difficult, not to mention the stigma of working in the "bughouse." Anoka had very high patient-to-staff ratios, and staff numbers declined in this period while the patient census grew. The shortages meant that often one attendant would be responsible for a hundred women.[11] Engla graphically described the consequences in terms of patient care:

> We worked fast and mechanically again. Pushing patients around to the toilet, pulling off nightgowns, unlocking and locking their handcuffs, lacing camisoles and generally operating like cow hands on some ranch. We didn't talk to the patients except to give orders and they seldom talked to us. I don't think we were altogether to blame. It was the system. I don't know how else we could get the patients dressed in the time allowed.

Aerial view of Anoka State Hospital, 1937. The hospital opened in 1900 as an asylum for "hopeless cases." It was built on the cottage plan, a popular alternative to the Kirkbride model. Connected by underground tunnels, cottages were considered more homelike, and patients were grouped by behavior or condition. The term *asylum* was dropped in favor of *hospital* in 1937, though conditions did not change as a result. Photograph by Leo A. Moore, *St. Paul Daily News*. Courtesy of the Minnesota Historical Society.

Upon touring Anoka, Dr. Royal Gray, head of the Mental Health Unit in the Division of Public Institutions (the DPI, the state agency that oversaw mental institutions), wrote to his boss, Carl Swanson, "The Anoka State Hospital certainly needs an upward revision in its numbers of attendants. There are too many patients stagnating in the cottage for the disturbed and noisy group."[12] Such "revision," however, did not occur.

Anoka suffered from scarcity and deferred maintenance. Specific deficiencies included lack of maintenance, fire hazards, and a heating system so old and worn that it was likely to fail.[13] The Depression meant increased limitations on many necessities, and restrictions and curtailment of many other needs. Everywhere there were not enough

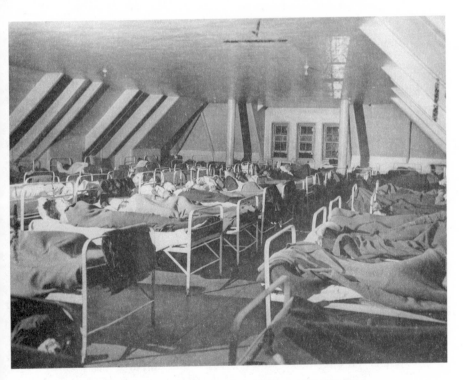

One hundred men slept in overcrowded attic rooms like this one, unventilated and poorly insulated. Lacking dressers or closets, they stored their clothes on the floor. In some hospitals, beds were so close together that the patient could not climb out on either side but had to crawl over the foot. Photograph by Arthur Hager, *Minneapolis Tribune*. Courtesy of the Minnesota Historical Society.

shoes, coats, underwear, socks, toilet paper, soap, and reading materials. There were no radios. The food quality and preparation were poor,
the food service was even worse. In the 1940s, one volunteer reported:

> When I visited the central kitchen, I was thoroughly nauseated. At
> two-thirty in the afternoon the patients' suppers were already dished
> out on open carts, ready to be pushed through the underground tun-
> nels to the different cottages. The plates had once been white enamel,
> but the paint had long since chipped off so that they were almost
> totally black and half rusted. The supper consisted of watery gruel
> with apples in it, coffee, and rolls burned black on the bottom. When
> I asked the head cook who planned the meals, he said he did, accord-
> ing to the money he was allowed.[14]

In these unpromising conditions, Engla worked her forty-eight hours
per week, managing the wards, cleaning, feeding, and caring for patients' needs. She kept her eyes open, learned the ropes, and looked for
opportunities to make improvements in the lives of patients.

When she wasn't working, Engla was driven to learn more about
mental illness. Despite the long working hours with limited time off,
she managed to take the bus down to Minneapolis, twenty-five miles to
the south, to attend courses at the University of Minnesota. She completed six credits in abnormal psychology, a course in mental hygiene
in the Department of Family Nursing Service, and a course in dynamic
behavior.[15] An attendant taking university courses was unprecedented,
and inevitably raised suspicion in the mind of the Supervisor of Nurses.
What was Engla up to now?

Engla also spent time with her cousins Emma and Jennie Schey.[16]
All three were unmarried working women in their midforties during
this period. After an enjoyable visit from the cousins, Engla confided
in her journal: "I am proud of these two girls. They are wide-awake and
love their work and people. It was nice being with people who were
so understanding of the tragedies of my youth. They know how it has
colored my life and make allowances for some of my attitudes."

Cousin Emma took Engla to the First Unitarian Society (FUS) of
Minneapolis, an introduction that would have a profound effect on
Engla and would connect her to people sympathetic to her cause.[17] Unitarianism had flourished in New England during the mid-nineteenth
century. Unitarians rejected the harsh and judgmental theology of the

Puritans, and embraced the centrality of the essential goodness of all people. Unitarianism was considered a "liberal" religion because it subscribed to no fixed creed; adherents applied their own reason to matters theological. The faith expanded west to Minnesota. Unitarians in St. Paul formed Unity Church in 1872, a traditional and robust congregation that thrived despite being considered "misguided unbelievers" by some of their neighbors.[18]

The First Unitarian Society of Minneapolis, founded in 1881, had more political and activist roots than the congregation in St. Paul. In fact, the Liberal League, a group of Minneapolis intellectuals interested in new scientific advances and progressive thought, formed the nucleus of the new FUS. They were more distinctly secular and nonecclesiastical than the St. Paul group. In November 1887, after the opening of its first church, the FUS joined with St. Paul's Unity Church, along with some smaller Universalist congregations, to form the Minnesota Unitarian Conference (MUC), which represented liberal coreligionists across the state.[19]

The FUS Women's Alliance was socially active from the outset. As historian Colette A. Hyman writes, "Churchgoers actively pursued current affairs through the Women's Alliance and the Promethean Club, both of which were open to the public. Alliance members were 'public spirited women' who had 'done valiant duty in battle for the great reforms of the day.'"[20] The Alliance supported a wide range of women's issues and is credited with the establishment of a birth control clinic in 1929.[21]

In the 1930s FUS operated out of the Unitarian Center on Harmon Place in downtown Minneapolis. The church embraced both radical theology and radical politics. Sunday services were called "a secularization of the Sunday morning liturgical experience," and took place in the commodious Shubert Theater to accommodate the large audiences. Often over a thousand people flocked to hear the longtime FUS minister John Dietrich and his associate minister Raymond Bragg.

Rejecting the term *sermon*, Dietrich intended that the Sunday lectures not impose any religious approach but rather "stimulate and guide you in your thinking that you may work out your own conceptions of religion and mortality."[22] Dietrich and Bragg both embraced humanism and evolution, dismissing creationism and abandoning theism in favor of the affirmation of human life. The Unitarian message embraced social action as fundamental to any concept of religion.[23]

This building at 1526 Harmon Place in Minneapolis served as the Unitarian Center from 1926 until 1957, housing the First Unitarian Society's offices and meeting space. Sunday services were held in theaters to accommodate the crowds. Courtesy of Hennepin County Library Special Collections.

Both were antiwar and peace activists, and Harmon Place also hosted the left-wing Theater Union.[24]

Bragg, who succeeded Dietrich in 1938, was deeply involved in social issues in Minneapolis and in liberal politics. He chaired the Children's Protective Society board and worked with Minneapolis mayor Hubert Humphrey on a number of committees, including the Mayor's Council on Human Relations. He was active in the founding of the Unitarian Service Committee and spent every summer at the Boston headquarters of the American Unitarian Association, working on issues of displaced persons and medical missions in Europe in the years before America entered the war.[25]

Engla resonated with the Unitarian religious message that embraced the world and rejected the judgmental fire and brimstone of her youth, putting social action front and center. How different from the message in the Newfolden Mission Society! Engla officially joined FUS in 1943 and remained a member throughout her life.[26] She had to struggle to attend services regularly due to her work schedule and living situation. But in FUS and its humanist message, she had found a spiritual home.[27]

Not surprisingly, her mother was a staunch critic of Engla's Unitarian predilections. In her diary, Engla commented:

> There was Sunday for instance. I had a good, old Lutheran friend take me to the Unitarian church for services and home to dinner. I had accidentally left around a copy of the church bulletin. It mentioned the weekly square dances and instructions in square dancing. Mother was all set for us at the dinner table. . . . "What do you think of this church?" she flings at him. "Do you know that they dance there? . . . I want you to take E to the Billy Graham meeting and try to get other ideas into her head." . . . I wouldn't want to become further disturbed by going to hear a fanatical tirade on Billy's atrocious interpretation of the devil and hell and said so."

On her time off, Engla was learning about mental illness in her university coursework and exposed to the liberal Unitarian humanitarian perspective. She began to feel empowered to make suggestions for improvements. She was consistently rejected or ignored. She continued to speak her mind, and her supervisors considered her views insubordination or worse. Privately, she wrote about her frustrations:

Patients were awakened at night several times to help the night nurse clean the untidy patients. They also worked at more or less objectionable work all day long. In only one cottage in this institution, while I was there, did the patients who worked even harder than most of the attendants have a day a week off as the attendants did? I suggested to the supervisor of nurses in this other hospital that we give the workers afternoon lunch as a token of appreciation for their services. She said this would cost the state $200 a year. We attendants got together and out of our own meager salary furnished the lunch. It was pitiful to see how the patients appreciated this. They more than made it up to us by helping us with the work. Then we furnished some reading materials and brought our newspapers after we were through with them. They appreciated the newspapers most of all. They were anxious to read about the war and affairs of the world.

Engla's frustrations increased, but she held on to her dream of promotion. She took the civil service examinations and received Attendant 1, 2, 3, and 4 civil service ratings. She expected to be promoted to Attendant 2 and put in charge of a cottage. She knew the culture could only change with a position of leadership. She had seen it happen when she was given a chance:

I later for brief periods between graduate nurses had the opportunity to be in charge of cottages. The waxed floors were then scrubbed to eliminate the problem of fragile and confused patients falling and injuring themselves on the floor. Mechanical and chemical restraints were reduced to a minimum. The attendant will generally follow whoever is in charge. The most important thing, as I see it, is to get conscientious psychiatrically trained supervision. The underlings will usually follow, to the best of their ability.[28]

Despite her skill in relating to patients, or perhaps because of that ability, Nelson thwarted Engla's efforts. There would be no promotion. She told Engla, "The patients like you and when you run a cottage I must say it is run well but the charge nurses don't like you or the way you do things and when I promote someone to take charge of a cottage it will be one the other charge nurses like. This is the only way to have harmony on my staff."[29]

Superintendent Gardner could have overruled Nelson, but he chose not to do so. While he seemed sympathetic to Engla, he cautioned, "The life of a crusader is hard. You should learn to swallow a few things. It takes time to do things. You have to learn to go slow." Dr. Gardner, who never rocked any boats, retired to open a private practice treating "nervous disorders" in St. Paul in 1944.[30]

His successor, Dr. Edmund Miller, was even more impassive to Engla's concerns. Miller was an enormous man with a hands-off attitude. A young doctor who served at Anoka in the late 1940s recalled, "He was a huge man. I would say well over 300 pounds, so he was not very mobile and he spent most of his time in the office in administrative work, and did not get too involved in day-to-day patient care."[31] Shirley Lynch, a secretarial and administrative employee at Anoka for forty years, recalled Dr. Miller sitting in his office chair as if it were "a throne"; he had a large black dog that guarded the doorway, menacing all who walked by.[32]

Following Dr. Miller's arrival, Miss Nelson ratcheted up her war on Engla. At one point, she ordered, "Either you go to the TB or you leave." This was a serious threat. The tuberculosis cottage had poor infection control and attendants risked contracting the disease.[33]

Engla raised even more hackles in a letter to the *Minneapolis Tribune* in the fall of 1945. In response to a story about an orderly mistreating a mentally ill patient at Minneapolis General Hospital, she criticized the lack of qualifications for attendants in mental hospitals: "Since attendants have more intimate contact with the patients than any other employee in mental hospitals, one would assume that an attendant should have some scientific knowledge of the care and treatment of a patient under his supervision."[34] Such a public critique no doubt infuriated the "higher-ups" at Anoka and across the system.

Engla began experiencing bouts of severe migraine headaches from the stress, suffering episodes of misery where she lay helpless in the ward office while on the job. It was increasingly difficult for her to continue. An event in 1945 may have been the catalyst for her departure from Anoka. She wrote:

> When I came back from my vacation I found twenty-one senile women tied like dogs in a kennel on benches in two small bedrooms. The night nurse, Mrs. Hannah Anderson, who still works as an attendant in Anoka, was weeping. The charge nurse said to me, "There is nothing you can do about it, Miss Nelson likes it this way and I like it. That is all that is necessary." "What the patients like doesn't matter,"

I retorted. The charge nurse then said, "Mrs. Anderson, how do you like it?" Mrs. Anderson choked back her tears and said "It depends on what you think these institutions are run for, the convenience of the employees or the welfare of the patients." The following day the kind elderly Dr. Rogers came in. I followed him out of the door and pleaded with him to do something. I caught a tear glistening in his eye, as he shook his head and said, "I can't go over the supervisor of nurses' head." . . . Dr. Miller finally came over, looked at it and left without comment. Later while discussing my conflict with the supervisor of nurses, Dr. Miller said: "As an executive I will almost have to back up the supervisor of nurses." [35]

Blocked for promotion, harassed, threatened, and bereft of allies, Engla felt cornered. She decided to transfer to another Minnesota hospital in hopes of finding opportunities for promotion and additional special training with nursing affiliates. She wrote to superintendents at other institutions and haunted the office of Royal Gray, the chief of the Mental Health Unit at the Division of Public Institutions. She told Dr. Gray's assistant that she wanted to transfer to a more modern receiving hospital, and that she was interested in the rehabilitation of patients, not just custodial care. She described her education and course work and noted her interest in promotion to a higher classification in civil service for which she was qualified.[36]

Engla discovered that the superintendents controlled the system of transfers from hospital to hospital, and transfers were possible only with permission from the superintendent. They had a "code of honor" that discouraged recruiting attendants working in other hospitals. She also learned that there were no opportunities for advancement beyond the Attendant 1 classification in any of the hospitals, regardless of training or experience. The higher classifications intended for attendants had been, in practice, "reserved" for some categories of nurses only.[37] Male attendants did receive promotions, in large part because there were no male nurses with whom to compete.

Through her dogged efforts, Engla finally received an interview at Rochester State Hospital. The superintendent there, Dr. Magnus Petersen, was considered an enlightened administrator, at least compared to Dr. Miller. She wrote to Dr. Peterson and got a prompt reply. According to Engla, there were no "alibis about professional ethics between superintendents." Rochester was a receiving hospital, mental and physical treatment was provided, and its proximity to the Mayo Clinic assured the presence of well-trained physicians and nurses. Engla met with Mrs. Lorna Bullard, the nursing supervisor, and reported, "She was the first person I had met up to now who seemed interested in the professional courses I had had at the university."[38]

Although there were no opportunities for higher classification than

Women patients in straitjackets, euphemistically called camisoles, were tied to wooden benches with leather straps, bound at their ankles, and left unattended for hours at a time. Photograph by Arthur Hager, *Minneapolis Tribune*. Courtesy of the Minnesota Historical Society.

Attendant 1 at Rochester, Engla decided to take the job that she had to fight so hard to land. She had high hopes for greater opportunities for education and advancement there. She took a month off, moved into the Yngve home during the interim, and began work at Rochester State Hospital in late 1945.

FOUR

Spreading the Gospel

I had to do something about it or go mad.

■ *Engla Schey*

Engla was on the move again. She traveled the nearly ninety miles southeast from Minneapolis to Rochester in the late summer of 1945, through rolling green hills and farms with fields high with corn and soybeans. Rochester, no longer just a little railroad village, was a bustling town of twenty-nine thousand, nestled in a lovely valley on a fork of the Zumbro River. From the train station, Engla took the short cab ride to Rochester State Hospital on the outskirts of the city. The hospital was an immense and imposing structure of red brick. The tall tower of the central administration building, looking more like a college hall than a hospital, dominated the landscape for miles.[1]

Rochester State Hospital was a big operation, growing steadily since opening in 1879. When Engla arrived, there were nearly sixteen hundred patients. The grounds included seventeen hundred acres encompassing a large farm with orchards, field crops, and greenhouses. Patient labor supported canning and preserving of produce, raising and slaughtering cattle, along with tailoring and sewing, shops for blacksmith and carpentry, laundry, soap production, grounds keeping, and cleaning and cooking services for the inmates, administrators, and staff doctors.[2] Able patients also assisted the attendants. Unique to Rochester was a quarrying operation for limestone and gravel production situated on a sand bluff on the property. Male patients provided the backbreaking work in the quarry, and the revenue helped defray hospital expenses.[3]

Unlike Anoka, Rochester was a receiving hospital that admitted new patients, who were evaluated, diagnosed, and sent to the appropriate ward based on their behavior. The hospital had established a nursing school on the campus in 1889, one of the first mental hospitals in the nation to do so. Proximity to the Mayo Clinic provided greater access to physicians and nurses than was possible in Anoka. New staff quarters were constructed in 1938, allowing employees to have their own space on the campus.[4] Engla had been attracted to Rochester because of the opportunity for advanced education and the focus on treatment.

The Depression and the war had been hard on Rochester as it had on all the mental hospitals in Minnesota. The large building was over-crowded, outdated, and in significant disrepair.[5] Although better than at the other hospitals in many ways, Rochester's physician and nursing staff ratios did not meet the American Psychiatric Association's (APA) minimum requirements.[6] Nevertheless, Engla was impressed by con-ditions in the lower wards, where the most disturbed patients lived. One patient parlor had pictures on the walls and vases of flowers, all items not permitted in Anoka for fear of breakage. She was pleased that the ward also had drinking fountains, rolls of toilet paper in the lava-tories, and other amenities unheard of at Anoka. She also approved of the comparative freedom given to patients and the absence of chemi-cal restraining, the term used to describe drugs administered to keep patients in prolonged sleep. A few weeks after her arrival at Rochester, Engla telephoned the office of Dr. Royal Gray in the Department of Public Institutions (DPI) Mental Health Unit. She told Dr. Gray's assis-tant, "There is no comparison between the two institutions."[7]

Dr. Magnus C. Petersen was the superintendent at Rochester State Hospital. A Danish immigrant, Petersen was a formal man, ramrod straight, gracious and courtly. Trained in psychiatry at the University of Nebraska, he served as superintendent at Willmar State Hospital before coming to Rochester in 1942. He lived in the superintendent's home on the hospital grounds.[8] It was a large, impressive edifice with public rooms for entertaining and was well staffed by hospital patients.

Dependent on public funds, many superintendents engaged in the active promotion of both themselves and their institutions. The men-tal hospital system was entrenched in state budgets, but received lit-tle oversight. A superintendent's external role was to curry favor with the DPI and the politicians who made financial decisions for the state. Inside the institutions, however, they held absolute sway to run their institutions as they saw fit. Individual superintendents varied in their inclination and skill in managing the political environment, and also varied in the culture they chose to impose within their own hospitals.

Magnus C. Petersen was a man in charge. He abhorred outsiders meddling in the hospital's business. He saw himself as a benign leader. Petersen was well liked by the patients. In Engla's journal, upon her arrival at Rochester, she wrote that a patient had volunteered to her, "We are lucky to have a superintendent who speaks to us." Another patient had said, "Dr. P. sure is swell. [He] talked to me like I was somebody. I wasn't so scared any more." On her second day at Rochester, a local doctor told her, "This used to be a rough house before Dr. P came, but he put a stop to it in a hurry." Petersen was also politically effective. Unlike

Minnesota mental hospital leaders, circa 1949–50. From left: Dr. Royal Gray, Mental Health Unit of the State Division of Public Institutions (DPI); Carl Jackson, head of DPI; and Dr. Magnus C. Petersen, superintendent of Rochester State Hospital. Courtesy of the Minnesota Historical Society.

Dr. Ralph Rossen at Hastings, who disliked politics, or Dr. Walter P. Gardner at Anoka, who was ineffectual, Petersen was an ardent advocate for his hospital. He felt it was his responsibility to persuade politicians and bureaucrats to send more money by whatever means necessary. He knew how to work the system.

Petersen boasted of his political skills. Around the time of Engla's arrival, a legislative building committee was on its biennial tour to evaluate the needs of state institutions. The procedure, especially in the lean war years, was to "shine the place up" to impress the legislators at how wisely funds were being used. Engla had experienced such visits at Anoka, where the distinguished visitors were quickly steered to selected cottages that had been prepared for them, then whisked away to see the farm operations, more familiar territory for rural legislators. Dr. Petersen, however, decided to shock rather than impress his visitors. He arranged for an evening visit, waiting until patients were in bed, some needing a change of sheets, and then toured the committee members through dark, overcrowded, and smelly wards. Of this shocking tour, Petersen wrote that it was "just as exhausting to some of them as the midnight ride was to Paul Revere."[9]

■ ■ ■

During the first two decades of the twentieth century, psychiatry had little to offer mental patients. Medicine was expanding dramatically, with anesthesia, sterile techniques, X-rays, and the emergence of complex surgery.[10] Psychiatry, unlike medicine, had not advanced as rapidly, however. Training in psychiatry had lagged behind some of the other medical fields, in part because the science of the brain was rudimentary at best. Medical schools, including the University of Minnesota, added psychiatry to the regular curriculum as early as the 1890s, but it was offered in association with neurology in the Department of Nervous and Mental Diseases.[11] It was an uneasy alliance with neurology, however, because neurology was advancing knowledge of organic brain and nervous disorders, but there were few scientific treatments for "mental" disorders that showed no physical abnormalities.[12]

Most psychiatrists went to work in mental institutions. They were called alienists, and were truly alienated from their medical colleagues and the rest of society "keeping watch over inmates who had little hope of recovery."[13] Dr. Emil Kaepelin, one of the founders of the application of science to psychiatric research, noted in 1917: "We can rarely alter the course of mental illness. We must openly admit that the vast majority of patients placed in our institutions are forever lost."[1] Engla, who related to patients as people, saw firsthand how the feeling of hopelessness had, many years later, curdled into callousness, indifference, and often cruelty toward them.

Clifford Beers, an 1897 Yale graduate, spent three years (1900–1903) as a delusional patient in mental institutions in Connecticut, where he was beaten, restrained, and reviled by attendants. Following a spontaneous recovery, he began a quest to improve institutional conditions. In 1909 he formed the National Committee for Mental Hygiene with progressive reformers from the fields of psychiatry, medicine, and social work.[15] The term *mental hygiene* applied to the movement that viewed every patient as unique, and aimed to bring education about and prevention of mental illness into the community. → N ASW

Acute episodes would be treated in new psychopathic hospitals for short-term confinement. The committee reluctantly recognized that mental institutions were still necessary for chronic patients, though it recommended improvements in the institutions. Historian David Rothman argues that the superintendents could embrace the mental hygiene movement because it acknowledged a place for them in the new mental hygiene approach, thereby assuring their own continued existence.[16]

Many in academic psychiatry looked down on the mental institutions, and focused their research and training on acute short-term care. Mental hygiene advocates promoted psychopathic hospitals. The University of Minnesota struggled for eighteen years to get the state to fund a freestanding psychopathic hospital. The university settled for more limited funds that supported a unit with thirty-seven beds in the existing hospital. The first patient was admitted in 1937.[17]

■ ■ ■

Rochester's Superintendent Petersen strived to engage with the psychiatric profession and to be at the forefront of new ideas in the field. When he was superintendent of Willmar State Hospital he had been instrumental in the founding of the Minnesota Mental Hygiene Society, a state chapter of the national organization, in 1939. Dr. George Freeman, superintendent of St. Peter, was also involved, along with social workers and psychiatrists in private practice. Their stated goals mirrored those of the national organization, and included public education, prevention, and improvement in mental health services.[18]

Unlike some of the mental institutions that were isolated from major medical centers, Rochester State Hospital had a close relationship with the nearby Mayo Clinic for decades.[19] Mayo influenced Rochester's early adoption of some of the newer treatments for mental patients in the 1940s, primarily electroshock treatment and lobotomies.[20]

Dr. Frederick P. Moersch, a Mayo neurologist, had become familiar with convulsive therapy for the treatment of schizophrenia in Europe before World War II. He introduced electroshock and insulin shock at Mayo in May 1937. Shock treatments were subsequently employed at Rochester State Hospital.[21] Dr. Petersen had jumped on the new therapies bandwagon when he arrived at Rochester in 1942. In the 1944 *Biennial Report* he noted, "We have greatly extended the use of electroshock." Out of a total population of 1,500 to 1,600 patients, nearly 800 had received shock treatment, some with more than one course, and often on the day of admission.[22] Two years later, occurrences of shock treatment had increased even further: "We continue to use electroshock treatments—altogether we have treated 1,342 patients, with a total of 25,357 treatments administered."[23]

These are astounding statistics because the numbers imply that patients across the spectrum at Rochester received shock treatment regardless of the severity of their conditions. Electroshock at the time resulted in fractures, dislocated jaws, and chronic neck pain from the convulsions. The voltage to the brain was unregulated and was hit or miss in its power. Patients who received shock treatment were dazed and disoriented after the procedure. Repeated shocking led to permanent memory loss. While some patients were considered improved, many were permanently impaired.[24]

Dr. Petersen was also a big proponent of lobotomies, which he supported long after the procedure had been discredited. Dr. Walter Freeman, a neurologist and psychiatrist, had refined and promoted the procedure that involved cutting a patient's frontal lobes to relieve psychiatric disorders.[25] He later pioneered the transorbital lobotomy, in which an ice pick was inserted through the eye socket to damage the frontal lobes. In Dr. Freeman's early years as tireless advocate for the procedure, Petersen, then superintendent at Willmar, brought in a neurosurgeon who lobotomized forty-six patients in seventeen months starting in January 1941.[26]

The first lobotomies performed at Rochester occurred in 1941–42. In the 1944 *Biennial Report*, Petersen noted that there were fifty-eight prefrontal lobotomy operations at Rochester, with improved results "after better criteria for selection and slight modification of surgical procedure."[27] Two years later, he reported that 138 cases had been performed, with "improvements" that he found "gratifying."[28] Petersen encouraged the spread of lobotomy treatments to Hastings State Hospital, where Dr. Freeman performed several transorbital procedures.[29] Petersen's overzealous use of the operation, despite growing concerns about its safety or efficacy, caused him to come "near being cited before the ethics committee of the Minnesota State Medical Society, not so much for carrying out the procedure but for doing too many."[30]

As an attendant during the heyday of shock and lobotomy treatments at Rochester, Engla saw all this firsthand. Although she did write about some instances of severely violent and delusional patients relieved through lobotomy, she also saw patients whose emotional reactions were destroyed by the procedure, a cruel outcome. She also participated in marching hundreds of terrified patients through a long underground tunnel to the "shock room."

Petersen, like many doctors of his day, desperately wanted effective scientific treatments, and would only reluctantly admit any limitations of these new therapies. A more cynical view was that these procedures were effective means of punishment and control.[31] Lobotomy fell into disfavor and was generally abandoned in the 1950s. Electroshock, rebranded as ECT (electroconvulsive therapy), was also highly controversial and declined in use, although it has made a modest comeback for limited conditions. At a National Institutes of Health Consensus Conference to evaluate the procedure in 1985, David Rothman argued, "ECT stands practically alone among the medical/surgical interventions in that misuse was not the goal of curing but of controlling the patients for the benefits of the hospital staff."[32]

As her first year at Rochester wore on, Engla began to see similar systemic problems to those at Anoka, beyond the issues related to new treatments. There was serious overcrowding and understaffing. Conditions were so bad that it was hard to keep new staff. She noted in her journal:

I met a new attendant, Mrs. A. She was sick about overcrowded conditions, lack of adequate help and the sordid environment that patients had to live in. She had been unable to sleep, wept most of the night, and had been so emotionally upset about the whole business that she thought she would quit.

On the assaultive wards, there was no recreational therapy, no occupational therapy, and very little physiotherapy. The dayroom was filled with beds, so for most patients, there was no room for activities of any kind. Some wards had no night nurses or staff attendants. Patients were put in charge of these wards, and often they performed all the duties of attendants and nurses. Engla commented:

> The patients in charge of these wards who were not paid except as they shared the board and room with other patients were on duty quietly getting the more preoccupied patients up and dressed. I couldn't help seeing the contrast between their superior quiet dignified techniques as compared with the average attendants rough handling of patients. These are some of the things the public seldom hears about and probably would never believe.

Staff shortages meant limits on walks for patients, even in the lovely setting and on beautiful days. Engla noted:

> As I write I am sitting with my back to the mental hospital and my eyes towards the lovely hills and the gorgeous foliage on the huge trees. It is a warm lovely autumn day. But during the two hours I have sat here, I haven't seen any patients. They are all sitting inside on the stuffy crowded wards. It's a long time ago since sunshine and fresh air and outdoor exercise was recommended as having great therapeutic value for the mentally ill.

Worse still, she observed the same culture of cruelty toward patients that had plagued Anoka. The old "warhorses" frequently used the camisole and other restraints as punishment. Patients were belittled, cursed, ridiculed when they were incontinent, and called "lower than animals." She described one painful scene: "Patient H had an idea that she had no means of elimination and refused to eat. After trying forcibly to feed her she was put in a camisole over a muslin state nightgown and tied to the radiator. There she sat barefooted all day. She was forcibly tube fed twice."

Engla continued to use the skills she had developed over the years to manage patients. She described her efforts:

On the most assaultive ward, no student nurses assigned. Said they could be injured. There wasn't much I could do in self-defense with my 102# [pounds] if anyone should decide to mop me up. I had always maintained that the best weapon to use on any ward for protection was rapport. I had great confidence in this weapon and had no fear. . . . I was not afraid of these people because I had learned from past experiences that patients like dogs and cats seem to instinctively sense who is for and against them. "They know you're for them," a doctor in another institution had told me. "This is why they don't attack you as they do some of the attendants."

The dilapidated shower rooms at Rochester State Hospital also served as storage closets for mops, brooms, and chairs. Showers had no towels or soap unless supplied by the attendant, and the patients' clothing was tied in a bundle and handed back as they exited. Courtesy of the History Center of Olmsted County.

Engla urgently wanted to get advanced psychiatric nursing skills, and waited over a year for her chance. She was elated when Dr. Petersen personally gave her permission to take a training class with the nurses:

> The great day had at last arrived, but still I had a premonition some-thing would go wrong at the last minute. But how could it? The Superintendent had told the director of psychiatric nursing that he was in favor of letting me take the three months course in psychiatry given the student nurses. There was no problem with prerequisites even though I was not a graduate nurse. I had more university cred-its in mental hygiene and related subjects than the average student in the class. The year before the supervisor of nurses had said she couldn't spare me from the ward. "Can I report to class?" I asked the head of psychiatric nursing on the ward.

This time around, Engla was allowed to attend the first class. Then she discovered she had been scheduled to work during class hours. When she complained, she was told she was needed on the ward and could only attend class when off duty, making it impossible for her to partici-pate. It was a bitter blow.

Engla's frustration grew. Rochester was better than Anoka, but still full of problems. She lamented: "the patient lingering in a living hell in a mental hospital, deprived of their life, liberty and pursuit of happiness reminds me of someone who has fallen in a well and all around him people go about minding their own business and refusing to look into the well." She began by trying to work from within. No one inside the system seemed willing to look down the well. Engla approached them all. The caste system within the hospitals was impervious to her quest for improvements. Attendants were the lowest caste with no job secu-rity or influence. The good ones left, and the worst among them often took out their frustration on patients. She believed that nurses had all been "carefully taught to keep their place." Many nurses and attendants were ashamed of where they worked too. "It seemed to be the consen-sus of opinion among many that no one who could get a job anywhere else would work in a mental hospital."

She continued fearlessly to approach doctors and nursing leaders within the system. The caste system was so rigid that Engla could get little respect or response from them. She wrote bitterly:

The professions apparently couldn't have any truck with non-professionals like me. "Who are you anyway" seemed to be the attitude—"just an attendant in a mental hospital—Who do you think you are? What do you know about mental illness and patients? You're just wasting your time—who would ever listen to an attendant? Now if you were a nurse it would be different. People listen to nurses. Its just a lot of tom-foolishness for a non-professional to work on things that are professional."

Engla even went up the chain of command to leaders in the political system. She called upon Dr. Walter P. Gardner, who had retired from Anoka in 1944, hoping he would take up the cause. No such luck:

> He was in private psychiatric practice now and I assumed would not have anything to lose from an economic and social point of view if he would lend his influence in interpreting the cause for the terrible conditions in Minnesota, which I think is the lazy lacksidazical [*sic*] attitude of the political administrations and politically dominated division of public institutions. He sang me the same old theme song that he tried to lull me to sleep with when I worked as an attendant in his state hospital. "Well, we have to restrain them when we have so little help. We can't do any better until we get more and better trained help." "Hell, what's the use to fool around with psychiatrists and nurses" I said to myself. "It will take too long if we are going to depend on them."

Fearless, Engla went to the top. She made an appointment with the deputy director of the Division of Public Institutions. Dr. George Orr had been appointed in 1939 as the number-two man. He was a dentist by training, but had chaired Governor Stassen's election committee in 1938.[33] That was apparently his qualification for the job. Her account of the meeting was chilling:

> I never could figure out how being a dentist could qualify one for next to the highest authority in the state on mental hospitals. However, I never understood politics generally. Maybe politicians are supermen and understand all about mental illness and management of mental hospitals without having to spend years in preparation and training for their work as the average man had to do, I said to myself....

I told this dentist about the abuses that existed in the state institution I worked in at the time. The excessive use of morphine, sodium amytal and other drugs they were needlessly subjected to. I told him how patients were pushed around, insulted, talked down to, and tied down because of the untrained nurses and almost illiterate attendants that worked in that hospital. . . .

I sat there petrified at his stupid remarks about how insane people have to be "drugged and tied down for their protection." Finally he began to stroke his hands. I sat there and stared at him. So this is the standard of training the people in the state thinks sufficient to put in charge of mental patients I thought. Any politician will do. Well, there wasn't any point in wasting my breath talking to the Division of Public Institutions then—that seemed obvious. Finally he said, "Now what do you want me to do. Let these people run loose and kill each other?" There was no sense in talking to a man so illiterate about mental illness anymore. I thanked him for listening to me and went out.

The apathy of the public, including those with relatives in the institutions, was particularly frustrating. From Engla's point of view:

Relatives of patients won't show their interest because they are afraid someone might find out that there is mental illness in their family. The taxpayers who support these institutions leave it up to the politicians to run them. They never come in here to see how the mental patients are treated. They stay away from mental hospitals as if they were houses of prostitution. In fact it is more of a disgrace to have been in a mental hospital than an inmate in a house of ill fame.

What an act of courage and persistence it was to go all the way to the top with her concern! How challenging for a woman of intelligence, compassion, and action to confront relentless complacency, and to be dismissed as too lowly to be heard.

Change was in the wind, however, and coming from an unexpected source—conscientious objectors (COs) of World War II.[34] In the period immediately before the war, traditional peace churches—including Quakers, Mennonites, and the Brethren—advocated for alternatives to conscription in the armed forces. President Roosevelt signed the Selective Training and Service Act in September 1940. The act included provisions allowing those with religious objections or belief to be assigned to noncombatant service, or if opposed to noncombatant service, to be assigned "to work of national importance under civilian direction." A subsequent executive order allowed the Selective Service authority to determine the work and prescribe the rules and regulations. The Civilian Public Service (CPS) program was born.[35]

Over the course of the war, 10 million men were drafted, and 37,000 were exempted under the 1940 act. Of these, 25,000 served as noncombatants and 11,996 performed alternative service in the CPS.[36] At the start of the program, the men were assigned to work camps that included forestry service and soil conservation activities. Selective Service wanted these men out of sight, given the widespread public hostility to this small minority who refused to fight.

However, as Alex Sareyan, former CO and scholar of the movement wrote, "As the nation became almost totally absorbed in its commitment to World War II, serious disruptions began to be felt in the delivery of services to the nearly 600,000 persons confined in America's public mental institutions."[37] In 1942 the Selective Service approved "special service units" allowing COs to serve in hospitals, mental hospitals, and training schools that faced labor shortages when staff were drafted or left to take higher-paying jobs in the wartime economy. The first CPS unit of COs arrived at Eastern State Hospital in Virginia in June 1942. Overall, sixty-one institutions benefited from CPS men over the course of the war. None of these hospitals were in Minnesota.[38]

This labor pool of COs was significantly different from the population from which male attendants were generally drawn, especially the "bughouse drifters," who were rough and prone to violence toward patients.[39] The COs as a group came from humanitarian, pacifist churches and had been raised idealistically to have compassion for all. They were also better educated than most army recruits, and clearly more educated than the attendants, as there were few if any credentials required. Sareyan observed: "At the time of their induction, many of the men had been employed as teachers at the high school or college level. Quite a few had been trained as research scientists, lawyers, artists, and musicians and in other similar professions."[40]

It is not surprising that the COs assigned to mental hospitals found the cruel treatment of patients in deprived living conditions intolerable. Deeply troubled by what they witnessed firsthand, the COs began to communicate with each other and collectively document the abuses. As early as 1943, a small group assigned to Cleveland State Hospital reported to local religious leaders the serious mistreatment, including beatings, excessive restraint, and isolation, that they witnessed there. The abuses became public through stories in the local press. Widespread publicity, grand jury investigations, and indictments followed. At the request of the state of Ohio, however, the CPS unit was closed, the men were reassigned elsewhere, and much of the furor died down thereafter.[41] These COs learned the limits of sensationalism as opposed to lasting institutional change.

Another activist CO group formed at the Philadelphia State Hospital. Called Byberry for the neighborhood in which it was located, the facility had 6,100 patients and was the second-largest institution of its kind in the country. It was here that four COs, Willard Hetzel, Harold (Hal) Barton, Philip Steer, and Leonard Edelstein, developed a plan to reform the mental hospital system.[42] With the permission of the CPS, they created the Mental Hygiene Program (MHP) within the CPS. The only official constraint was that the MHP work under the supervision of medical experts.

The MHP's first goal was to print a newsletter and develop training manuals for attendants and other staff. The introductory issue of the *Attendant,* their quarterly newsletter, appeared in May 1944. This was the first time anyone had paid attention to the attendants, like Engla, who performed the day-to-day work at mental hospitals. By October 1944, CPS allowed the MHP men to work full-time on the project. In 1945–46, as the war was concluding, the MHP group began traveling to other CPS units serving in mental hospitals, gathering information and sharing their materials. They worked on training handbooks for attendants and public relations materials to educate the public about conditions around the country.[43]

May 1946 was a pivotal month for COs. On May 6, *Life,* the popular and widely circulated magazine, published "Bedlam 1946: Most U.S. Mental Hospitals Are a Shame and a Disgrace."[44] The COs had participated directly in the development of the article. CO Justin Reese accompanied *Life* reporter Albert Q. Maisel on his tour of hospitals in preparation for the story. The article relied on data collected by the three thousand COs who had worked as mental hospital attendants. The text and pictures documented beatings, starvation, slave labor, mistreatment, drugging, and excessive restraint. "Hundreds are confined in 'lodges'—bare, bed less rooms reeking with filth and feces—by day lit only through half-inch holes in steel-plated windows, by night merely black tombs in which the cries of the insane echo unheard from the peeling plaster of the walls."[45] Maisel cast blame on the states: "Through public neglect and legislative penny-pinching, state after state has allowed its institutions for the care and cure of the mentally sick to degenerate into little more than concentration camps on the Belsen pattern."[46] This was an incredibly damning indictment as the horrors of the Holocaust were now known to the world.

Other publicity followed in some local press, articles in the widely circulated *Reader's Digest,* books, and even a movie.[47]

The COs wanted more than publicity, however. MHP leaders decided to create a national organization to ensure continuation of their work after the war. Information about the COs had begun to reach important people throughout the nation, including former first lady Eleanor Roosevelt, Supreme Court justice Owen J. Roberts, and author Pearl S. Buck among other prominent figures. On the same day as the *Life* exposé, the *Philadelphia Inquirer* officially announced the formation of the National Mental Health Foundation:

> NMHF has arisen both as a cause and as a challenge toward permitting the public a larger place in this problem. The Foundation is a citizens' lay organization based upon democratic principles. It endeavors to inform the public of conditions in state hospitals, to improve these conditions, and in various other ways to improve the lot of the mentally ill.[48]

While the NMHF board was made up of luminaries, former COs from the MHP filled the administrative positions in the new organization. Harold Barton, one of the founders of the CPS mental health program, ran the education division. With the assistance of a psychiatric and nursing advisory board, he developed a series of popular leaflets on mental health. The *Attendant* journal was renamed *Psychiatric Aid* (later *Aide*), "reflecting the goal to upgrade the status of direct-care staff with a proper title and training requirements." Circulation soared from 1,446 to double that in six months.[49] The *Handbook for Psychiatric Aides*, described as Barton's pride, was a widely distributed orientation manual for all institutional employees.[50]

The NMHF also developed a wide range of public relations materials, including entertaining radio programs designed specifically to create new and better attitudes among the public. There was demand for

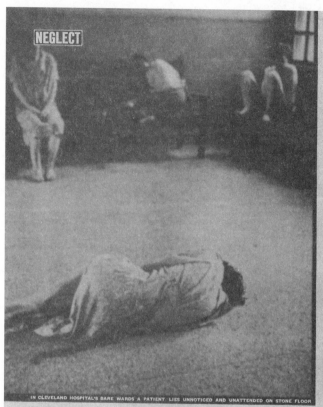

NEGLECT

IN CLEVELAND HOSPITAL'S BARE WARDS A PATIENT LIES UNNOTICED AND UNATTENDED ON STONE FLOOR

THIS CLEVELAND STATE HOSPITAL BUILDIN

BEDLAM
1946

MOST U.S. MENTAL HOSPITALS
ARE A SHAME AND A DISGRACE
by ALBERT Q. MAISEL

The author of this article, through his previous writing and his testimony before a congressional committee, helped instigate important improvements in the Veterans Administration's mental hospitals. The Ohio photographs were taken by Jerry Cooke with the permission of Frazier Reams, Ohio State Commissioner of Public Welfare, and the cooperation of the Ohio Mental Hygiene Association, an affiliate of The National Committee for Mental Hygiene.

In Philadelphia the sovereign Commonwealth of Pennsylvania mair a dilapidated, overcrowded, undermanned mental "hospital" know Byberry. There, on the stone wall of a basement ward appropriately k as the "Dungeon," one can still read, after nine years, the five-word le "George was kill here 1937."

This pitiful memorial might apply quite as well to hundreds of Georges in mental institutions in almost every state in the Unio Pennsylvania is not unique. Through public neglect and legislative p pinching, state after state has allowed its institutions for the care an of the mentally sick to degenerate into little more than concentr camps on the Belsen pattern.

Court and grand-jury records document scores of deaths of patien lowing beatings by attendants. Hundreds of instances of abuse, fallin short of man-slaughter, are similarly documented. And reliable evic from hospital after hospital, indicates that these are but a tiny fract the beatings that occur, day after day, only to be covered up by a conspiracy of mutually protective silence and a code that ostracize ployes who "sing too loud."

Yet beatings and murders are hardly the most significant of the nities we have heaped upon most of the 400,000 guiltless patient-pris of over 180 state mental institutions.

We feed thousands a starvation diet, often dragged further belo low-budget standard by the withdrawal of the best food for the staff c rooms. We jam-pack men, women and sometimes even children into dred-year-old firetraps in wards so crowded that the floors cannot be between the rickety cots, while thousands more sleep on ticks, on bla or on the bare floors. We give them little and shoddy clothing at Hundreds—of my own knowledge and sight—spend 24 hours a d stark and filthy nakedness. Those who are well enough to work slave in many institutions for 12 hours a day, often without a day's re

"Bedlam 1946: Most U.S. Mental Hospitals Are a Shame and a Disgrace," *Life*, May 6, 1946. Conscientious objectors in World War II who were assigned to mental hospitals provided information for this article that informed the American public about conditions in hospitals across the country. Author's collection.

RESTRAINT

RESTRAINT

ECTED IN 1885, METAL SCREENS BAR WINDOWS   THIS WOMAN WEARS A CAMISOLE WITH SLEEVES TIED BEHIND HER. ULCERS ON LEG ARE UNBANDAGED

ears on end. One man at Cleveland, Ohio—and he is no isolated excep-
on—worked in this fashion for 19 solid years on a diet the poorest share-
ropper would spurn.

Thousands spend their days—often for weeks at a stretch—locked in
evices euphemistically called "restraints": thick leather handcuffs, great
anvas camisoles, "muffs," "mitts," wristlets, locks and straps and
straining sheets. Hundreds are confined in "lodges"—bare, bedless
ooms reeking with filth and feces—by day lit only through half-inch holes
1 steel-plated windows, by night merely black tombs in which the cries of
he insane echo unheard from the peeling plaster of the walls.

Worst of all, for these wards of society we provide physicians, nurses
nd attendants in numbers far below even the minimum standards set by
ate rules. Institutions that would be seriously undermanned even if not
vercrowded find themselves swamped with 30%, 50% and even 100%
ore patients than they were built to hold. These are not wartime condi-
ons but have existed for decades. Restraints, seclusion, and con-
tant drugging of patients become essential in wards where one attendant
aust herd as many as 400 mentally deranged charges.

Paid wages insufficient to attract able personnel, even by prewar stand-
rds, and often working 10- and 12-hour days, these medical staffs have
lmost ceased (with some significant exceptions) to strive for cures. Many
ave resigned themselves, instead, to mere custodial care on a level that
d one governor to admit that "our cows in the hospital barns get better
are than the men and women in the wards."

Thus thousands who might be restored to society linger in man-made
ells for a release that comes more quickly only because death comes
aster to the abused, the beaten, the drugged, the starved and the neglected.
n some mental hospitals, for example, tuberculosis is 13 times as common
s in the population at large.

Such conditions cannot be explained away as a result of wartime per-

sonnel shortages; the war merely accentuated long-existing failings. Most
hospitals have never had enough personnel, even by their own low sched-
ules. Wages have always been desperately low. Even a year before Pearl
Harbor we had already crowded 404,293 patients into buildings built to
hold only 365,192.

Nor can any of these horrors be excused on the grounds of "common
practice" or as "the best that can be done for the insane." For some states
have managed to eliminate overcrowding. Some states discharge, as cured
or improved, three and four times as high a proportion of patients as
others. A few, notably tiny Delaware, have managed to secure an adequate
or nearly adequate number of doctors, nurses and attendants.

Even within individual states some outstanding superintendents have
managed to raise their institutions to a decent level despite low pay scales
and heavy overloads. By ingenuity, leadership and hard work some have
succeeded not merely in discountenancing beatings and restricting the use
of restraints and solitary confinement but in eliminating these relics of the
dark ages entirely.

The sad and shocking fact, however, is that these exceptions are few and
far between. The vast majority of our state mental institutions are dreary,
dilapidated excuses for hospitals, costly monuments to the states' betrayal
of the duty they have assumed to their most helpless wards.

Charges such as these are far too serious to be based solely upon the
observations of any single investigator. But there is no need to do so. In
addition to my own observations in a dozen hospitals, in addition to court
records and the reports of occasional investigating commissions, there is
now available for the first time a reliable body of data covering nearly
one third of all the state hospitals in 20 states from Washington to Virginia,
from Maine to Utah. A by-product of the war's aggravation of the long-existing personnel shortage, this data represents the collated reports of more
than 3,000 conscientious objectors who, under Selective Service, volun-

CONTINUED ON PAGE 105   103

these programs, and by mid-1947, the NMHF had completed *The Tenth Man*, a thirteen-episode radio program, designed to stimulate the public's interest in local mental health services.[51]

The NMHF also prodded the American Psychiatric Association (APA) to speak out. In October 1946, the organization issued a statement:

> The Association called on its entire membership, including state mental hospital superintendents, to call forcefully to the attention of the public and their legislators all of the shortcomings and deficiencies in state hospitals, and to demand the assistance and backing necessary to maintain mental hospitals in fact as well as in name.[52]

The efforts of the NMHF caught the attention of the president of the United States. In July 1946, Harry Truman sent a letter of commendation to the Honorable Owen J. Roberts, chairman of the NMHF, sharing the concern for the "ever-increasing number of mental patients needing hospital care" and the "effort of your organization in seeking to improve the quality of psychiatric aides and attendants throughout the country."[53] That same month, President Truman signed the National Mental Health Act, the first entry of the federal government into the field. Calling mental illness the "nation's number one health problem," the act created the National Advisory Mental Health Council and promised to increase research, training of personnel, and mental health services.[54]

One might conclude, that with all this national activity, conditions in mental institutions would rapidly change in Minnesota and elsewhere. Because mental health was the responsibility of each state, change occurred at the state level. In Minnesota, entrenched bureaucracy and an uninformed and unsympathetic public were significant barriers to reform. The COs found that sensational press was never enough. A ground game "in the trenches," as it were, was required.

Engla had been fighting a one-woman trench war since 1939. For seven years, she had encountered complacency, intransigence, and hostility in the mental health institutions of Minnesota. Once Engla caught wind of the NMHF, she jumped on the bandwagon. She worked to get the informational materials into the hands of the public. She also tried to get the organization's *Handbook* and newsletters designed for institutional personnel into their hands as well. Most importantly, the NMHF provided Engla with moral support. For the first time, she had an ally with important connections and credibility to help her fight for her cause.

For Engla, 1946 was a heady year. She became the NMHF's key link in Minnesota and was in frequent contact with Harold Barton, who sent her literature and contacts. In her journal, she noted, "Talking to a nurse who said, 'I was in Philadelphia and I saw a chap from NMHF.' He said, 'We have someone from Minnesota' and we both said in unison—'Engla Schey'. I felt good and important."

Her passion became, as she christened it, "spreading the gospel of NMHF." After fourteen years in the Salvation Army, she knew how to spread a gospel! Engla had always been a crusader, but now she had support for her cause. Having given up on insiders, she identified liberal churches like her own First Unitarian Society in Minneapolis, organized labor, and writers as the key forces to mobilize the public.

Engla was incredibly active in the summer and fall of 1946. With the NMHF on her side, she approached all levels of employees in the hospitals. She fought to get the literature from the NMHF into the institutions, and she called the DPI to get the central office to promote the sale of the *Psychiatric Aide* and furnish the *Handbook* to all new attendants. She informed the office of Dr. Gray in DPI's Mental Health Unit that the information was important and that Raymond Bragg, her minister, would try to obtain funds for the NMHF to "see to it that the literature is distributed."

The professionals threatened attendants like Engla who became activists. One of the old warhorses told her, "The state draws them from such a low economic and social group that losing their job would be a major catastrophe." Engla responded, "We attendants don't need to be scared anymore. Thanks to the 3,000 conscientious objectors that worked in mental hospitals during the war, we now have the powerful NMHF that we can join forces with and march with on to victory."

Engla's journals in this period document her activity with outside organizations. While working her grueling shifts at Rochester, she found time to communicate frequently with the NMHF. She mailed the organization's literature to influential contacts in the Twin Cities, urging them "to join hands with NMHF to educate the public about mental illness and conditions." Engla hitchhiked into the Cities and brought literature to the office of the *Public Employee*, a union newspaper, calling on the union to demand in-service training for attendants. She visited the Volunteers of America, spoke out at a labor convention of institutional employers, and visited a county welfare agency and a union for hospital employees. She lobbied a Catholic priest, a Lutheran Sunday school, and even buttonholed strangers she met hitchhiking to the Twin Cities on her days off. Her journal reflected a new tone of empowerment:

> They won't like to get labor/liberal groups in on their racket. But they asked for it. If they showed any inclination to clean things up we'd sit around and wait awhile. They have ignored it long enough. Our patience is wearing out—It was after trying in vain to get some action from psychiatrists and the professions that I finally turned to this liberal humanitarian church, writers and organized labor.

Engla believed writers could have a major influence on public awareness, and she aspired to become a writer herself. She sent articles to the NMHF describing the conditions patients endured, and the "slave labor" they were forced to perform.[55] Engla met with Meridel Le Sueur, a well-known left-wing writer in the Twin Cities, to help her with her own work. Le Sueur, an ardent feminist and socialist, published prolifically from the late 1920s until the end of World War II. After the war, she was harassed and blacklisted by many of her publishers, and turned to freelance teaching for income. She called this period "her dark time."[56] Bragg, who had served on the advisory committee of a left-wing theater group with Le Sueur in the 1930s, undoubtedly made the connection between the two women.[57] Engla recalled:

> I got a letter from Meridel Le Sueur inviting me to meet her at 4 pm in St. Paul Oct 7. She was beginning classes in short story structure. She would talk with me about the two manuscripts I had sent her. I was elated. If such a busy woman in the midst of novel writing will take time out to see me I must have something after all. I thought she had said she would like to teach structure to people who had a social message the world needed to know—I felt sure I had such a message.

At the meeting, Le Sueur told Engla that while she got favorable comments on Engla's articles, they didn't sell. "Writing was a highly professional skill like figure skating. One couldn't learn it in 6 months." Engla, who had been a lifelong private journal writer, vowed to continue her journals and to submit articles about her experiences to magazines. There was a list of submissions—and rejections—in the flyleaf of one of her journals. There is no evidence that she ever did get her articles published.

In October 1946, Engla was invited to the Minnesota Unitarian Conference (MUC), the fifty-ninth annual gathering of all Unitarians and other liberal churches in the state. Its purpose was to "foster religion through organization and support of liberal churches and educational and other activities to that end." The conclave was set for October 17–19, 1946, at Camp Ihduhapi, a YMCA facility west of Minneapolis in Maple Plain.

Through Bragg, Engla undoubtedly knew that mental health would be on the agenda, and he personally encouraged her to attend. She saw an opportunity to distribute NMHF literature and, though it was challenging to get the time off, she succeeded. She wrote to Harold Barton, "I can think of no better soil to sow the literature in than a Unitarian Conference."

Engla hitchhiked up to Minneapolis, then rode the bus to Maple Plain, where shuttles ferried participants to the YMCA camp. As she arrived in the evening, the setting sun illuminated the glistening lake, surrounded by maples vibrant with golden and crimson leaves. The pastoral setting was far from the chaos and stress of her life on the wards. She had the excitement of a crusader. She had trod a long hard road from Newfolden and her pietistic roots to this meeting of liberal church people to plead the cause of mental hospital reform. She yearned for reform, not just for her beloved father, but also on behalf of all fifteen thousand people residing in Minnesota's institutions. She did not foresee that this meeting would be a turning point in Minnesota history.

FIVE

The Modest Visionary

Even as a young mother must have invincible patience with
her bawling babe, refusing to get angry and insisting on
learning instead what is the cause of all this grief, so must we
listen . . . in a way that can help bring as prompt a correction
of wrongs . . . as is humanly possible.

■ *Arthur Foote,* Taking Down the Defenses

The morning of October 18, 1946, dawned crisp and cool at
Camp Ihduhapi, the rising sun illuminating the colorful foliage of the
maple trees. On this day, more than one hundred Unitarians had gathered for the Fifty-Ninth Minnesota Unitarian Conference (MUC). As participants emerged from their cabins and walked toward the rustic, log-
sided lodge, there was a palpable feeling of excitement among them. The
war was finally over. A new era was beginning.

The Reverend Arthur Foote from St. Paul's Unity Church joined the
throng. Foote, thirty-five years old, was boyishly handsome, with rich
brown eyes and thick dark hair. Just eighteen months into his ministry, he had been elected vice-chairman of the MUC in 1945 and he was
scheduled to lead the morning service.

As Foote strode energetically up the path, he reflected on the contrast between 1945 and 1946. The MUC Conference in the fall of 1945,
in deference to wartime and with limited funds, was only a one-day
meeting at Unity Church.[1] The Great Depression and World War II
had significantly depleted resources and demoralized congregations.
Membership in Unitarian churches across the nation fell.[2] As Foote
later opined, the denomination was "rent with theological controversy,
and seemed badly bogged down with dwindling membership and lag-
ging enthusiasm."[3]

Minnesota was no exception. Out of a state population of two and a half million, there were just twenty-five hundred people who identified as Unitarians in 1945.[4] The two strongest congregations were the First Unitarian Society in Minneapolis and Unity in St. Paul. Though both experienced decreased membership during the Depression and World War II, each had remained large enough to stay afloat.[5] The smaller churches in Duluth, Willmar, Underwood, and Hanska struggled, some unsuccessfully, to survive.[6]

The MUC meeting in 1946 was poised to move beyond its traditional focus on religious and organizational issues. During the Depression, American Unitarian Association (AUA) president Frederick May Eliot led a team that devised a postwar revitalization program under the banner "Unitarian Advance."[7] With this program, the denomination would expand by making a difference in the world. The AUA encouraged congregations to take action as Unitarians. "Mankind is buying with its blood and agony, the chance to build a better world. Let

Reverend Arthur Foote, circa 1945. Courtesy of the Minnesota Historical Society.

us begin to build it. The time of opportunity is now."[8] Minnesota Unitarians were exposed to the program through a widely circulated pamphlet titled *Dynamic of Unitarian Advance,* a call to action from Dr. Winfred Overholser, a prominent psychiatrist and respected Unitarian.[9]

Unitarian Advance caused trepidation, particularly among parishioners from Unity Church. Unity had a different history from its more activist brethren across the river in Minneapolis. Traditional Unitarians from New England formed Unity Church in 1872. As early as 1876, Reverend William Channing Gannett, the godson of the famed Unitarian leader William Ellery Channing, arrived at Unity. He was an ardent abolitionist and women's suffragist. His statement of belief, "Things Commonly Believed among Us," joined traditional Unitarian Christians and the more liberal theists.[10] Unity Church retained some Christian traditions while being tolerant of a range of beliefs, but did not go as far as FUS by rejecting theism and embracing humanism.

Unity did not carry its theological liberalism into political controversies as FUS did either. As a more traditional church, Unity was stable and grew quietly, particularly under Frederick May Eliot's leadership from 1917 to 1937. In the tumultuous 1930s, Unity maintained a more reserved stance toward church involvement in liberal or left-wing social and economic causes.[11]

The political reticence of Unity's congregation surfaced when Reverend Wallace Robbins replaced Eliot, who left to lead the AUA in 1937. Robbins's outspoken pacifism and his role as a "great agitator" and civil rights activist divided the congregation.[12] Church members did not share Robbins's controversial positions, and he was forced to leave in 1944.[13] The congregation selected Arthur Foote in 1945 with the expectation that he could heal its wounds. At the time of the 1946 MUC Conference, Foote had been on the job for only eighteen months. His inclusive theological stance reassured the congregation, as did his patient manner and insistence on civil discourse. At this point, some felt Unitarian Advance might lead back into political waters.

In the spring of 1946, the MUC planning committee began to design a meeting to inspire Unitarians to social action. The participants included Raymond Bragg, Foote, and several others.[14] There is no extant record of their conversations regarding possible projects to pursue, but Bragg probably initiated the possibility of mental hospital reform. Though they were all undoubtedly aware of the controversy in the national press, there had been no exposés of institutional failings in Minnesota.[15]

Bragg knew better. He had worked with Dr. Overholser on the Unitarian Service Committee, the humanitarian arm of the AUA active during the war.[16] Overholser was the superintendent at St. Elizabeth's Hospital, a federal mental institution in Washington, D.C. He was known for his efforts to improve patient care and as an advocate for mentally ill patients accused of crimes. And, of course, Bragg was familiar with the NMHF and had helped Engla finance distribution of its literature.

Word was out that Bragg was planning to move to Boston to head the Unitarian Service Committee. His departure meant that Foote would lead any effort under Unitarian Advance. Bragg was not yet sure what Foote's commitment to an activist agenda or his skills in that role might be. As the attendees gathered at the lodge, Engla, with a bulging bag of NMHF materials at her feet, eyed Reverend Foote. No doubt she, along with others in the conference pondered, Who is this young, serious newcomer from "out east," and what can we expect from him?

■ ■ ■

Given his upbringing and temperament, Foote was not likely to be a social activist. He came from a long tradition of genteel New England Unitarians. His ancestors were among those who broke with the harsh Calvinism at the end of the eighteenth century, questioning fundamental tenets including the concept of the Trinity (hence the later name "Unitarian"), original sin, and eternal punishment.[17] They did not reject Christianity but, influenced by liberal thinkers like John Locke and Isaac Newton, they saw reason and tolerance as the underpinnings of religious faith. Their benign view of a loving God led naturally to a focus on love toward one's fellow human beings.[18]

In the 1820s, the charismatic and popular Reverend William Ellery Channing set forth the foundation of Unitarian principles—belief in the goodness of God, Christ as a moral example, and love for all people.[19] By the mid-1820s, one-third of Congregational churches in New England were avowedly Unitarian, including most of the wealthiest and prestigious ones. As Harriet Beecher Stowe recalled, at the time of her father's arrival in Boston in 1826:

> Calvinism or orthodoxy was the despised and persecuted form of faith . . . where once it had held court. . . . Unitarianism reigned in its

stead. . . . All the literary men of Massachusetts were Unitarian. All
the trustees and professors of Harvard College were Unitarians. All
the élite of wealth and fashion crowded Unitarian churches.[20]

The theological tenet of people's inherent goodness inspired social reforms to make the world a better place. Early Unitarian reformers included Horace Mann, who created the first statewide system of public
schools and teachers colleges in Massachusetts; Samuel Gridley Howe,
who crusaded for the blind; and Joseph Tuckerman, who worked to help
the poor in Boston. During this time, Dorothea Dix led a one-woman
fight across the nation for improved care for the mentally ill.[21] The
Foote family lived near Boston in Salem, Massachusetts, and traveled
in Unitarian social and religious circles, but did not engage in reform
efforts. They concentrated on gentility, modesty, self-improvement, hard
work, and tolerance of others.[22]

Foote's grandfather Henry Wilder Foote I (1838–1889) and his father, Henry Wilder Foote II (1875–1964), became Unitarians ministers.
Both were quiet, cautious, and modest men cut from the Channing
cloth and Boston through and through. Henry Wilder Foote I, longtime
minister at King's Chapel, a prestigious Boston Unitarian church, led a
quiet faith-filled life. During the Civil War, when many fellow religion-
ists stood on the ramparts as abolitionists, he declined to take a stand,
though his church did raise funds for wounded Union soldiers.[23]

His son, Henry Wilder Foote II, followed a similar path. The Unitarian denomination grew more liberal as it moved westward, pressing for
a more inclusive and less creedal church.[24] At the start of his career,
Henry Foote II served two churches outside New England. Arthur was
born in Michigan in 1911, but the Foote family returned to the Boston
area in 1913 and remained firmly rooted in the New England Unitarian
tradition.[25] The family was financially comfortable and lived graciously,
with a lovely home in Cambridge and a seaside cottage in Maine.

Foote's father tried assiduously to pass on his values to his children, defined as a life of integrity and honor embodied in New England
Unitarianism, and expressed in the family as modesty, tolerance, dili-
gence, and goodness. In the last two generations, the choice of the
Unitarian ministry was the way to live out these values, and thus became part of the family tradition as well. With his two brothers either
not interested in, or unsuited to, the cloth, Arthur, the dutiful son, was
the likely choice.[26]

A shy child with a pronounced stammer, his prep school headmaster described young Arthur as "thoroughly dependable, capable and willing to do good work."[27] He received only "gentlemen's Cs" at Harvard, ran track, and had no strong professional vocation. Despite his concern that his stammer would impede him, but with his father's strong urging, Foote chose to enter the ministry.[28]

His teenage romance with Rebecca Clark, the lively harbormaster's daughter from Southwest Harbor, Maine, was Foote's early and perhaps only act of rebellion against his family. He firmly resisted their dogged efforts to discourage his relationship with a country girl from a respectable but working-class family. Love prevailed, and in the summer of 1933, after his Harvard graduation, Foote married Rebecca when she was twenty, and he but twenty-two years old.

The pair went off to Meadville Theological School in Chicago, a break with the family's Harvard Divinity School tradition.[29] Though the Depression was deepening in 1933, Arthur and Rebecca were insulated from financial worries. His father financed his education and supported them during their three years in Chicago. Foote thrived at Meadville. He later wrote, "Once at Meadville, my inner doubts vanished. With a clear goal before me, I at last found studies that captured my total interest."[30] He was still enmeshed in his family heritage, and even wrote his graduate thesis on his grandfather Henry Wilder Foote's ministry. His father kept a close eye on his son's progress, and arranged a preaching tour in Europe after graduation in 1936, assiduously opening professional doors for him.

Fresh from five months in Europe, a rare extravagance in 1936, Foote was ordained in King's Chapel, one of the first Unitarian churches in New England, where his grandfather had served as minister and his father had also been ordained.[31] Family pride and expectation pervaded the solemn event. The church itself was steeped in family history; a marble bust of his grandfather stood on the altar.[32] As the dignitaries processed down the aisle, garbed in the black robes and symbols of office befitting their station, the weight of the family was palpable. His father participated in the service, along with two other relatives who were ministers with high standing in the Unitarian universe.[33] Guests included elderly Great-Uncle Arthur, a distinguished American composer, beaming at his beloved namesake.[34] Foote's gentle Quaker mother, Eleanor, sat quietly with his four siblings.

Foote glowed with youth, in contrast to his elders who preceded him. He was twenty-five years old, tall, dark, and handsome. A former Harvard track star, his step radiated athletic energy as he climbed the circular stair to the raised lectern. All who knew him undoubtedly hoped that when he spoke he would not be afflicted with the stammer he had endured since his childhood. A hush fell on the congregation. He paused, gathered himself, and his voice rang out, loud and clear.

Following Foote's benediction, the church bell, which had once been repaired by Paul Revere himself, began to toll. The organ burst forth. He was on his way to his future in the west. No doubt, the family expected him to return to the New England fold after a few years. But this earnest young man, naive and privileged, insulated financially from the Great Depression, fresh from a five-month European tour preaching to large crowds, and basking in the glow of his ordination in grand King's Chapel, was leaving the orbit of his family and about to come face to face with the brutal realities of life in America.

■ ■ ■

The Great Depression had significantly depleted resources and demoralized congregations, and Unitarian membership across the nation fell. Positions for new ministers were scarce as Arthur and Rebecca "set their hearts on the golden west."[35] With the help of family connections at the AUA, Arthur chose to serve at a small church in Stockton, California. Because the church had insufficient resources for a full-time minister, he also agreed to simultaneously lead another struggling congregation in Sacramento, forty-eight miles to the north. With high hopes, the Footes set off for the long drive in the fall of 1936. They shared Route 66 with thousands of desperate migrants moving west to escape the terrible drought that had devastated the midwestern and southern Plains states and turned the area into what came to be known as the Dust Bowl.

Stockton and Sacramento were farming and food-processing towns in the fertile Delta region of Central and Northern California. But this was no Garden of Eden. By the 1930s, small farms had given way to large agribusiness conglomerates, unemployment was high as demand for canned goods fell, and thousands of impoverished migrants camped in shanties on the outskirts of town. Conditions deteriorated and union organizers moved in, vying for members, dividing the labor force, and riling up the powerful growers and processors. Strikes and violence broke out a few months after Arthur and Rebecca arrived.[36] Welcome to the Golden State!

The two churches Foote was expected to serve were on shaky ground. The First Unitarian Church of Stockton was a small, charming brick church with a lovely wood-paneled art deco interior; it had been built in 1930.[37] The Stockton parish, founded in 1892 but never robust, had only thirty-three members and a minuscule budget.[38] His second parish, the Unitarian Society of Sacramento, had been without a minister for three years, had rented its church out to others, and had essentially ceased operations by the time Foote arrived.[39] In response to an unsolicited applicant for the pulpit in 1935, a board member had written, "Relative to your inquiry concerning the vacancy in the pulpit here, I might say that we nearly have a vacant church also. . . . I cannot offer you any encouragement as to coming. People seem more concerned as to getting food than as to their salvation, here as elsewhere."[40] Only ten people were interested in reviving the Sacramento church in 1936.

These were the inauspicious circumstances facing Foote, the twenty-five-year-old, newly minted minister. Arthur dug deep. Despite the few and often fractious parishioners, he took seriously his role of ministering to the meager flock in both churches. He assiduously prepared sermons each week that were well received.

On Thursday evenings, he drove the nearly fifty miles to Sacramento, a long journey on the rutted rural roads. Of that challenge, he wrote, "We persisted holding services for the handful that came out, sometimes as many as a dozen, usually less than ten; and on one dismal, rainy night, only one hardy soul showed up. . . . So we were never skunked. But there was very little to encourage us that first year."[41] Foote was relentlessly optimistic. To those who wanted to close the Sacramento church, he insisted, "Our group is small, and some of you seem to think that because it is small, it cannot justify its existence. But institutions are not justified by their size, but by their vitality and usefulness."[42] He strove to meet that challenge.

Foote's belief in tolerance was put to the test as soon as he arrived. Within Unitarian congregations, there were theological fissures between the more conservative members and those who leaned toward less traditional approaches to worship. Again, he later reminisced:

> I viewed my job as one of healing and uniting, especially in the first several years. And my theological position has always been one that

emphasized the inclusive and catholic nature of Unitarianism and I strove then (as I have steadily since) to make sure that the whole theological gamut could feel at home—from the agnostic and humanist across the board to the traditional theistic religious liberal.[43]

Members of the churches in Stockton and Sacramento were also sharply divided on the role of the church in politics, divisions that were intensified by the dire economic and social conditions of the time. Some wanted the church to take explicit positions on capitalism and socialism. Others did not want to be forced into taking sides on social issues of the day. Arthur tried to calm the waters, and set an example of civil and respectful discourse. In writing to an irate parishioner, rather than responding in kind, Foote praised him for speaking out and counseled that "such differences of opinion as may exist would be talked over in a quiet way instead of becoming hidden sources of grievance."[44]

Foote emphasized the importance of freedom of conscience; one side could not impose its views on the rest. Under his leadership, the two churches would not take formal positions on political or social issues; they would encourage discussion and dialogue. His wise counsel kept the congregations from fracturing. As a result, an early critic of Foote's in Sacramento later praised him as "one of the ablest we have ever had. He is well liked by everybody and shows a real deal of wisdom and tact."[45] Foote survived by keeping conflict in check.

As Foote later confessed, the stresses of working two jobs and the challenges of each, in a place far removed from the life he and Rebecca knew, were exhausting. He later wrote, "The discouragements and heartbreaks of those Depression years in California have long slipped into the background of my mind. Only the resiliency of youth saw us through."[46] It must have been particularly hard, we can be sure, on his plucky young wife from Southwest Harbor, Maine, living three thousand miles from home. The Footes had their first child, Frances, in 1937, followed by Nathan in 1940, and Caleb in 1943.

The lead up to and outbreak of World War II was a heartbreaking time for the nation. The advent of war generated an economic boom in Stockton and Sacramento. Given California's proximity to the Pacific Theater, the federal government activated army and air force centers in the state. The deep-water port of Stockton supplied components to shipyards in San Francisco, and thousands found work in war industries or served in the armed forces.[47]

Patriotism was the order of the day. Personally, Foote had to confront painful and difficult choices. Like his father before him, Foote declared himself a pacifist but had an automatic deferment from the draft because he was a practicing minister. In the wartime environment, pacifism was no longer theoretical; there were ramifications in the community. Support for the war was popular in Stockton, as it was throughout the nation, and most Americans did not view pacifists favorably. Foote wrote, "Few in the congregation shared my pacifism, but they lived with it; and I, for my part, was careful (while making my position on war plain) not to shove my conviction down their throats." He kept the peace by his respectful and unobtrusive demeanor. Like other pacifists, he sat on the sidelines as the war unfolded.

Anti-Japanese hysteria spread on the West Coast after the bombing of Pearl Harbor. President Roosevelt authorized the forced relocation of Japanese Americans, and both Stockton and Sacramento were designated as temporary detention centers from May to October 1942. In the little town of Stockton, 4,390 Japanese internees were forced to live in the horse stalls at the fairgrounds awaiting transfer to "permanent" relocation centers farther inland.[48] Foote watched powerlessly as humanitarian principles were violated in his own backyard.

In contrast to his quiet pacifism, Foote's younger brother, Caleb, carried his beliefs to the ramparts. Brilliant, outspoken, and combative, Caleb was often at odds with his family's quiet ways. In 1941 he joined the Fellowship of Reconciliation, a pacifist organization that did not sanction war or violence, and ran its Northern California office. He refused to register for the draft or to apply for conscientious objector status. In August 1942, he went to trial in federal court in San Francisco on draft evasion charges and was ordered to serve six months at McNeil Island Penitentiary.[49] Arthur wrote an impassioned letter of support for his brother, and he attended the trial and sentencing.

After Caleb was released in early 1944, he wrote a hard-hitting critique of the Japanese relocation. His pamphlet, *Outcasts!,* called for justice for interned Japanese Americans.[50] The federal grand jury reincarcerated him.[51]

Their father did not approve of Caleb's activities. Pacifism was fine, but attacking the United States government and going to jail for noncooperation went too far. Henry refused to speak to or of his son during this period, much to the chagrin of his Quaker wife.[52] Arthur Foote suffered through the family rift. Up to this point, he was secure in his family's bedrock values that had always guided him, and deeply admired his brother, whose antiwar views had taken him along a different path. The world was in turmoil and people were suffering. Foote engaged in painful soul-searching in this difficult time.

The Stockton church grew during wartime and began to agitate for a full-time minister. Arthur and Rebecca's baby, Caleb, was suffering from an undiagnosed condition and was slowly dying of malnutrition. The only pediatrician in Stockton was mystified, and the alarmed parents felt an urgent need for more sophisticated care. It was time to think about moving on.

When Unity Church came knocking in the fall of 1944, Foote was interested. The St. Paul congregation was a vibrant one, and the search committee had identified him as the best candidate.[53] After a visit in December 1944, an offer came. Foote readily accepted and planned to leave in the spring of 1945. Frederick May Eliot wrote to Foote that "the church was filled with unanimous and most enthusiastic delight . . . that you have accepted."[54]

The nearly nine years in California had a profound effect on Foote. He arrived as a sheltered, naive, well-intentioned young man of twenty-five. As the family began the long drive back across the country, Arthur and Rebecca were no longer the idealistic couple with dreams of the west. Foote had experienced heartache and frustration, but also honed his skills as a minister—dignified, tactful, inclusive, tolerant, and wise. Yet, he was now facing the dilemma of how to live out those principles in the real world. When was tolerance of differences enough, and when was it imperative to take a stand? Following the family tradition of quiet pacifism felt limited, but was angry dissent the only option? He would have to carve out a new path.

When the Footes arrived in St. Paul in early April 1945, the snow was still flying. Because of the postwar housing shortage, they lived in a series of temporary quarters until permanent housing was ready in September. Eighteen-month-old Caleb was immediately admitted to St. Paul Children's Hospital, diagnosed with celiac disease, and remained in the hospital for three long months.[55]

In the midst of these family challenges, Arthur prepared to deliver his first sermon at Unity.[56] He found a church full of several hundred parishioners who had gathered expectantly. As he stood before the packed house—looking up at the huge red cedar beams arched over the sanctuary, standing behind an ornate pulpit, with a fine organ behind an elaborate hand-carved screen—he surely felt exhilaration that he had finally arrived.[57] He later wrote, "It is wonderful to have so many facilities, such as a movie projector and an excellent stenographer, with which to work."[58]

Alongside the challenges of adjusting to a new position, Foote experienced a mental health crisis in his own family. The Children's Hospital policy forbade parental visits so that young patients could adjust to institutional routines. Rebecca was separated from her sick baby, living in temporary housing with two small children in a new community, and expected to participate in social functions required of the new minister's wife.

When the hospital discharged baby Caleb in the fall of 1945, Rebecca broke down from emotional exhaustion. She was not hospitalized, but was unable to care for her family. Caleb, by then two years old and be-

Unity Church-Unitarian, St. Paul, Minnesota, circa 1960. The church, located at Portland and Grotto Streets, was built in 1905. A parish hall and the Ames Chapel were added in 1921. Courtesy of the Minnesota Historical Society.

ginning a slow recovery, had a full-time nurse at home. There was additional household help for the older children. Foote experienced the fragility of his wife in crisis, and knew he was fortunate that his parents provided financial resources so she could recover. He knew others without family support were not so fortunate.

With a nurse in tow, the Footes traveled to Maine in the summer of 1946. Living with her parents in her hometown, Rebecca decided to stay with the children through October. Arthur drove back alone to begin the fall church calendar and to attend the Minnesota Unitarian Conference meeting. He had much to think about on the long drive.

■ ■ ■

Thus, having reflected on his past experiences, as he surveyed the crowded lodge at Camp Ihduhapi, he knew that this meeting was an important step for Minnesota Unitarians and for him. He admired Eliot and the Unitarian Advance concept, while reserving judgment about the consequences of taking sides. He listened intently, as was his wont, to the speakers.

The Reverend Leslie Pennington from First Unitarian Church in Chicago spoke of the importance of the church in the creative shaping of the social order.[59] AUA representative Ernest Kuebler gave a passionate plea for Unitarian Advance. Minnesota activists were also at the ready. Along with Bragg, Peggy Taylor, an involved leader in the FUS Women's Alliance, represented the statewide organization. Another activist, Genevieve Steefel, came from Unity Church. Steefel had a long history working in social welfare, and served on Minneapolis mayor Hubert Humphrey's Human Relations Council and Fair Housing Commission.[60] She was a friend of Bragg, who also was active with Mayor Humphrey. Steefel had no doubt that immediate action was necessary to address the crisis in Minnesota's mental institutions.

Bragg led the afternoon session during which the issue of mental institution reform was put on the table. Engla noted in her diary that he gave "a splendid appeal for the cause." He spoke of Unitarian Dorothea Dix and her crusade for mental hospital reform decades before. He reiterated the goals of Unitarian Advance and urged the MUC to take up the issue.

Discussion followed. Some attendees questioned Bragg, arguing that the conditions were not as bad as he said. In response to the *Life*

59th Annual

Minnesota Unitarian Conference
1946

October, 17 - 18 - 19

AT CAMP IDHUHAPI, MAPLE PLAIN, MINNESOTA

"The Minnesota Unitarian Conference has as its purpose the fostering of religion through the organization and support of liberal churches in the state of Minnesota . . . and the promotion of educational and any other activities to that end."

(Constitutional statement of purpose)

Unitarian churches are dedicated to the progressive transformation and ennoblement of individual and social life, through religion in accordance with advancing knowledge and the growing vision of mankind.

Cover of the 1946 Minnesota Unitarian Conference program. At the conference, Minnesota Unitarians voted to study the conditions in the state mental hospitals under the leadership of Reverend Arthur Foote. Courtesy of the Minnesota Historical Society.

magazine exposé, state officials and hospital superintendents denied that Minnesota's hospitals were like those in other states. A story in the *Pioneer Press* titled "No Snake Pits in Minnesota Asylums" reflected their party line. The article stated that in Minnesota institutions, the food was good, the wards spotless, restraints never used for punishment, recreation was plentiful, and remarkable results were obtained with electroshock. The conclusion: "Such conditions may exist in other parts of the country. But it should give the people of this state a feeling of pride that there are no snake pits in Minnesota."[61]

Not intimidated, Engla Schey reacted strongly to the debate and rose to her feet to speak. She later described the scene:

> When someone said, "We have gone to the highest authority. We have talked to the Superintendents," I stood up and volunteered, "You have not gone to the highest authority. These men are so far removed from the patients and low level personnel that they don't often know what is cooking. Take a dance band out and dance with the patients. Then you will get an idea about what needs to be done in mental hospitals."

Foote's version of the debate corroborated Engla's recollection:

> The Minnesota Unitarians were reinforced by a state hospital attendant who appealed to the sense of responsibility of community leadership. She had had years of staff service in two different Minnesota mental hospitals and knew, first hand, of the conditions which prevailed there. . . . Riled by the frequency with which individuals to whom she appealed, even among Unitarians, tried to reassure her about conditions in Minnesota state hospitals which, they were sure were not as bad as those in other states, she made some pretty frank disclosures.[62]

Engla's remarks electrified the crowd. A committee was chosen to draft a resolution that would then be considered by the whole group the next day. Foote was on the drafting committee. He had been quiet during the meeting. He listened to the impassioned pleas, and to those who had their doubts about the facts. He knew he would be asked to play a key role. What was the right path?

The resolution presented the following morning bore Foote's influence and reflected all he had learned during his difficult years in

California. He supported action, but effective action was not necessarily immediate action. Effective action required restraint. Despite the rousing appeals at the sessions, Foote knew that there were divisions among the attendees on the true nature of the problem. He had experienced such divisiveness before and his instinct was to go slowly. Facts needed to be gathered not just to bring everyone together but also to determine a reasonable course of action, and to have the credibility to persuade others. The final resolution read:

> Whereas, the care of the mentally ill has been the concern of Unitarians since the time of Dorothea Dix,
>
> And whereas, deplorable conditions resulting from overcrowding and understaffing in our mental hospitals have been charged by various recent publications, and that these conditions are said to exist in Minnesota,
>
> Be it resolved: that the Minnesota Unitarian Conference request that the Board of Directors of the Conference institute an investigation of conditions in our Minnesota State Hospitals and present their findings to the member societies with recommendations for action.[63]

As expected, Foote was chosen to chair the MUC Committee on Mental Hospitals. Genevieve Steefel accepted the role as committee secretary, and committee volunteers would be assembled in due time. A year of study lay ahead.

Engla returned to Rochester State Hospital and reported to work. Upon her return, she recorded in her journal:

> I've had a week. Holidays. I took it for the purpose of introducing NMHF at a Unitarian State conference. Dorothea Lynde Dix was a Unitarian. It was in line with their traditions I reasoned to concern themselves with conditions in mental hospitals. There were 102 delegates present. My own pastor, Raymond Bragg gave a splendid appeal for the cause. A resolution was passed to study conditions in mental hospitals and demand social action.

Engla's presence at the meeting was the catalyst for the resolution. Her one-woman crusade was about to pass into the hands of a new movement led by Foote. He had embraced action as an end, but the means would be on his own terms. As he later reflected:

It was doubtless assumed that a knowledge of conditions would result in action for improvement. The arduous climb over the road from anger and protest, through indignant challenge to responsible study and analysis and cooperative sympathetic service was not even dreamt of by most of those who took the action.[64]

The arduous climb had begun.

SIX

The Arduous Climb

The danger was great, however, that protest alone would
characterize its approach to the problem.

■ *Arthur Foote, Minnesota Unitarian Conference, 1946–49*

On the freezing afternoon of December 17, 1946, the campus of the University of Minnesota was quiet, the students having gone home for the winter holidays. Genevieve Steefel hurried along the path, past deserted stately academic buildings, until she came to Nolte Hall, home to the Center for Continuing Education.[1] She didn't want to be late. She was responsible for this meeting of key state and university leaders with the newly organized MUC Committee on Mental Hospitals.

Steefel quickly climbed the stairs to the entrance and was greeted with a warm blast of welcoming heat. In the ladies' cloakroom, she slipped out of her winter coat, adjusted her hat, and confidently emerged to ensure that the details were in order. Arthur Foote as chairman and Steefel as secretary of the MUC Committee on Mental Hospitals, along with George W. Jacobson, the new MUC president, would be representing the Unitarians at this meeting.

Steefel would, of course, take and transcribe the notes. This job was a familiar one, usually assigned to a female participant if there was one on hand. But Steefel intended to play a much more pivotal role in shaping and defining the committee's work. In truth, she had already done so. Steefel insisted the committee begin its work at once, and not wait until after the Christmas holidays. Though she recognized that Foote was the chair, he was a relative newcomer to Minnesota. She had been on the Unity board of trustees committee that selected Foote as minister. She liked him well enough, but feared he might be too cautious for this challenge. It was time to get going, she thought, and so she did.

Steefel had the network, the contacts, and influence throughout

Minnesota. Through her university and political connections she was responsible for organizing this first meeting of the MUC Committee on Mental Hospitals. The invitees were few—only eight would join the Unitarians—but each was a critically important player. She had landed Carl Swanson, director of the Division of Public Institutions (DPI). That was a coup. In addition, Dr. Magnus Petersen, superintendent of Rochester State Hospital, would also attend. From the university, three key leaders—Dr. Harold Diehl, dean of the Medical School; Dr. Donald Hastings, chair of the Department of Psychiatry; and Roy Amberg, who ran the University Hospitals. Finally, there was Dr. Alexander Dumas, a Minneapolis psychiatrist, longtime consultant to the Veterans Administration, and medical director of the Minnesota Mental Hygiene Society. A university regent and a state legislator rounded out the distinguished group.[2] Everyone Steefel had invited had said yes, despite the fact it was the week before Christmas. She made things happen.

Formidable is the best word to describe forty-seven-year-old Genevieve Fallon Steefel. Formidable in intellect, she had been an honors graduate at Radcliffe, the prestigious and demanding women's college affiliated with the all-male Harvard University. Formidable in style, she was not tall but carried herself with confidence, dressed smartly, and was full of irrepressible, impatient energy. She had social status in the Twin Cities.

Women, by the conventions of the time, were addressed by the names of their husband. She was Mrs. Lawrence D. Steefel, wife of a well-respected member of the History Department at the university. Steefel knew she was a woman in a man's world, but that didn't stop her. As Mrs. Lawrence Steefel she worked hard to establish her own credibility and her own influence. She had a long résumé, including both paid and volunteer work. She had always been active in social services and increasingly in postwar politics, but now that her children were nearly grown—Lawrence Jr. was in college and Nina in high school—she was running on all cylinders. She was on the board of Family and Children's Services, state president of the American Association of University Women, a member of the United Nations Association, the Citizens League of Minneapolis, cochair of the Minnesota Council for a Permanent Fair Employment Practices Commission, and had just been reappointed to Mayor Hubert Humphrey's Council on Human Relations.[3]

Though not from Minnesota, Steefel had made her mark in the Twin Cities. She met her future husband when he was a graduate student in history at Harvard and she at Radcliffe. With his new Ph.D., he had joined the University of Minnesota's history faculty in 1923, while she had a one-year fellowship in France. She followed him to Minnesota in 1924 and took a job as a research assistant in the History Department.

Genevieve Fallon joined Unity Church in St. Paul in February 1925, and a few months later, she and Lawrence married. As she had been raised a Roman Catholic and her husband was Jewish, Unity may have been the only church that would bless the union.[4] Steefel landed leadership roles wherever she went, and Unity Church was no exception. She eschewed the traditional women's role, however, and did not join either the long-standing Women's Alliance or the newer Elizabeth Eliot Club for working women at Unity.[5] The board of trustees was more her style.

The Steefels were a prominent and influential couple. They had a lovely home, staffed by several servants, on West River Road in Minneapolis. They often hosted meetings and dinners there for the many organizations they supported. The Steefels spent summers at their house

Genevieve Steefel, active in social work, civil rights, and fair housing, was secretary and later vice-chair of the MUC Committee on Mental Hospitals, 1940s. Courtesy of Sarah Steefel.

on Star Island in northern Minnesota along with many other university families.

What forces drove the energy, passion, and commitment of Genevieve Fallon Steefel? She later credited Radcliffe for her relentless activity and community involvement:

> I learned the tools of continuing education in new fields of endeavor and standards of workmanship applicable to such jobs as the community asked me to do. Aside from the intellectual disciplines I was given an ideal to work toward: the mark of the educated woman, to be able to place herself in the other fellow's place with understanding without regard for his status in life, his race, his creed or his temporary loss of dignity.[6]

Her words ring of noblesse oblige. At the finest women's college she learned empathy for others less fortunate. But appearances can be deceiving. Steefel harbored a dark secret, even now not fully known or knowable, that provides a clue to her passion to make the world a better place, and her intense interest in the mentally ill.

■ ■ ■

Genevieve's past paints a very different picture. She was born into a poor Irish Catholic family in Cambridge, Massachusetts, in 1899, the second child of Christopher and Gertrude Fallon, both first-generation Irish immigrants. Her father was a bookbinder and her mother a seamstress. Tragedy struck the family in 1906, when her thirty-one-year-old father died of tuberculosis, leaving his widow and two daughters, eight-year-old Gertrude and seven-year-old Genevieve Rose. By 1910 the girls were living with their paternal grandmother, Isabella Fallon, in Malden, a modest town outside Boston. The household included the widowed Isabella, who had borne thirteen children, and three of her youngest sons, who were all laborers in the Boston area.

Where was the mother of the Fallon girls? In 1910 she was an inmate in Worcester Insane Asylum. Gertrude Fallon was assigned to ward work there. Perhaps, like Anders Schey, she was able to function at a level that kept her from being relegated to the back wards. Was it grief, mental illness, poverty, or all three, that caused a young mother to lose her children, with whom she would never live again?

Genevieve and Gertrude spent their girlhood with their grandmother Isabella and various uncles in Malden. Little is known of their living conditions, though Genevieve's grandson remembers his grandmother saying that she carried a hot potato to school each morning both to keep her hands warm and to serve as her lunch at noon.[7] Despite hardships, Genevieve was an exceptional student at Medford High School during her three years there from 1915 to 1918. The principal of the school wrote on her nearly perfect transcript: "This is part of the story, but not all. Miss Fallon is choice, very, very choice."[8] What was the rest of the story?

Perhaps the principal was referring to the next tragedy that befell the Fallon girls, though the details again remain unclear. Genevieve's grandmother lost her home during this period, as a result of old age or poverty, and moved in with one of her sons in Malden. The granddaughters did not go with her. Young Gertrude had just graduated from high school and became a domestic, living in her employer's home. Genevieve was sent to Lancaster, a town fifty miles from Malden, and a place without known family connections, possibly to a foster home. Despite these troubling circumstances, she was a star student once again in her senior year at Lancaster High School in 1919. She attended Simmons College for one year (1919–20), boarding with a family near the campus, before applying to transfer to Radcliffe in 1920.[9]

How did an impoverished young woman, with no family support, accomplish this feat? The answer is on her 1920 Radcliffe application. Genevieve did not list her mother or her grandmother as the adult to receive communications from the school. Instead, she referred the college to a Mrs. E. M. S. (Edith) Baylor, a social worker from Newton. On the same application, she listed her father as deceased, and provided her mother's street address. The address was the Home for Working Girls, an institution for impoverished workingwomen run by a Catholic charity.[10] Clearly her mother was in no position to assist her daughter, and the two may not even have been in contact at this time.

Under the wing of Mrs. Baylor, who undoubtedly found a benefactor for scholarship support, the bright young Genevieve Rose Fallon changed her life. In little more than five years she would become the educated spouse of Professor Steefel and devote herself to many worthy causes in the Twin Cities. And now, in 1946, she had an opportunity to affect the care for mental patients. She had overcome tremendous odds and appeared to have erased her tragic past, but carried forever deep in her heart a drive to help the unfortunate, less from noble obligation than from an intimate knowledge of true misfortune.

■ ■ ■

Steefel had put the past firmly behind her. She smiled as she entered the lounge at Nolte Hall, with its mahogany trim, coved ceiling, brass sconces, and comfortable sofas. Yes, she thought, a gracious place for the participants to gather. The staff indicated to her that the refreshments were in order. She turned to the library, where the group would hold its three-hour session. Adorned with built-in bookcases, paneled wainscoting, and ample light, the room was welcoming, with a scholarly feel. Wide windows looked out upon the lightly falling snow. The mahogany conference table, around which they would assemble, had been polished to a brilliant shine.

At the meeting, there were five individuals representing the Unitarian contingent. In addition to Foote and Steefel, George W. Jacobson took his seat at the table. Jacobson was a longtime member of FUS, and incoming chair of the MUC. He was a tall, dapper man, who sported bow ties, pomaded hair, and a pencil-thin moustache. Born in 1900, he was the youngest of six children of Norwegian Lutheran immigrants. Jacobson had attended teachers college in Duluth, taught in rural schools in small Minnesota towns, and held other odd jobs. At age twenty-four he attended the university and received his B.S. in business administration.[11]

His passion was cooperatives and, after graduating from the university, he plunged into Minnesota's vibrant co-op movement in the 1920s.[12] He attended the Northern States Cooperative Training School in 1927, and had a variety of leadership positions in cooperative organizations. In 1939 Jacobson was the chief founder, along with his wife, Dorothy Houston Jacobson, and a nucleus of credit union leaders, of Group Health Mutual. In 1946 he was serving as executive president, fighting the long uphill battle to offer prepaid health plans to members in Minnesota.[13] Jacobson was used to difficult fights against sophisticated opponents, including those in the medical profession. He was a valuable part of the work of the MUC Committee on Mental Hospitals.

Unitarian Frank Rarig Jr., who was experienced in welfare and social services, was one of the expert speakers. In 1946 he was chairman of the Legislative Committee for the Minnesota Welfare Conference, and executive secretary of the Wilder Charities.[14] His father, Frank Rarig Sr., was a well-known professor in the Speech Department at the university and a longtime FUS member. Frank Jr., a graduate of the university and its Law School, was raised up at FUS and was now a member of Unity Church.

Frank Jr. was also known as a man of high principle. In 1932, when he was only twenty-five, he ran the Emergency Relief Administration for the state of Minnesota and was responsible for putting one hundred thousand Minnesotans to work in 1933. However, when Governor Floyd B. Olson put the agency under the newly created Board of Control in 1934, Rarig resigned in protest against Olson's political appointees.[15] After stints in Indiana and Washington, D.C., he returned to Minnesota to become executive secretary of the Ramsey County Board of Public Welfare. During the war, he did double duty overseeing the War Manpower Commission for five states and the Wilder Charities.[16]

Last, there was Dr. George Ruhberg, also a member of Unity Church and a noted St. Paul neurologist, who was on the staff of Gillette Children's Hospital and the university's Medical School.[17]

Where was Engla Schey, the attendant who had galvanized the conference with her impassioned appeal, and who knew the true conditions in the institutions? Engla was working. Attendants toiled forty-eight hours per week. She had received grudging permission to attend the MUC conclave at Camp Ihduhapi in October and had to use scarce vacation time. With no car and little time off, Engla could not participate on the official committee.

She stayed connected, however. Steefel was impressed with Engla and knew she had important inside information. Engla wrote to Steefel after the MUC meeting, and a correspondence began. Engla was an inveterate letter writer, and the flurry of letters to "Mrs. Steefel," as she always addressed her, were full of suggestions, contacts, and advice.[18] Engla had Steefel's ear, but was never at the table.

These two women shared both a passion for mental health reform and an impatience for action. They also shared the limitations of their gender; women faced many barriers to credibility in the patriarchal world of 1946. They likely did not know, however, that they shared something else—similar childhood tragedies including the mental illness of a parent, family strife, and poverty. Engla, known in her community as a girl with promise, had earned her own way, with limited education and no assistance from anyone. Professionals found the low-paid, low-status attendant easy to overlook or dismiss despite her years of experience and commitment to the cause. In contrast, Genevieve had benefited from the intervention of an interested social worker and the gift of her own prodigious intellect. She had received a prestigious education and married well. Class differences now separated these two women. Genevieve was in a position of influence; Engla worked the wards.

Steefel may have planned the meeting, but Foote set the tone. The invitation communicated the Unitarians' sincere concern for "state hospital needs and their desire to inform themselves reliably through consultation with those best informed on basic problems."[19] They were undertaking a study of the care of the mentally ill in Minnesota "with the hope that lay citizen support may be developed for a sound program."[20]

The Unitarians had also prepared themselves by immersion in background research. Though sophisticated in their fields, they had only rudimentary knowledge of mental health care in the state. They all read the biennial reports to the governor prepared by the DPI as well as the USPHS survey of Minnesota mental hospitals.[21]

The attendees seated themselves around the commodious conference table. Foote opened the meeting. He was cordial, earnest, and soft-spoken, his style consistent with the educational and nonconfrontational tone of the invitation. He read aloud the Minnesota Unitarian Conference (MUC) Resolution adopted just a few weeks earlier, and reiterated the goals of its Committee on Mental Hospitals.

The first two speakers represented the status quo. DPI chief Carl Swanson was a longtime administrator in Minnesota's public institutions. Governor Harold Stassen had appointed him to the DPI post in 1939. Swanson embodied the bureaucratic institutional perspective. Steefel's notes from the meeting capture Swanson's defensive posture. He blamed the legislature's penury for infrastructure breakdowns, overcrowding, and the lack of resources needed to expand and maintain facilities. He bemoaned the shortage of personnel, calling out the civil service for setting uncompetitive salaries. He told the group that the DPI would be asking for more money for buildings and cost-of-living adjustments in the 1947 legislative session. His mantra was "Give us more money for buildings, ask no questions, and conditions will improve."[22]

Rochester superintendent Magnus C. Petersen had a smoother,

more approachable demeanor, but he too had been raised in the institutional culture. He believed the superintendent was the man in charge
and abhorred outsiders meddling in the hospital's business. His responsibility was simply to persuade politicians and bureaucrats to send
more money, and he was pleased that Swanson cited Rochester State
Hospital as most in need of large investments for building repairs and
upgrades.

Hoping that the Unitarians would dutifully lobby for more generous appropriations, Petersen invited the group to visit his hospital
to see the "unbelievably overcrowded" conditions for themselves. He
also sought funds to increase salaries for doctors so they could compete with the Veterans Administration, but dismissed the idea of better on-the-job training for attendants, an issue of pressing concern to
Engla. For Peterson, such training was "out of the picture now for staff
is needed too much for routine care."[23]

There was a stark contrast between the views of Swanson and
Petersen and those of the university leaders. Academic psychiatry
was on the cusp of a wave of new postwar opportunities. Before World
War II, there was little public interest in, or knowledge about, psychiatry. Public perceptions of its importance and the need for more research and training accelerated when the mental health problems of recruits and active-duty servicemen became apparent. At the beginning
of the war, psychiatry had only a minimal presence in the armed forces;
by the end of the war many psychiatrists and other physicians trained
in neuropsychiatry were in the service.[24] In the postwar period, over
60 percent of VA patients were considered "neuropsychiatric," requiring
the administration to scramble to try to address their needs. The VA
embarked on rapid expansion of mental health services and began to
seek affiliation with medical schools, winning modifications in the civil
service system to attract talented physicians.[25]

The postwar period also saw new federal recognition of the importance of mental health research and training for civilians. On
July 3, 1946, President Truman signed the National Mental Health Act,
which called for the creation of the National Institute of Mental Health
(NIMH) to provide financial support for research and professional
training, and to make grants to states for mental health facilities. The
National Institutes of Health began awarding grants in July 1947, although the new NIMH was not formally established until 1949.[26] Psychiatrists, including those at the University of Minnesota, believed they

were on the ascendancy. As historian Ellen Herman has noted, "Clinicians . . . mounted persistent advocacy efforts on their own behalf, convinced that gains in professional visibility and prestige would result from increased federal funding."[27]

The University of Minnesota was anxious to take advantage of these new postwar opportunities. Training in psychiatry had lagged behind some of the other medical sciences, in part because the science of the brain was rudimentary at best during the first half of the twentieth century. The university added psychiatry to the regular curriculum as early as the 1890s, but it was offered in association with neurology in the Department of Nervous and Mental Diseases.[28] The department, with its emphasis on neurology, hired its first full-time faculty psychiatrist in 1921, but struggled to get legislative support to build a neuropsychiatric hospital on the campus.[29]

Dr. Donald Hastings, hired in March 1946 to lead the department, was one of the new postwar breed. Hastings had served as chief psychiatrist of the U.S. Army Air Forces after his training in Wisconsin and Pennsylvania. Soon after his arrival, and reflecting the growing consensus that psychiatry and neurology were different fields, Hastings separated neurology and psychiatry into two departments, elevating psychiatry as a result.[30]

Dean Harold Diehl spoke for the Medical School. His remarks revealed a starkly different perspective from the leaders of the state mental hospital system. Diehl rejected Swanson's emphasis on buildings. Rather he insisted that "we would need fewer buildings and staff if we focused on preventive work."[31]

Diehl acknowledged little or no collaboration between the mental institutions and university faculty, and little inclination to pursue it. He explained that, among other things, psychiatrists were not attracted to practice in mental institutions, especially when the training and pay were significantly better at the VA. In fact, he stated that the Medical School would participate in training for mental hospital staff only if done at a new psychiatric institute, located on the university campus, funded by the state, and staffed by Medical School faculty. It was hard to miss his condescending tone toward state mental institutions.[32]

Dr. Alexander G. Dumas, a psychiatrist in Minneapolis, longtime consultant to the VA, and medical director of the Minnesota Mental Hygiene Society, was also on the agenda.[33] The society included psychiatrists who worked in the institutions as well as those in the community and academics.[34] Reflecting the range of society members' views, Dumas reported that the group had a short-term plan to persuade the legislature to provide more money for building projects and for full staffing. Its longer-term vision was to educate the public to support more money for research into prevention and treatment in the 1949 legislature and beyond. Thus, he challenged the DPI view, as articulated by

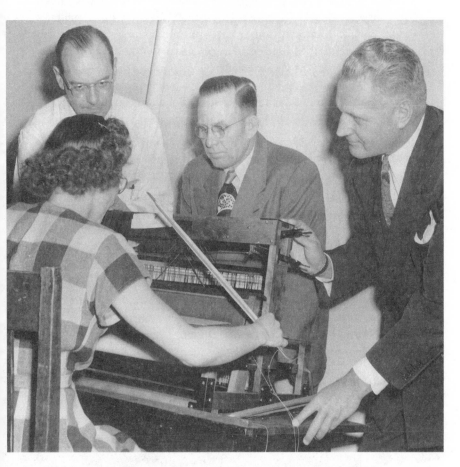

In 1949, Dr. Donald Hastings (far left), head of the University of Minnesota's Psychiatry Department, shows Governor Youngdahl and State Senator Gerald Mullin (center) one of the occupational therapy treatments at University Hospitals. Mullin, a North Minneapolis Democrat, was a strong supporter of the university and the mental health reform effort. Photograph by the *Minneapolis Star*. Courtesy of Hennepin County Library Special Collections.

Swanson, stating, "Buildings cannot cure patients, only improved treatment methods and adequate well-trained personnel."[35]

Frank Rarig, the last speaker, argued that the current state organization created silos for delivery of services that did not address the welfare of the individual. "What is needed," he stated, "is a single welfare service with mental hygiene service for all citizens in or out of institutions." Reflecting the perspective of social welfare, Rarig understood the consequences of a fragmented system, a situation that still plagues mental health treatment today. Carl Swanson, as might be expected from an institution man, rejected Rarig's ideas to rationalize state services, calling them "unrealistic and needing further study."[36]

The meeting lasted only three hours, but it provided Unitarian participants with a valuable glimpse into the differing perspectives between state officials and the field of psychiatry. While they under-

Informational displays like this one, produced by the Minnesota Mental Hygiene Society, stressed the importance of public education in reforming mental health care, late 1940s. Courtesy of the Minneapolis City Archives.

stood the potential benefits to patients as a result of increased funds for buildings and for more research and better medical training, the Unitarians knew something important was missing. Where were the calls to remediate inadequacies of food, clothing, medical care, psychiatric care, and reliance on patient labor? What about the need for better recruiting, training, and compensation for attendants, about which Engla had spoken so persuasively? As laypersons, the Unitarians could see beyond the self-interest of professionals and bureaucrats. But who spoke for the voiceless? It was also clear that the issues were complex, the bureaucracy entrenched, and the politics challenging.

As Foote later summed up:

> The committee members came out of that conference with the conviction that the sum total of the programs proposed could not be that of the [MUC] Conference Committee. While the committee would back a building program, higher salaries and in-service training programs, it felt it must extend its own projects well beyond these into the area of selection and advanced training of highly qualified personnel and to the effort to develop a sound study and research program to extend the knowledge as to how to deal with the problems of mental illness itself.[37]

As they left the meeting room, stepped out into the cold air, and scurried to their automobiles, each participant carried with him or her impressions of the day and its implications for the future of the effort. For Foote, the holidays were fast approaching with their multitude of ministerial tasks—the Christmas pageant, sermons and services to prepare, and many holiday events. The Unitarians had not established a structure for their new committee or developed a strategic plan. Work, Foote reasoned, could begin again after the Christmas holidays. Steefel, however, felt there was no time to waste. Given Minnesota's biennial legislative calendar and short legislative session, without action in 1947, there was no chance at securing reforms until 1949.[38] To Steefel, such a delay was unconscionable. She worried that Foote might procrastinate, so she stepped aggressively forward.

■ ■ ■

On December 26, 1946, Steefel called a second meeting of the MUC Committee on Mental Hospitals at her home. She served as chair and took notes. Only five individuals attended; Foote and Jacobson were not there. She began by describing the Nolte Center meeting. Then, at her urging, they agreed to put together a flyer to lobby legislators. Elsa Krauch, an insurance company copywriter, offered to draft it.[39] Steefel requested that it include statistics on a wide range of mental hospital issues and be completed before the 1947 legislative session began.[40]

Steefel was on a roll. On January 2, 1947, she called a third meeting of the committee at her home. A slightly larger group attended, including Foote and Bragg. She had also invited Robert C. Stover, the civil service commissioner.[41] Stover clarified what he thought were Swanson's misstatements on the role of civil service requirements for mental hospitals. He also recommended professional managers at each hospital so that superintendents could focus on treatment, a position Dr. Magnus Petersen strongly opposed.[42]

The Nolte Hall meeting in mid-December of the previous year revealed fissures among the medical professionals and the state. The meeting with Stover revealed that state agencies were rife with internecine quarrels. To Foote, the discussion was yet another signal not to dive in unprepared. He also had concerns that the MUC had authorized its Committee on Mental Hospitals to investigate, but not to take any action.

Then, a bombshell hit. On January 13, the *Minneapolis Star* ran a story captioned "Unitarians to Ask Help for State's Mental Hospitals."[43] The story stated that George Jacobson, president of the MUC, "announced today that his group has already begun a campaign aimed at improving institutional standards." The text, however, quoted Jacobson, emphasizing "the fact that his group has only just begun its study of the problem." Who had placed this story that implied imminent action by the Unitarians?

Jacobson was not pleased. He had asked for an organizational meeting, but it had not been held. On January 17, Steefel wrote to Jacobson, "I am sorry it was not possible to have the get together you suggested for the purpose of planning how we could set up something of a structure within the Conference for the development of this work. . . . But I trust some way will be found to follow through to a thorough well-rounded plan for work on this job."[44] She enclosed her outline of the issues that were currently under study for the flyer.

After another conversation just ten days later, Genevieve again wrote to Jacobson:

I am rather puzzled, after our conversation today to know how to plan in relation to the study on the Care of the Mentally Ill. Perhaps when the committee meets something will develop in the way of a use for our findings. I shall be crowding other things and myself to get these facts together. Unless they lead straight to something in the way of practical application I doubt that I shall undertake to do more on it now.[45]

Steefel was moving too fast, way out ahead of the MUC Committee on Mental Hospitals, and without authorization from the MUC. Jacobson had to rein her in. No contemporaneous record of Foote's opinions has survived, but he summarized the period in a later report:

At its outset, the Committee had no clearly defined program or agenda. It was made up of laymen and ministers totally uninformed on channels of authority and administration of the state's program for the care and treatment of mental illness, but it was of the disposition to protest the evils known to exist.[46]

Foote was especially concerned that action in the name of the Minnesota Unitarian Conference be done judiciously. "Any errors in judgment might lose the confidence of the community before it had been won."[47]

Even action-oriented Engla Schey urged caution. Getting wind of the flurry of Unitarian activity, she wrote to Steefel:

Citizens can raise the money for personnel and get publicity in the newspapers etc. They can make surveys, pile up questions, recommend changes, but they have to get right in on the wards for days and days and live this thing to really understand what needs to be done in human relations inside the mental hospital. I hope some of the Unitarians who have time on their hands can get into Anoka and work as attendants. . . . Even trained people aren't permitted to see anything on these carefully supervised trips at Anoka. When the Legislative committee came through they often spent most of their time at the dairy barn and farm when I worked at Anoka.[48]

Steefel got the message. A full three months went by before the fourth official meeting of the MUC Committee on Mental Hospitals on April 2, 1947. Bill Keeney, a key leader of the National Mental Health Foundation, spoke. Engla had urged that such a meeting take place because of her great respect for the NMHF. She told Steefel that she hoped the Unitarians would give "these educated, sincere boys who started the ball rolling to clear up conditions in both the Veterans and civilian hospitals" a warm reception.[49]

Daunted by the complexity of the reform task, some of the Unitarians had hoped to find a ready-made policy solution from affiliation with NMHF or the Mental Hygiene Society. At the April meeting, Keeney explained the work of NMHF and criticized the Minnesota Mental Hygiene Society as "largely professional in its outlook and its appeal, and not geared to laymen."[50] More disagreements had surfaced.

After weeks working through how to collaborate, the Unitarians realized there were no ready-made solutions, and their insistence on independence required them to develop their own views and design their own solutions. There was no shortcut to the hard work that was necessary.

Then, in early May, Steefel informed Foote in a letter that she had agreed to join the Mental Hygiene Society board. She argued that "it puts our committee into the main current of development of programs in the state," clearly trying to anticipate Foote's concern that her membership might compromise the independence of the MUC Committee on Mental Hospitals. Genevieve did not discuss her decision with Foote before she accepted: "It's too bad there wasn't a chance to talk this through, but if I delayed acceptance until discussions were possible, the first year's work would have been done and first policy laid down before I could share in it."[51] While she assured Foote that she would leave the society if she felt it compromised the Unitarian committee, her unilateral decision and after-the-fact notification no doubt rankled Foote once again as he worked to develop the committee's mission and identity.

The 1947 legislative session came and went. Carl Swanson's DPI lobbied for more money and worked the press.[52] A March 7, 1947, article in the *Minneapolis Tribune* bore the hand of Superintendent Petersen. In "State Mental Hospitals Crowded Like Slave Ship," the reporter described overcrowded wards, staff shortages, and dilapidated buildings. But, he concluded:

> On the credit side of the Rochester ledger, Dr. Petersen is considered one of the outstanding men in such a position: the institution has excellent operating facilities and operations are performed by mem-

bers of the Mayo Clinic staff. There are excellent facilities of administering the important electric shock treatment, the food is good and the institution is immaculate.[53]

In the session, the legislature finally allocated funds that had been deferred in 1943 and 1945 by the economic constraints of wartime. Foote commented that the 1945 request had been "scotched by inflationary costs and forced to lie dormant until two years had passed and another legislative session came round."[54] While the money was sorely needed, he knew there were "no positive results for the state hospital system . . . in terms of real reform."[55]

The inability of the Unitarians to mobilize for the 1947 legislature, while undoubtedly disappointing, was a blessing in disguise to the MUC Committee on Mental Hospitals. The reprieve gave Foote time to build a solid group committed to clear principles and unassailable facts. When the opportunity arose to influence the policy environment, they would be ready.

His first task was to establish the character of the MUC Committee on Mental Hospitals. Independent laypeople were key; those "whose religious humanitarian values prompted them to inform themselves about the problems at the root of state hospital conditions" with "no other purpose to serve than the disinterested purposes which spring from his religious motives, can speak with more authority on the need for reform than any other group."[56]

The committee would study the issues and build consensus among themselves through discussion and debate. They would confer with professionals working in the mental institutions and other experts outside government. They would show respect for those who had "year-in-year-out experience with personnel, budget, professional practice, labor unions, civil services, state administrative problems which bring a full realization of the interplay of forces out of which a program for the care of the mentally ill must finally come."[57] Under this line of thinking, only the well-informed layperson has the right to propose reforms, and to be heard and taken seriously by legislators.

In that spirit, members of the committee interviewed fifty persons active in the field, and visited state institutions, VA hospitals, and institutions out of the state. Subcommittees began to focus more deeply on a wide range of issues, including recruiting, staffing, pay, training concerns for attendants, and specifics of conditions for patients themselves.

Steefel, despite the inevitable disappointment at the lack of action in the 1947 legislature, swallowed her frustration and labored on. She worked tirelessly, attending committee and subcommittee meetings, taking and typing up minutes, and putting together the findings that pointed out vital needs.[58]

In mid-September 1947, the Sixtieth Annual Meeting of the statewide MUC took place once again at Camp Ihduhapi. Foote chaired a panel discussion on the committee's findings that Steefel had painstakingly compiled. The MUC renewed its commitment in the following resolution:

> *Whereas:* The Minnesota Unitarian Conference Committee on Mental Institutions has been invited in the past and first year of its existence, to cooperate with state and other officials to assist in developing an education program on behalf of state mental institutions; and
>
> *Whereas:* the future development of the program of improvement in the care of the mentally ill will require cooperation with these officials; and
>
> *Whereas:* there is a need to revise and develop a more adequate program for diagnosis and preventive work in the treatment of the mentally ill;
>
> *Be it therefore resolved:* that the state conference committee, after conference with and approval by the Board of the Minnesota Unitarian Conference shall take such action as is necessary to express and implement an improved program for the care of the mentally ill.[59]

The findings of the MUC Committee on Mental Hospitals persuaded the assembled Unitarians to authorize "such action as is necessary to express and implement an improved program." They had overcome the inclination to rely on protest and outrage alone, had willingly listened to experts, and armed themselves with facts and figures. Foote's Unitarian principles guided their work and shaped the committee's character. Steefel gamely continued to organize meetings, drafted notes and recorded the findings. And when opportunity to act arose, the deliberate Arthur Foote and the action-oriented Genevieve Fallon Steefel, flanked by an exceptionally committed group of Unitarians, rose to the challenge.

While the Unitarians made their arduous journey toward commitment to mental health reform during 1947, the newly elected Governor Luther Youngdahl was engaged in a very different learning process of his own, one that would put him on a collision course with the Unitarian reformers.

SEVEN

Where There Is Smoke

You and I know that where there is smoke, there is fire. People
don't just generally have such a dread to take a loved one to an
institution like this without a reason therefor.

   ■ *Judge Frank J. Rosemeier to Governor Luther Youngdahl*

On a blustery Sunday in early February 1946, a sedan pulled
into the driveway of a stately brick home perched on the bluff overlooking the Mississippi River in South St. Paul. A few miles from the capitol to the north, South St. Paul was a working-class town, populated by
Eastern and Southern European immigrants. It was home to the Union
Stockyards with its thousands of pens for incoming livestock. In the
summer, the smells of manure and slaughter permeated the air, though
residents claimed to be accustomed to the stench. But on this crisp late
afternoon in winter, lights were twinkling from the downtown below
and shone through the leafless branches of the trees framing the view.
The wide, meandering Mississippi River flowed peacefully by.

   Bernhard LeVander, a lanky young Swede fresh out of the navy,
sauntered up the curving walkway to the dark wood-paneled front
door. Known to his friends as "Pete," he had just been asked to serve
as organization director for the Republican State Central Committee.[1]
LeVander was at the home of Harold Stassen, former governor of Minnesota. Stassen was only thirty-nine years old, tall, charismatic, with
dark eyes and a rapidly receding hairline. He had begun his career as a
lawyer in South St. Paul. At age thirty-one, he had been elected governor and served from 1938 until 1943, when he resigned to join the navy
under Admiral William Halsey. In 1945, President Roosevelt appointed
Stassen to serve as U.S. delegate to the United Nations.[2]

   By 1946 Stassen resided at home in Minnesota. But having had a
taste of national politics, he wanted to be free to operate nationally

and internationally as a "springboard," as LeVander put it, to a run for the presidency.[3] He also intended to protect his legacy and find suitable Republicans who shared his views to hold positions of power in Minnesota.

Stassen had quite a legacy. He and his Young Republican colleagues had challenged the hegemony of the old guard from the right, who had increasingly become the party of big business—milling, logging, banking, and railroads. He had also defeated Elmer Benson, a leader of the Minnesota Farmer-Labor Party, a left-wing amalgamation of farmers and workers who rose to power in this period of agrarian and labor unrest.[4] Stassen found a new middle ground between the right and the left. When asked how his philosophy, dubbed the New Republican Liberalism, differed from the New Deal, he responded:

> I think the difference is a matter of emphasis. Individual opportunity and social security are the two great considerations of a people's government. The New Deal sought security above all else. I think now a new balance must be worked out between security and opportunity.[5]

During his tenure as governor (1939–43), Stassen reduced the state's indebtedness, reformed the civil service system, supported longer old age assistance and better standards for relief for the poor, extended the moratorium on mortgages, and passed an anti–loan shark bill. He also brought a system of financial control, with a state business manager accountable directly to the governor. He created a "cooling-off period" for labor disputes, employed a state labor conciliator for direct negotiations, encouraged settlements, and reduced the number of strikes by 70 percent. He won reelection twice with substantial majorities.[6]

Stassen opened his front door, smiling at LeVander, and stepped aside to let him in. Stassen's wife, Esther, took his coat, and hustled back into the kitchen to put the coffee on. Soon, other cars pulled up the drive, parking haphazardly at the end of the cul-de-sac. The group included Governor Ed Thye, who as Stassen's lieutenant governor had assumed the office when Stassen enlisted and had been elected in his own right in 1944. Thye was considered "Stassen's man."[7] The others were lawyers and political operatives from around the state. The group, known as the Stassen "machine," had been meeting regularly, holding "noodling sessions" as LeVander called them.[8] They had one goal at this meeting. Tonight was the night they would pick the man who would be the next governor of Minnesota.

The men stepped down into the cozy living room with its heavy, hand-hewn beams and broad windows with views of the Mississippi. A fire crackled in the fireplace. Coffee was served, pipes, cigars, and cigarettes lit. In this quintessential "smoke-filled room," the guys got down to business.

The 1946 election was approaching. Henrik Shipstead, a United States senator since 1923, had broken with the Democratic Party in 1940 and was running again as a Republican. Shipstead was one of only two senators to vote against the United Nations Charter. His isolationist stance was unacceptable to Stassen. Shipstead had to go. As LeVander recalled, Stassen felt that

> Shipstead really wasn't representative of the feeling of the people of Minnesota here. So we decided that one of the chores that the guys that came out of the service had to get done was to get Shipstead out of here. So the move then was to get Ed Thye to run against Shipstead, and that was going to uncover the governorship. So we had to figure out who was going to go in there.[9]

By the end of the evening they all agreed that Judge Luther Youngdahl was the right man. He had a Scandinavian name and was a devout Lutheran, valuable political assets in Minnesota. He had attended Gustavus Adolphus College, a respected Swedish Lutheran school in St. Peter, the Minnesota College of Law in St. Paul, and served in World War I. He also had campaign experience running for municipal judge and now sat on the Minnesota Supreme Court.

Personally, Youngdahl was athletic, gregarious, competitive, and stubborn, with a deep laugh and rollicking sense of humor. Importantly, he had demonstrated an interest in human problems consistent with the Stassen tradition. Because of their friendship, LeVander was tapped to talk to Youngdahl as soon as possible. The meeting ended, and the boys went out into the night, satisfied with a job well done.

LeVander called Youngdahl that evening and arranged to meet him in his chambers at the Supreme Court the next day. While the judge was putting on his robes, LeVander acknowledged that his purpose was to ask whether Youngdahl would consider running for governor. Understanding that LeVander was representing Stassen, Youngdahl wanted to speak with Stassen personally before he made a final decision. A meeting was arranged at the Youngdahl home the following Saturday. The three men met, and Youngdahl agreed to run.[10]

Having put the right candidates in place, the 1946 campaign began. Stassen's Republican Party operatives ran the show, and the Thye-Shipstead race for the Senate seat dominated the news, framed in part as a contest between isolationism and internationalism. But because Stassen's presidential aspirations were well known, the press reported that his "prestige depends upon the outcome of the Republican race for the senatorial nomination."[11] A lot was on the line for Stassen and his particular brand of Republicanism.

The Stassen organization also ran the Youngdahl campaign, or as Robert Esbjornson, Youngdahl's biographer, noted, "the Stassen organization took him over."[12] The strategy was to avoid controversies and highlight Youngdahl's personality and qualifications. He was an energetic campaigner, visiting over 150 towns and villages, and an effective speaker who connected personally with the people he met. LeVander's job was to "keep those two guys [Thye and Youngdahl] in the same harness." Thye resented any new ideas that candidate Youngdahl proposed, assuming they implied the failure of Thye's governorship to solve them. Tension between the two was high.[13]

Hjalmar Petersen, the fiery Farmer-Labor Party man, who switched to the Republican side after losing to Stassen in 1940 and 1942, challenged Youngdahl in the Republican primary.[14] Petersen triggered a controversy involving the Faribault School and Colony for the Feeble-Minded, as it was known at the time. Established in 1879 with 15 children, by the 1940s the school was overcrowded, with a population of more than 2,600 in an institution equipped to care for 2,200.[15] While the school for the intellectually disabled at Faribault differed from the seven hospitals for the mentally ill, the Mental Health Unit in the Division of Public Institutions (DPI) oversaw them all. Carl Swanson, whom Stassen appointed in 1939 and Thye had subsequently reappointed, ran the DPI.[16]

On June 10, 1946, four weeks before the July primary, Petersen demanded that the Rice County attorney, John Coughlin, immediately convene a special grand jury investigation of the school. Petersen's allies had submitted sworn affidavits to Coughlin alleging patient mistreatment, including children tied to toilets and left out all night, food unfit for human consumption, and widespread sterilizations. On June 19, the headline in the *Veterans' News,* a pro-Petersen paper, screamed "Cruelty in State School Charged" and was accompanied by a cartoon captioned "Smash the Machine with Petersen."[17]

Within days, the Republican powers that be closed ranks and came out swinging. Coughlin, who had served in the legislature, persuaded Thye to take a tough stance. On June 28, the *St. Paul Dispatch*'s headline read, "School Staff Libeled—Thye."[18]

Coughlin sent the sheriff to interview those who had sworn to affidavits; Petersen alleged intimidation of witnesses.

Governor Thye took an aggressive tone in a KSTP radio address the following day. He asserted that many of the affidavits were false, that Swanson was a fine Christian man, and that Faribault's superintendent E. J. Engberg had served admirably since 1937. Thye said the grand jury should meet, but not until its regular session in the fall, and insisted that the investigation would determine whether additional legal action against those who submitted the affidavits was called for. His response was biting:

I knew that in the heat of the political campaign there would be false and malicious rumors circulated and unfounded charges made, but

Faribault State School for the Feeble-Minded, circa 1900. At that time, the school housed up to fifteen hundred intellectually disabled children and adults in overcrowded conditions. The building was razed in 1957. Photograph by Henry H. Altschwager. Courtesy of the Minnesota Historical Society.

I never thought that unscrupulous supporters of desperate candidates would stoop to measures whose chief result is to bring anguish to innocent persons and accusation against state employees.[19]

The Stassen forces had experience with Petersen based on his two unsuccessful bids to defeat Stassen, and they did not shy away from hardball tactics. They decisively dispatched the issue. Since this was an attack on the current administration, Thye himself took the lead in responding. Youngdahl stayed in the background, even though Petersen was his opponent, not Thye's.

The strategy worked. Both Thye and Youngdahl trounced their respective primary opponents on July 9.[20] Esbjorson concluded that Youngdahl continued his "campaign for election . . . laid stress on good government, youth conservation, law enforcement, and tolerance and understanding in human relations; but it was no crusade. . . . He aroused no fears, or hopes, of a reform administration."[21]

Thye did not want this issue hanging over his head in the general election. Carl Swanson, hoping to stay on in the next administration, was still hurting over the attack on the Division of Public Institutions. He wrote to the governor on August 2, 1946, requesting that the Council of the Minnesota Medical Association be asked to appoint a special committee of qualified specialists to investigate "thoroughly and completely" the care and treatment of persons at Faribault.[22] Swanson didn't stop there. He also asked Thye, "In your request and in any publicity connected therewith, I believe it only fair to ask that you, Doctor Engberg, and the writer [Swanson] be given credit for requesting such an investigation."[23] The governor made the request to the medical association and, by October, it assembled a committee of seven doctors who would report their findings in the spring.[24] Given the frosty relations between Thye and Youngdahl, it is likely that Youngdahl was not informed of the pending investigation. The campaign promptly moved on.

The election on November 4, 1946, led to big victories for Thye and Youngdahl, who handily defeated his Farmer-Labor opponent, Harold H. Barker.[25] Conveniently, ten days later, the grand jury in Rice County reported:

We have investigated the conditions at the Minnesota School for the Feeble Minded by questioning numerous witnesses and a thorough inspection of the Institution. From such investigation we found that the charges of mistreatment of inmates, wholesale and authorized sterilization and unsatisfactory food conditions were unwarranted and not substantiated. We further found that in general the conditions at the Institution were very satisfactory, especially so in view of the difficult help situation during the past few years.[26]

Coughlin sent a personal note to Swanson and enclosed copies of the grand jury report for Governor Thye. Coughlin, who had a close personal relationship with Swanson, wrote, "Probably a more detailed report on the School could have been made, but they wanted it clear, definite and without any possibility of misinterpretation. Hope it will relieve the parents and relatives, and be a warning to politicians in the future."[27] Swanson, in turn, sent a supportive note to Superintendent

Three of Minnesota's governors, circa 1950 (from left): Harold Stassen (1939–43), Edward Thye (1943–47), and Luther Youngdahl (1947–51). Courtesy of the Minnesota Historical Society.

Engberg expressing the DPI's confidence in and respect for Engberg's work. He also commented, "With the resignations of many of those responsible for the misinformation that was publicized and the conclusions of the Grand Jury, I hope the matter is settled once and for all and that you will never again be subjected to such a disagreeable experience."[28]

Senator Thye went off to Washington, D.C., and Governor Youngdahl took office in January 1947. The Republican Party had successfully put the final nail in the Faribault controversy coffin, or so they thought.

The politicians may have set the issue aside, but those familiar with the state institutions knew conditions at Faribault were wretched, just as they were at the other mental hospitals. Engla Schey, ever the fearless activist, wrote to Petersen after the election, "The outcome of the Faribault investigation grieved me, knowing the low status of care we have in Minnesota institutions. . . . The politicians thru the press labeled it a smear campaign, the professions who must have known better, were as usual silent."[29] She also confided to Petersen: "The patients watched your primaries with enthusiasm. They were as sorry at the results as I was."[30]

On January 8, 1947, Luther Youngdahl gave his inaugural address before a joint session of the legislature. He stated his priorities in this first postwar governorship. Protecting "human resources," defined as addressing the needs of the people, was closest to his heart:

> An enlightened citizenry, showing concern for its handicapped and needy members, courageously attacking the problems of education, housing, public health, youth conservation and racial discrimination—here is a goal that is worthy of all the thought and energy at our command, and if the faint heart should object that the difficulties lying in our course are insuperable, our answer must be, "We have no alternative; we have got to launch out."[31]

His budget proposal sought to balance Minnesota's financial problems with the urgent needs of the people. The proposed spending, higher than the previous two years, included increases for education, the aged, blind, and the needy.[32]

In his address, Youngdahl described the principles upon which he would govern—morality and independence. In his view, "Politics is the machinery by which society makes its moral decisions."[33] For the new governor, morality was inextricably linked to his Christian faith. As an Augustana Lutheran, he believed drinking, gambling, and dancing were immoral acts. However, unlike many pietistic Lutherans who stressed subjective religious experience and were indifferent to social and political issues, the Augustana Synod emphasized the role of Christians in society and active engagement in political and social concerns.[34]

Youngdahl declared that he would be independent and not beholden to his political party or other organized interests. "Although I believe in the two-party system of government, the governor is elected to serve all the people. . . . I will endeavor to serve you without reference to blocs or pressure groups and without regard to political consequences. I shall attempt to follow my own convictions on any matter that comes before me."[35]

His two key 1947 initiatives reflected those principles. Within a few weeks of his inauguration, Youngdahl launched what became known as his "anti-slot machine" bill, seeking to enforce the laws against gambling that the state and local police ignored.[36] There was immediate opposition from owners of resorts, men's clubs, and other organizations, many of whom were loyal Republicans, and who relied on slot machine income to finance their activities.[37]

Red flags went up among the Stassen Republicans who had invited him to run for the office. Republican Party leaders who had not been consulted were shocked by Youngdahl's zealotry. LeVander, now party chairman, told Youngdahl that he was pushing his anti–slot machine bill "out of all proportion," and damaging relationships with loyal Republicans.[38] Unmoved, Youngdahl appealed directly to the people and to the churches. He aggressively twisted many legislative arms. The bill passed at the end of the session. As the *Des Moines Register* concluded, "Youngdahl has a trait puzzling to professional politicians: he means what he says. . . . The Minnesota record proves that old-fashioned civic morality can still be sold to the public."[39]

Youngdahl's second major initiative of 1947, the Youth Conservation Act, provides more clues to his governing style. While he was on the bench, he was involved in addressing the problems of juvenile delinquency. During this time, youth with serious psychological problems, often due to parental neglect, alcohol abuse, and poverty, were punished and incarcerated in reform schools rather than treated and rehabilitated under the law.

Youngdahl's religious and moral values bristled at the callous treatment of young people—they were a human resource to be "conserved." He worked with Dr. Alexander Dumas, a Minneapolis psychiatrist, to find ways to provide guidance and support for these young offenders, and saw firsthand what constructive intervention could accomplish. He even took several boys under his wing personally, and was pleased with the progress these young men made.[40]

As governor, Youngdahl wanted a more understanding approach to delinquency based on a model law already in place in four other states.[41] The Youth Conservation Act he proposed would establish a five-member commission invested with extensive authority over youths under twenty-one found guilty of felony or gross misdemeanors, and supplement local resources, including rehabilitation, probation services, and public education.[42] He pressed forward despite the fact that many church leaders issued, as Steefel observed, "dire warnings that Youth must be punished and atheist psychiatrists prevented from interfering with the will of God."[43] He found support from the State Bar Association, county attorneys, and other civic groups.[44] The bill passed.

Youngdahl was driven by moral principles and cared deeply about vulnerable people. For issues that mattered to him, he ignored party concerns and special interests.

How did mental hospitals fare? The status quo prevailed. Youngdahl reappointed Carl Swanson in March. The state mental institutions were not on his priority list in 1947. That year the legislature did approve the report of an interim committee requesting the 1945 authorization of $5 million for a building program for aged patients in mental institutions to reduce overcrowding.[45] All state employees received modest cost-of-living increases under the civil service, but the DPI's biennial requests for repairs and equipment were only partially funded.[46]

Swanson crowed about results in a May radio interview. The interviewer concluded that "Mr. Swanson has outlined a far-reaching program of improvement and expansion, especially in so far as mentally ill people are concerned, as a result of action by the 1947 Legislature."[47] But, as the Unitarians knew full well, there was no far-reaching improvement; this was business as usual for the public institutions.

Behind the scenes, however, the Faribault issue resurfaced. During the legislative session, Youngdahl had relied heavily on the advice and support of his friend Dumas. That the Minnesota Mental Hygiene Society, where Dumas was medical director, did everything possible to secure the passage of the Youth Conservation Act no doubt strengthened their relationship.[48] Dr. Alan Challman, the president of the society, worked closely with Dumas and was also one of the doctors on the team investigating conditions at Faribault.

In the first week of March, Dr. Challman and the president of the Minnesota Medical Association met with the governor, perhaps at the urging of Dumas. No doubt they told Youngdahl that the report would not contain good news. During that same week, Youngdahl asked for recommendations for individuals to serve on an advisory council "to help in the solution of state problems in connection with the mental institutions."[49] Dr. Dumas also was asked to join as an author on the forthcoming report about Faribault. The confluence of these activities suggests that the creation of the advisory council was a defensive move on the part of the governor, arming him with experts if the bad news about Faribault broke.

On April 16, 1947, before the Governor's Advisory Council on Mental Health was made official, Youngdahl officially received *A Report by the Special Committee Appointed by the Council of the Minnesota State Medical Association at the Request of Governor Edward J. Thye.*[50] Youngdahl had not been directly involved in the controversy over conditions at Faribault during the campaign, and indeed he may not have even been informed of its existence, but as sitting governor he would be accountable for the results.

After months of thorough investigation, the Minnesota State Medical Association's report was a damning indictment.[51] The findings: severe overcrowding of children; "woefully inadequate, poorly equipped, obsolete and unsafe" buildings; a kitchen so meagerly equipped that it was "impossible to supply, prepare and serve a balanced and palatable diet"; significant understaffing in all departments; underpaid and unprepared workers, resulting in inadequate vocational, recreational, or educational training; inadequate medical care and clothing, especially for the very youngest ones; large numbers of children in restraints (e.g., one-third of patients in one building); and children tied to toilets.

The recommendations: the administration should urge the legislature to increase the budget for the physical plant, with special attention to food preparation facilities; an *"immediate and urgent need"* for upgrades of the kitchen for proper preparation and distribution of food; the legislature must raise the budget for payroll and revise civil service laws to permit hiring and pay of trained personnel; reasonable sums should be appropriated for this school (and other institutions for care of the unfortunate wards of the state). In sum, the special committee concluded that there could be no appreciable improvement of the physical plant or staff issues "until an adequate operational budget has been furnished." Again, with underscoring, *"This is a serious responsibility of the people of this State."*[52]

These findings actually corroborated many of Petersen's charges the Thye administration had denied, and the Rice County grand jury had summarily dismissed. There was no evidence, however, that the report was made public.[53] Knowing Youngdahl's moral compass and his passion for the conservation of human resources, he must have been saddened and angry at the findings of these well-meaning, independent physicians. But Youngdahl was now a politician, and these politics were risky for the sitting governor. His own party had been complicit in a cover-up, including Swanson, a man Youngdahl had reappointed. What now?

His first step was to officially launch the Governor's Advisory Council on Mental Health in June. The panel included Dumas and Challman, along with Dr. Francis Braceland, chair of psychiatry at Mayo, Dr. Donald Hastings, chair of psychiatry at the university, and former Anoka superintendent Walter P. Gardner. Frank Rarig Jr. was the only nonpsychiatrist on the council.[54] Unquestionably, Youngdahl had surrounded himself with the most influential and respected physicians and psychiatrists in the state. He did not, however, call the first meeting of the group until July.

Carl Swanson was on the hot seat. During the campaign, he had declared that the charges against Faribault were false, and he, ironically, had sought credit for requesting the Medical Association investigation, though he clearly did not anticipate the result. The DPI's official response to the report did not arrive on the governor's desk until June 10. Dr. Royal C. Gray, chief of the DPI's Mental Health Unit, signed the cover letter to the governor on Swanson's behalf.[55]

With classic bureaucratic defensiveness, the letter began by extracting the one arguably exonerating phrase in the report: "The institution is being conducted as well as can be expected under the circumstances." While it was true that lack of resources accounted for deficiencies in the physical plant and the staffing, the DPI had vociferously denied any assertions of inadequacies during the campaign. Instead, it had alleged that the individual complainants unduly and unfairly upset inmates' loved ones with their charges. Privately, they had shared smug satisfaction that those employees who had testified to dismal conditions were forced to resign.

Now the DPI insisted it had been cognizant of the deficiencies, arguing that they were set forth in prior biennial reports, and complained that their budget requests had not been fully funded by the legislature in 1947.[56] It was an interesting argument, since Swanson had touted the sufficiency of the funds on the radio just a few weeks before.

Luther Youngdahl had a big problem on his hands. Granted, there were financial deficiencies and personnel shortages at Faribault. But the problems clearly went much deeper. His own leadership had misled him about the abject conditions there, dragged their feet in response to the report, and then blamed others. Whom could Youngdahl trust?

The governor turned to his new Advisory Council for help. By mid-September 1947, the council stated that its mission was to determine how to "proceed to develop a constructive and realistic program for the improvement of our state mental hospitals and the whole mental health system of the state."[57] The council called meetings with the superintendents of the state mental institutions, and also invited representatives of employee unions and some local citizens to testify about problems. In keeping with council members' physician-oriented perspective, however, they did not consult patients or lower-ranking staff. The superintendents felt vulnerable and under attack. The bureaucrats and their employees began to take sides.

One such superintendent was Stanley B. Lindley M.D. of Willmar State Hospital. Willmar began in 1912 as a hospital farm for inebriates. Renamed the Willmar State Asylum in 1917, and intended for hopeless or custodial care cases, the facility later became Willmar State Hospital. It was now severely overcrowded with a population of nearly fifteen hundred.[58]

Lindley had been called to one of the council meetings where there was discussion of issues related to Willmar. He wrote to Swanson in November 1947, "Shame and resentment have forced me to write this letter. I cannot forgive myself for sitting quietly while you were unfairly criticized during the governor's conference with the superintendents and the advisory committee." He spoke of frustration at the presence of union members who implied that Swanson was untruthful and obstructionist, and whose remarks Lindley called "both stupid and evil." He concluded by stating to Swanson, "You have my full respect and you have been a great help to me and anything that you wish I shall try to carry out."[59]

Youngdahl faced another case that provided him with even more disturbing evidence of problems at the state institutions. The governor received lots of mail from constituents. His files were bulging with letters from patients and families regarding their experiences. Each letter was referred to the superintendent of the relevant institution to respond to the complainant, with a copy of the response forwarded to the governor. The responses were formulaic and generally polite, but firmly dismissed the concerns.

One letter caught the governor's eye. On September 3, Youngdahl received a letter from Frank J. Rosemeier, a judge in the Municipal Court of the City of Virginia, on official letterhead.[60] The judge told a tragic tale in a fair and balanced manner. The case involved John Davidson, Rosemeier's brother-in-law. A gentleman advanced in years, Mr. Davidson began to deteriorate physically and mentally, becoming, in the judge's words, "a mental case toward the last."

Mrs. Davidson, the judge's sister, cared for her husband at home because she feared sending him to an asylum. But over time she was unable to cope, and was reluctantly persuaded to do so. The judge himself had assisted in the paperwork to facilitate the transfer. John Davidson entered St. Peter State Hospital on August 2, 1947.

Rosemeier's sister visited her husband eight days after his admission. He was bruised, dressed in rags, had his head on his chest, and appeared unconscious. The attendant told her that Davidson "was a mean fellow." She insisted her husband be given medical help. Davidson was taken to the medical ward and died on August 12, two days after his wife's visit. The judge's grieving sister did not want to report this situation, being so full of humiliation and guilt, or as the judge put it, "ugly thoughts she will carry with her to her grave." Rosemeier, however, believed he had a duty to society to report this situation "to the proper source." He wrote:

> I recall some time ago, reading about treatment of patients at this same institution, but I regarded that as a political matter, which eventually it developed to be. You and I know, however, that where there is smoke, there is fire. People don't just generally have such a dread to take a loved one to an institution like this without a reason therefor. I feel particularly guilty in this instance because I had initiated the proceeding.

After calling for this case to be "very, very thoroughly investigated," Judge Rosemeier concluded graciously, "Please regard this letter in the spirit in which it is written. I am doing this on my own initiative."

The governor precipitated a furious correspondence.

September 4: Youngdahl, deeply moved and concerned, immediately sought answers from Swanson. Swanson called Dr. George H. Freeman, the superintendent of St. Peter.

September 8: Swanson forwarded a report from Freeman. The superintendent concluded that "the whole thing was a matter of [the attendants] using poor judgment." In the cover letter from Swanson forwarding the Freeman report, Swanson stated that Freeman visited the central office and they explored the issue with Dr. Gray. Swanson explained: "Doctor Freeman stated that seemingly the attendant in this case was not too careful in his handling of the situation" and that "the undersigned [Swanson] impressed upon Doctor Freeman that he should call in the persons concerned and advise them regarding being more alert in situations of this kind."

September 15: The governor wrote to Judge Rosemeier, telling him that he would be referring the matter to his Advisory Council on Mental Health for investigation, and expressing deep sympathy and grave concerns.

September 18: Youngdahl fired off a stern letter to Swanson stating that he was "very much disturbed" about the admission of improper care and demanding "a further and more complete report as to just what supervision the superintendent makes over employees and all the details in connection with this case, so the whole matter can be submitted to the Advisory Council."

September 18: The governor sent Royal Gray a copy of his September 18 letter to Swanson, with a note asking for Gray's opinion on the lack of care.

September 23: Swanson responded to the governor, offering a new version of the events. "Dr. Freeman states that he is convinced that Mr. Davidson received the kindliest and most considerate treatment while he was a patient at the hospital. He also stated that the attendant in charge at the time the complaint was made is an old employee, and an employee that Dr. Freeman had complete confidence in, and the last person to be unkind or inconsiderate of patients." He went on to state that superintendents check on their employees frequently and that "I am personally of the opinion that all of our superintendents are interested in the care and treatment given the patients entrusted to their care, and all of them have received many letters of thanks and commendation from relatives and patients."

October 6: Gray contradicted Swanson. He wrote, "I do not offer any excuse for the shortcomings in the care of Mr. Davidson." Gray acknowledged that state hospitals are sadly lacking in qualified nursing personnel; none of the attendants had nursing training and shouldn't be blamed. It is a personnel issue we must correct. "None of the attendants involved nor Doctor Freeman, the hospital superintendent, should be blamed for lack of care of Mr. Davidson. We should, instead, criticize ourselves for not being more insistent that there be provided sufficient qualified nursing personnel in the state hospitals."

October 9: The governor thanked Gray for his letter and agreed they must aggressively fight for necessary personnel.

October 9: The same day, the governor upbraided Swanson for the "inconsistent and conflicting statements" in his prior explanations, and insisted that he "get straight the facts in this case." In another rebuke, he noted that Gray, Swanson's subordinate, "hits at the nub of the situation," which was to get more funding for personnel.

October 24: Swanson tried to reconcile the conflicting statements that had infuriated Youngdahl. In order to deflect blame from the attendants, he now qualified the conclusion of "poor judgment" by the attendants as one in which the poor judgment was a result of a "desire to do their work well":

> Possibly the patient, after being dressed, and while being brought to the visiting room, turned worse and was, therefore, not in a condition to be brought to the visiting room. In that case, he felt that possibly the blame could not be placed against the attendant. In both reports Doctor Freeman states the attendants were kind and considerate, but perhaps in their desire to do their work well by bringing the patient to the visiting room, they used poor judgment.

October 31: The governor wrote to Judge Rosemeier. He used Swanson's language that the attendant's poor judgment stemmed from good motives. Then, Youngdahl assured the judge that he would be "exerting utmost efforts in improving the administration of these hospitals."

This explanation clearly altered the conclusions made earlier, and Youngdahl knew it. A man had died under questionable circumstances, a family grieved, and his director of the DPI and the superintendent of

St. Peter concocted conflicting versions of events. Two months of calls and correspondence and this was the best he could get. It wasn't good enough.

Youngdahl knew he had a serious problem. He was aware of unacceptable conditions in the institutions and of the cover-ups and infighting in his own administration. Unlike his signature issues—youth conservation and the anti–slot machine campaign—that he rode into the governorship vowing to address, the controversies in the state institutions were occurring on his watch and he would be held responsible. He now knew that his own party and his own people had quashed the evidence of scandalous conditions. How could he, the sitting governor, survive the political fallout of the truth?

While all these issues were swirling around the governor, a young reporter from the *Minneapolis Tribune* requested a meeting with him. Once authorized by the MUC to take action in September, the MUC Committee on Mental Hospitals looked to the press. Arthur Foote contacted Geri Hoffner, the cub investigative reporter he had met previously. He told her of the Unitarians' interest and preliminary findings, and suggested that the *Tribune* might want to run a story on conditions in the state's mental hospitals. Hoffner, intrigued, consulted with Bower Hawthorne, the urbane, sophisticated city editor of the *Tribune*. Bower knew she was just the person for the job.

Hoffner was a bright, confident, gracious young woman. She was the daughter of Sam and Edith Mack; her father was a Russian Jewish immigrant in the automotive business, her mother from St. Paul.[61] She had studied journalism and political science at the University of Minnesota, and graduated with honors in 1946. As managing editor of the *Minnesota Daily,* the university newspaper, she was considered one of the "big guns." Hoffner had a reputation as a hard-hitting reporter at the *Daily*—she "definitely pulled no punches in tackling such issues as the new Liberal group, the new University president, veterans' tuition and the U's housing problems."[62]

During her senior year, Hoffner had been asked to interview for a job at the *Tribune*. At first she resisted. She had set her sights on the *New York Times*! However, her friend and fellow editor persuaded her that there might be interesting work for her at the *Tribune,* so she agreed to consider it. The *Tribune* offered her a job doing in-depth, interpretive reporting, not just run-of-the-mill stories. Intrigued, she accepted the offer in 1946.[63] She was twenty-three years old.

Hoffner loved the job and found that the newspaper provided a great place to work. The newsroom was full of young people—the oldest was only twenty-seven—with lots of latitude for creative reporting. "We were all very green," she recalled. "But we were given great freedom to do challenging things—as long as we were accurate." She had been at the paper a little more than a year when Foote approached her with the idea of a story on the mental institutions. Even though the hospitals were technically public places, Hawthorne insisted that she inform the

From left, Minnesota Governor Orville Freeman (1955–61) meets with journalist and Unitarian reformer Ed Crane, *Minneapolis Tribune* reporter Geri Hoffner, and Arthur Foote, circa 1954. Author's collection.

governor of the plan to do a series. Hoffner recalled, "We didn't want to sneak in sub rosa. We wanted him to know we were there."[64]

So on a balmy October day, her dark eyes shining with excitement, Hoffner dressed in shirtwaist cotton dress and light sweater, and took the streetcar from the offices of the *Tribune* to the imposing Capitol building in St. Paul. She had butterflies. This was a tough assignment. But it was also a big opportunity for the young reporter. She had a good impression of the governor and admired his accomplishments. She waited in the elaborate anteroom, with its rich-grained, wood-paneled walls, enormous oil paintings in gilded frames, and ornate light fixtures.

A secretary ushered her into the governor's office. This young woman, bright and eager, found herself standing before *the* governor of the state of Minnesota. She made her pitch for a *Tribune* series on the institutions. She and a photographer proposed to spend several days in each of the seven mental hospitals over the course of the winter. They would write the story in the spring. Images of Faribault and St. Peter swirled in Youngdahl's mind. The face of the tall, outgoing, affable governor went from quizzical, to skeptical, to downright angry.

He rose to his feet from behind his desk, dwarfing the petite reporter. "If you try to do this," he bellowed, "I will have your job!"[65]

Heart pounding, Hoffner returned chastened to the *Tribune* office. Hawthorne was surprised and annoyed. He insisted they go back together to the governor's office. A few days later they returned. The governor was more controlled. Hawthorne told the governor that the paper would do the story no matter what. They agreed that Youngdahl could read her story before publication, but could not change the text.

The assignment was hers. It offered an opportunity of a lifetime. Foote offered background information and names of knowledgeable sources. The series would run in the spring of 1948. Youngdahl knew he couldn't prevent the press from nosing around in the dirty laundry of the public mental institutions, but hoped he could influence the outcome, or at least buy some time. He knew he was sitting on a political powder keg. But he didn't know when it might blow.

EIGHT

Political Dynamite

> We lock patients away, out of sight and out of mind. Ignorance
> plus indifference, and a false view of mental illness, have led to
> a veritable conspiracy of silence.
>
> ■ *Arthur Foote, "The Care of the Mentally Ill in Minnesota"*

On Saturday morning, November 8, 1947, Arthur Foote sat
at his kitchen table and sipped the last of his coffee. He flipped through
the morning paper. President Truman was calling a special congressional session to consider the Marshall Plan for postwar Europe, Harold
Stassen had announced his candidacy for president, the first to jump
into the 1948 race, and the world was buzzing about the impending
marriage of Princess Elizabeth. But, Foote's concern on this day was
the weather.

The *Pioneer Press* headline shouted "3 Dead, 4 Hurt in Storm's Wake."[1]
In the earliest and most intense winter storm in years, heavy winds
had downed trees and power lines throughout Minnesota. The paper
predicted blowing snow would snarl traffic and delay trains and
buses. Arthur scanned the gray, cloudy sky through his kitchen window on Goodrich Avenue in St. Paul. On this quiet street, it was a winter wonderland. Soon all the children would be outside at play in the
snowdrifts. Foote could hear the clatter of his children's footsteps
above on the second floor—Caleb had just turned four and was recover-
ing from his health challenges, and Frances would be ten years old in
nine days.

He sighed. Here it was, another weekend, and he was off to work.

On Saturdays he would usually walk over to the church to complete
his Sunday sermon. Today, however, he was to deliver his first public address on conditions in the state's mental hospitals. He was due in downtown Minneapolis before noon.

Calling good-bye to the family, Foote threw on his overcoat and boots and set out to shovel a path to his car in the unplowed alley. He cautiously ventured down to University Avenue, the wide boulevard linking Minneapolis and St. Paul. In the swirling snow, crews were feverishly shoveling the streetcar tracks. Slowly but surely he made his way west to his destination.

The Dyckman Hotel, one of the Twin Cities' finest, rose to over ten stories in downtown Minneapolis. Foote parked the car and stepped into the elegant Italianate lobby—all marble floors and gilded ceilings, with rich walnut and mahogany paneling throughout. He checked his coat, overshoes, and hat in the lobby, and entered the dining room. Tables were set with white linens under glittering crystal chandeliers. Tuxedo-clad waiters stood at the ready. He paused to consider the disparity between this lovely setting and the story he would soon tell.

The host was the Saturday Lunch Club of Minneapolis, of which he had heard so much. Stiles P. Jones, an early member of the First Unitarian Society, had founded the club in 1906. For over forty years, every Saturday noon, seven months a year, members gathered to discuss the issues of the day. The club was a voluntary "non-partisan open forum for free discussion of social, economic and political issues." Members included prominent university professors, professionals in law and medicine, and progressive business leaders. Foote was in good company. Former speakers included luminaries such as Louis D. Brandeis, Jane Addams, William Jennings Bryan, and Clarence Darrow. The club had admitted women in 1919, after several well-known female speakers on the women's suffrage movement applied for membership.[2] Frank Rarig Sr., University of Minnesota professor of rhetoric and recently retired chair of the FUS board, was a longtime member. He paved the way for Arthur to kick off the public face of the MUC's Committee on Mental Hospitals before this dignified group.

The attendees assembled and lunch was served. Foote rose to the podium. The clattering of silverware diminished and the audience turned its attention to him. The young minister cut a handsome figure behind the lectern. A reporter would note that he resembled the Hollywood star Robert Montgomery.[3] In the engaging cadence that served him well in the pulpit, Foote presented the facts about conditions in Minnesota's mental institutions in measured but unequivocal terms. He eschewed the protest and anger that the committee had worked to overcome, but did not hesitate to describe with brutal honesty what the committee had learned. He began:

> When, a year and a half ago, *Life Magazine* printed an article by Albert Q Maisel entitled "Our Mental Hospitals—a National Disgrace"[4] many of us were profoundly shocked. Were conditions in America as shameful as that article revealed? We simply could not believe it. But there were pictures, pictures whose brief captions summed up a tragic, heart-bending story:
>
>
>
> NEGLECT
> RESTRAINT
> USELESS WORK
> NAKEDNESS
> OVERCROWDING
> FORCED LABOR
> IDLENESS
> DESPAIR
>
>
>
> I wish I could tell you that, after a year's investigation, our Unitarian Committee has found that article false and ungrounded, but I cannot. The situation is not quite so unrelievedly bad as these pictures suggest, but such conditions as are here portrayed do exist, right now, and right here in Minnesota and probably in every other state in the Union.[5]

Foote proceeded to cite mental illness as the nation's number-one health problem, and related it in direct and personal terms to the audience: "Several of us here tonight will fall victim to this, the greatest single disability to which man is liable." He noted that society treats mental illness as "a disgrace, a crime, and incurable." He criticized the commitment process that treated the mentally ill like criminals. He noted, in response to questions, that a St. Paul doctor had confided that he had signed commitment papers without actually examining the patient, a clear violation of the law.[6]

Foote spoke of a lack of research, and cited facts and figures to support claims of serious underfunding of patients' basic needs. Drawing on the firsthand experience of Engla Schey, he described the dismal conditions for the attendant, who was "the most important person to the individual patient"—underpaid, hired without skills, and denied training or promotion, some fearful of patients and more than a few brutal in their treatment. He spoke of the culture within the hospitals—highlighting that many superintendents do their best, and specifically praising Dr. Ralph Rossen of Hastings State Hospital for limiting the use of restraints. "But that cannot correct the fact that even the best run mental hospital is not good enough." In regard to the building program approved in the 1947 session, "We need those buildings, BUT IT IS FOLLY TO SUPPOSE THAT WE CAN CURE PATIENTS WITH BUILDINGS, with brick and stone and mortar."[7]

The speech galvanized the members of the Saturday Lunch Club. A lively discussion period followed. The club voted to form a committee to support improvements for mental hospitals. Pleased with the reception he received, Foote drove home to his family. The next day was Sunday, and he knew he would be burning the midnight oil to prepare his sermon.

Unbeknownst to Foote, there was a young reporter in the audience whose story appeared in the *Sunday Minneapolis Tribune* the following morning. Margaret Allison, a recent Smith College graduate who was in her first job, wrote in breathless terms. Under the inflammatory banner "Pastor Calls Mental Hospitals 'Horrible,'" the story began, "A young St. Paul clergyman fired the opening shot Saturday in a campaign to clean up what he charges are 'horrible' conditions in Minnesota mental hospitals." Allison continued with details of the pastor's "charges."[8]

The careful effort of the MUC Committee on Mental Hospitals to move beyond protest and anger to constructive engagement was shattered by the reporter's bellicose characterization of the presentation. As Foote later wrote, "Although the address included full recognition of the handicaps under which the state hospital system was operating, and gave full credit for the work and effort of the superintendents, the newspaper publicity highlighted only the criticisms."[9]

On Monday morning, three telephone calls greeted Foote at the church office. The first came from a businessman with a daughter in a mental hospital who offered to contribute to the cause, starting with a check for five hundred dollars. The second call was from a judge who threatened to hold Foote in contempt of court unless he disclosed the source regarding doctors who had signed commitment papers without seeing the patients.[10]

The third call came from Governor Youngdahl's office, informing Foote that the governor was unhappy about his comments and was insisting on a meeting with him. A time was set for a few days later.

Fortunately, an MUC meeting occurred before the scheduled date. Foote reviewed the issues he would raise and, thanks to Genevieve Steefel, he had a printed memo of supporting facts and figures.

As Foote set off for the capitol building later that week, he was deeply concerned. All the good intentions, the care to engage professionals, not attack them, and the focus on fact finding, not name calling, seemed to evaporate in the face of the governor's anger. Foote was well aware of the governor's hot temper. Hoffner had told him of Youngdahl's threat to have her fired when she first informed him of the *Tribune*'s interest in writing about mental institutions. Foote had hoped that the Unitarians' accommodating style might forestall opposition, but he couldn't have known beforehand how fortuitous Allison's article turned out to be. The irony was that the dramatic verbiage, so antithetical to the Unitarians' agreed approach, was the catalyst that caught Youngdahl's attention.

Governor Youngdahl, a native Minnesotan and powerful personage, was prepared to dress down this Harvard man, a newcomer to Minnesota, and, judging from the press report, clearly a firebrand who had publicly attacked the Youngdahl administration and impugned the integrity of doctors.

As he entered the governor's office, Foote extended his hand in greeting. The governor wasted no time in confronting the young pastor. After listening quietly to the tirade, Foote was permitted to respond. The governor was surprised that the earnest, articulate minister was not the rabble-rouser described in the newspaper. Calmly and with great deference, Foote shared with him the data about the institutions. He explained patiently how the MUC Committee on Mental Hospitals had carefully undertaken its study, shown respect to the professionals and superintendents working under adverse conditions, and had based its conclusions on firmly held ethical and humanitarian principles.

Reverend Foote, serious, honest, and compassionate, moved the governor. Youngdahl also knew that what he said was likely to be true. He confided to Foote that the politics and timing for mental health reform were not good; raising the issue was politically explosive. Foote responded to Youngdahl's concern by suggesting to him that "the problems of the state hospitals were political dynamite only in other hands than his own."[11]

With no experience in Minnesota politics, indeed no politics of any kind, the young minister uttered words that immediately resonated with the politically savvy governor. Youngdahl immediately understood that if he took this issue as his own and got out in front of those who would expose the truth, he could turn the politics to his advantage. He recognized too that this pastor and his Unitarians shared his own belief in the value of each human being, and could help him make a difference for the "forgotten people." Like the proverbial lion and the lamb, the irascible Swede and the pacifist Unitarian, with mutual respect, knew they could work together.

Before the meeting was out, Youngdahl made one offer—to appoint Foote to the Governor's Advisory Council on Mental Health—and one request—that the Unitarians produce a "reliable and authoritative" report for him detailing evidence on the state hospital deficiencies. Foote agreed to consult with the Minnesota Unitarian Conference, and the men shook hands, each one aware that an important relationship was now in place. The two men maintained a remarkable rapport throughout the reform campaign. Youngdahl resisted efforts of his political advisers against "open identification . . . with a group 'thought in some rural areas to be atheistic'"; for his part, Foote admired Youngdahl:

> Years on the bench had developed in Luther Youngdahl an objective and judicial approach, and there was also that fine Scandinavian ability to take leadership, with dignity, in reform. In this, as in other fields he brought to Minnesota social values and leadership, which helped it to move forward to close a gap.[12]

Foote met with the MUC leadership. They agreed that it was critically important to preserve the independence of the Unitarian group. As chair of the MUC Committee on Mental Hospitals, Foote could freely provide information and advice to the Governor's Advisory Council, thereby channeling its own work into the "stream of administrative reform," but he would not be bound to the council's viewpoint and values, and would stand his own ground as part of the Unitarian effort.[13] With the conditions agreed to, Foote joined the Advisory Council the following week. The MUC Committee on Mental Hospitals accepted the assignment to prepare a report for the governor by early 1948.

News traveled fast in Unitarian circles. On November 17, just days after the Saturday speech, George Jacobson wrote to Raymond Bragg, former FUS minister and now executive director of the Unitarian Service Committee in Boston:

The Mental Institutions Committee under Arthur Foote and Genevieve Steefel's leadership is really going to town. They have done a great deal to prod public officials to become concerned about their responsibility.... The speech which Art Foote gave in Minneapolis last week aroused so much attention in the press that he had a call from the Governor to come and discuss the content of that speech with him.[14]

Bragg responded a week later:

I am particularly excited by your report of the Mental Institutions Committee. At the time that committee was appointed, I had a feeling and still have it, that that is the sort of thing that a movement such as ours could do with every chance of measureable success. Arthur is tremendously interested and has courage enough to state baldly his findings. .... Arthur I am sure will know how to handle situations.[15]

Thrust into a position of potential influence, the Unitarians discussed the format and content of the report. The group felt the study must be undertaken at once, during the month of December. Consistent with Unitarian values, the report must be fully grounded in demonstrable facts. The author had to be a credentialed layperson, not a self-interested professional, and responsible to the MUC Committee on Mental Hospitals alone. The investigator must have full and approved access to every hospital and the experience to evaluate all he or she saw and heard.[16]

Steefel knew just the person—Justin Reese, an applicant for the executive secretary position at the Minnesota Mental Hygiene Society. While a few states' mental hygiene societies had ventured into mental hospital reform issues, most notably Oklahoma and Ohio, the Minnesota society had not been very reform oriented. Perhaps owing to the influence of board members Challman and Dumas, both on the Governor's Advisory Council on Mental Health, and Steefel and Rarig on the Unitarian side, the Minnesota Mental Hygiene Society was considering hiring an executive director to become more directly involved. Justin Reese was the leading candidate, and Steefel was hoping to attract him to Minnesota.[17]

Pale and slender, with reddish-blond hair and soft features, Reese appeared to be a quiet and unassuming young man. But his lack of presence masked a dogged commitment to reform and deep experience in community organizing. Reese was currently employed as a field representative with the National Mental Hygiene Society, and had worked closely with state chapters. His application emphasized his experience with public education campaigns on mental health. Interestingly, he omitted the key fact that, as one of the activist conscientious objectors in the Civilian Public Service during the war, he had been responsible for exposing the shocking conditions at Cleveland State Hospital.[18] Undoubtedly Genevieve Steefel and others knew this background, though Reese kept that experience quiet given the continuing hostility to conscientious objectors in the postwar period.[19]

A deal was struck. Reese agreed to come to Minnesota. The MUC Committee on Mental Hospitals hired him, along with his wife, Christine, to conduct the investigation for the report the governor requested during the month of December, prior to joining the staff of the Mental Hygiene Society in January.[20]

The governor allowed the Reeses full access to the hospitals without restriction. Foote noted: "It was characteristic of the Governor that he granted this request in the spirit in which it was made, forthrightly and without quibbling."[21] The assignment was a difficult one. As emissaries of the Unitarians, the Reeses posed a threat to the state system's status quo. Wherever they went, hospital administrators viewed them with suspicion, resenting lay outsiders and fearing what they would find and what use would be made of the findings. As Foote later wrote, "It was not unnatural that they considered the Committee to be a headline snatching group of protesting citizens who would point out what was wrong, but have no sensible proposals for setting things right."[22]

From her insider's perspective, Engla Schey offered a less benign interpretation. She knew the "tricks of the trade" in which outsiders were shown only the most flattering aspects of an institution. In a letter to Steefel, Engla reported how the Unitarians were dismissed once word got out about the investigation. "The Unitarians won't find out anything. Let them look around all they want to I hear in Rochester. They're only a nosy church. Nobody believes church people. What do they know about mental hospitals?"[23] Engla told of hearing a nursing supervisor warn the staff at Rochester to refrain from beating patients—who were "locked in and whipped like helpless rats" prior to the "Reese appearance on the wards."[24]

The governor wasted no time preparing the ground for his reform initiative. His first challenge was to deal with the leadership in his own administration. During Youngdahl's first year, DPI chief Carl Swanson had shown himself to be defensive and unforthcoming—a roadblock to reform. Swanson may have seen the handwriting on the wall and voluntarily resigned; perhaps he was forced to do so. Whatever the motivation, Swanson sent Youngdahl a resignation letter on December 4, 1947.

Swanson's letter of resignation, like many of his communications, was blatantly self-serving. He recounted all the "major advances" in meeting the needs of the mentally ill since he took office, noted in great detail the building program that was under way, and the "continued" effort to fill existing open employee positions. After he touted his successful expansion of facilities and improvement in administration while conserving state funds, he concluded, "With the completion of the planning of the present program, and the imminence of its realization, it is with considerable reluctance that I have decided to sever my connections with the state service in order to accept another position."[25] His resignation was effective on December 31, 1947.

The governor had a ready replacement. He chose Carl J. Jackson, who, since 1939, had been the superintendent of the State Training School for delinquent boys in Red Wing. He was of Swedish Lutheran descent, had grown up in St. Cloud, and graduated from Gustavus Adolphus College in 1923, fours years behind Youngdahl. The two worked together on the Youth Conservation initiative. Jackson understood the Division of Public Institutions (the training schools were in its purview), but he was not entrenched in the existing mental hospital system. The governor announced Jackson's appointment on December 29 and he took office in January 1948.[26]

With new supportive leadership in the wings and a new ally in the Unitarians, Youngdahl was now ready to launch his state mental hospital campaign. He made the case at a dinner for the local press on December 22, 1947, at the Minnesota Club in St. Paul. Because the legislature met only biennially, Youngdahl said his plan for mental health reform would make "even more news" than his policies in 1947. Mental health reform was the priority for the 1949 legislature, which of course depended on his reelection in November. Youngdahl said to the assemblage, "I feel I have a trust to discharge for the people of Minnesota and if they continue to want the program we've begun, I'm willing to serve again as governor." In essence, his mental health campaign and his reelection were now inextricably linked. The mental health work would begin, the *Minneapolis Star* reported, "as soon as the governor gets back from his forthcoming mid-winter flying trip to the Scandinavian countries."[27]

The Reese team completed its investigation at the end of December, and Reese became executive director of the Mental Hygiene Society in January 1948. At the society's January board meeting, Reese plunged right in, assuming that the organization would be as ardent for reform and his methods as he was. Reese proposed that the society grant him time on its payroll to complete the report for the Unitarians, and in that way, the society could justify joint sponsorship of the report. The psychiatrists on the board replied that sponsorship would entitle them to "clear" the final version.[28]

As a lay board member, Steefel reacted with concern. She didn't believe anyone on the MUC Committee on Mental Hospitals had authorized joint sponsorship, and "stated baldly that this report had been contracted for solely by the Unitarian committee and that its complete freedom from censorship would be protected." The Unitarians would willingly work with all parties, including state agencies, the university, or other experts. Those activities, however, would never be allowed to compromise their independence. The Unitarians recognized early on that only independent laypersons could provide a voice for the voiceless—the mental patients and nonprofessional staff. There would be no "clearance" and no joint sponsorship.[29]

The tussle over sponsorship also revealed fissures among the professionals in the Minnesota Mental Hygiene Society. Superintendent Petersen was initially for "reform" if it meant more money for the hospitals without interference in his own professional autonomy and control. Others, like Dr. Dumas and Dr. Challman, psychiatrists with experience in private practice and the VA, and both of whom sat on the Governor's Advisory Council on Mental Health, understood that reform would entail fundamental changes in practices in the mental institutions. Yet even they also saw the world primarily through their own professional lens, with the highest priority placed on increased funds for psychiatric research and training.

In March, the MUC Committee on Mental Hospitals had quietly submitted its draft report to the governor. Titled *Summary of Conditions in Minnesota State Hospitals for the Mentally Ill*, the draft contained a litany of concerns, including staff shortages, lack of activities, overcrowding, insufficient clothing, unsanitary conditions, unpalatable food, excessive use of restraints, few available treatments, and a brief analysis of the personnel problems due to low pay, poor living conditions, and lack of training for staff.[30]

The new DPI chief Carl Jackson reviewed the report and forwarded it to the governor with handwritten comments:

> Governor—
>
> In general I feel the report is good—May be well not to make compari-sons of hospitals to avoid frictions—that is in the way of publicity— the emphasis of the things we are lacking is important—We had better be careful that we do not de-emphasize any progress that has been made—No doubt we have made some improvement over the period of years—Carl. In other words I believe the writer is fair.[31]

A final version would not be made public until April. Youngdahl, how-ever, used many of the findings, albeit unattributed at this point, in his dramatic public announcement one week later.

On Sunday, March 21, 1948, Minnesotans awoke to bold headlines: "Tours of Hospitals Shocking" in the *St. Paul Pioneer Press* and "Mental Hospital Campaign Opens" in the *Minneapolis Tribune*.[32] Youngdahl announced that he had made personal tours of some of the mental hospitals and called "our forgotten people . . . one of the greatest moral problems facing Minnesota." Using data taken from the draft Unitar-ian report, he cited facts and figures on low per-capita spending result-ing in inadequate living conditions and inadequate care. He praised his DPI chief Carl Jackson, his Advisory Council on Mental Health, the Minnesota Mental Hygiene Society, and the Minnesota Unitarian Con-ference Committee on Mental Hospitals.[33] The public awareness cam-paign had begun.

The following day, the *St. Paul Dispatch* reported that the Minnesota Mental Hygiene Society and the Minnesota Unitarian Conference pledged "full support" to Governor Youngdahl's proposal to improve conditions. The story quoted Challman as president of the Society and Foote, the chairman of the Unitarian group. Challman said "the Society . . . gives its full support to the program and urged all citizens and organizations to support appropriations asked for the purpose from the legislature." Foote lauded the governor for "the frankest state-ment of conditions we have heard from a high official," and said his committee "would do its best to arouse the public to support increased appropriations, particularly for personnel and food, at the next legislative session."[34]

The members of the Minnesota Mental Hygiene Society could all stand behind higher appropriations. However, deeper disagreements developed over more substantive reforms affecting hospital operations and patient care. Foote's emphasis on staffing needs and better food, both of which were patient care issues, was a subtle but important distinction between the two groups.

In just a few weeks, Youngdahl had successfully managed his political concerns. He claimed the mental hospital reform as his own and moved out ahead of potential critics. Mental hospital reform was now synonymous with his reelection campaign in 1948. He needed to energize the public and continue to stoke the flames to keep up the momentum.

A few weeks later, Youngdahl engineered more dramatic headlines. He called in reporters to a photo-op as he officially received the Unitarian Report. On April 26, the *Minneapolis Star* headline read, "All of the State's Mental Units Called Unfit: Report to the Governor cites misery, neglect."[35] The governor was seated with Dumas, his Advisory Council chair, Foote, and Reese. The governor acknowledged the Unitarians as sole author of the report, but Reese's presence implied the Mental Hygiene Society's concurrence.

Tensions soon began to surface. In a private meeting between Superintendent Petersen and the Unitarians' Committee on Mental Hospitals on May 12, Petersen attacked the committee and its report. He invoked the canard that had worked for the cover-up during the 1946 campaign—that any criticism of the hospitals led to "relatives worrying unnecessarily" and "staff ashamed and discouraged by the publicity." He justified the use of restraints and disparaged comparisons to the VA, "which deals only with battlefield problems" and whose patients are therefore quite distinct from the population in the state hospitals. In response to the concern expressed in the report that patients were required to work at "menial" jobs, Petersen claimed the Unitarians had a "chip on the shoulder attitude." Dismissing occupational and recreational therapy as "artificial," he praised the practice of using patient manual labor as "part of the life of the patient before he comes to the hospital and after he leaves." When Steefel asked why patients were forced to do the work of attendants, he likened ward work to "team work among patients developed by a skillful executive."[36]

In Petersen's view, the Unitarians' report was "not authoritative in its basic philosophy." The only goal of the Unitarians, he said, should "aim at the public's attitude" and direct it toward support for higher appropriations. They should not try "to revolutionize the profession." Nor should they try to alter treatment. "A change in the whole pattern of treatment is probably a bankrupting proposal. Ask for too much and you can be laughed out of court."[37] Petersen was "fiery" on the lack of funds, according to Steefel. The old arguments he used, however, which had worked well when politicians and state officials conspired to withhold information from the public, would crumble in the face of the governor's moral crusade.

Presentation of the report of the Minnesota Unitarian Conference to the governor, March 1948. From left: Dr. Alexander G. Dumas, chairman of the Governor's Advisory Council on Mental Health; the Reverend Arthur Foote, chairman of the MUC Committee on Mental Hospitals; Governor Luther Youngdahl; and Justin G. Reese, executive secretary of the Minnesota Mental Hygiene Society. Courtesy of the Minnesota Historical Society.

Youngdahl pressed forward. On May 5 he and Dumas appeared on WCCO radio. The governor expressed his moral and emotional commitment to the mentally ill, and spoke of his "anguish" after visiting mental hospitals: "Mental patients are human beings, each one endowed by his creator with something divine. The theologian calls it a soul. The psychiatrist may call it 'personality.' Whatever we call it—it is something so valuable that there is no means of limiting its worth."[38] He called for full public understanding of the need for, and full public support of, increased appropriations, concluding with reference to Scripture: "We must appeal to the soul and conscience of our citizens for the things which are required to bring hope and comfort to those most forgotten of all people—our mentally ill fellow citizens reminding you of one who said 'Inasmuch as ye have done it unto one of the least of these my brethren, ye have done it unto me.'"[39] For Youngdahl, mental hospital reform was not just a public policy issue; it had become a moral crusade.

The next public disclosure was a blockbuster. From May 13 to May 25, the *Minneapolis Tribune* ran "Minnesota Bedlam," Geri Hoffner's eleven-part series. It was every bit as powerful as the 1946 *Life* magazine exposé, but Hoffner brought the issue home to Minnesota. Accompanied by photographer Art Hager, she stayed several days in each of the seven mental hospitals.[40] They recorded with words and pictures the dismal conditions and the suffering and indignity the patients experienced. The timing of the *Tribune* series worked well for the governor. The series provided graphic and visceral documentation of the need for his crusade to reform the system.

Hoffner's searing and effectively written text described the sordid life in the institutions. Each installment focused on a specific problem, including unpalatable food, overcrowded and dilapidated accommodations, excessive use of restraints, idleness and inactivity, and understaffing, and highlighted overworked and underpaid attendants. Hager's photographs chillingly recorded the misery and despair of the patients. The impact is as compelling to the contemporary reader, nearly seventy years later, as it undoubtedly was in 1948. The headlines:

May 13 "Mentally Ill Need Care, Get Little Beside Custody"
May 14 "Mental Patients Sit in Untidy Loneliness"
May 15 "Attendants Hoe Hard Row"
May 17 "Mentally Ill Get Little Help"
May 18 "Patients Fed 8-Cent Meals"

May 19 "Chains Don't Cure Minds"
May 20 "Few Mental Patients Get Care They Need: TB strikes Hard at
Mentally Ill"
May 21 "Makeshifts Mark Hospital Care"
May 22 "State Put to Shame by US Mental Care"
May 24 "Hospital Needs Put at $6,000,000"
May 25 "Patients Need Sympathy"

In the final installment, Hoffner focused on what should be done to improve conditions and how the public could help. She had interviewed many leading doctors. Dr. Petersen said, "Give us the money to buy necessary services and we can do a better job." Dr. Dumas urged setting up small demonstration hospitals, and he and Reese advocated raising the standards for personnel. Dr. Rossen of Hastings recommended a consultant relationship with the University of Minnesota and research

The May 13, 1948, installment of the eleven-part *Minneapolis Tribune* discussion of conditions in Minnesota's mental hospitals. As part of the series, reporter Geri Hoffner and photographer Arthur Hager visited all seven hospitals. This blockbuster series galvanized public opinion toward reform. Author's collection.

facilities in every mental hospital. Among other needs mentioned were reform of unfair commitment laws, more modern treatments, and a prevention program that included mobile clinics.[41]

Dr. Petersen mounted an immediate attack. In a long "Open Forum" piece published in the *Tribune* on the last day of the "Bedlam" series, he lashed out, calling the series "a garbled mixture of truths and half-truths generously leavened with untruths. . . . We believe, however that the problem is too serious to be dealt with in a sensational manner. To do so only serves to intensify the anxiety in already fearful hearts of relatives." He impugned Hoffner's integrity, accusing her of ignoring facts and demanded a retraction from the newspaper.[42] Petersen had dug in to defend his terrain.

The shocking disclosures opened the eyes of the public, but there were no clear ways in the article for people to become more engaged. The *Tribune* opined that "none of us can escape responsibility entirely nor can any single individual remedy the situation by his own efforts."[43]

Youngdahl was ready. On May 27, two days after Hoffner's series concluded, he announced the appointment of the Citizens Mental Health Committee, which would be "entrusted with the responsibility for mobilizing public opinion and acquiring support."[44] The governor had been disappointed that few Minnesota churches or social welfare organizations endorsed the cause.[45] He had experience going directly to the people to build support for his initiatives, a tactic he had employed with both the slot machine and the youth conservation campaigns.

Dumas had argued that a citizens group could be an extension of the Mental Hygiene Society. However, disagreements among the society's professionals on aspects of broad-based reforms made its support of future legislation uncertain. Arthur Foote explained to the Unitarians: "The line may be narrow on the functions of the Hygiene Society and the Citizens Committee, but they would not be overlapping if the Minnesota Hygiene Society does not accept the legislative program or cannot follow through on it."[46] By early that summer, Reese left the Mental Hygiene Society to become director of the committee.

The committee was composed of forty-seven of the state's leading citizens, including religious leaders—a rabbi, a Catholic priest, a minister from the Evangelical Lutheran Church, a Congregationalist, and a Unitarian.[47] There were also farmers, labor organizations, newspaper publishers, and heads of women's civic and service organizations. Steefel,

Jacobson, and Foote were members. The Citizens Committee was also affirmatively nonpartisan. All were welcome:

> There are no dues or rules to join the citizens' mental health drive. Each one of us in his own way and in his own circle is a citizens mental health committee of one, able by his compassion and dedication to bring about a new era in our care of these forgotten souls—an era in which mental illness will be regarded and treated as a sickness—and not a disgrace.[48]

After the committee was formed, the governor sent its members off to raise money and undertake an education and public relations campaign. Arthur Foote had been appointed treasurer and was "instrumental in assisting with the meager financial support provided during its first year."[49] There were no official meetings with the governor in the early months as the public relations campaign developed.

With the governor's commitment to reform, the MUC Committee on Mental Hospitals could have rested on its laurels. As Foote wrote:

> To many committees this would have been "it." The facts revealed, it could have been assumed that "something would be done about it." The Committee was not of this opinion. It had educated itself sufficiently on the elements of the situation to realize that many answers remained to be found; . . . It felt a profound responsibility; . . . hope had been stirred in the patients who, better than anyone else, knew how much was needed. The Committee could not let these people down.[50]

Behind the scenes, the MUC Committee on Mental Hospitals continued its search for a deeper understanding of the issues and effective solutions to them. As Ed Crane, *Minneapolis Tribune* reporter and Unitarian committee member later wrote:

> Minnesota's Unitarians . . . knew that the increase in appropriations meant a chance for real reforms—but did not assure them. And they knew that such reforms would not be accomplished overnight. They realized that once the worst evils were corrected—the restraints removed, firetraps closed and food made edible—the fight to make state institutions into real hospitals would become less dramatic and so more difficult.[51]

Crane characterized their role as "gadfly"—to keep close watch on the entire program, to foresee needs before they arose, and to prepare plans to meet them—and then to persuade other, larger groups to do the job and to take credit for it.[52] And so the Unitarians quietly began to work, and Foote's philosophy of the well-informed, independent layperson was put to the test.

The Unitarians kept a close watch on the existing system, and they had the ear of the governor himself. The group's strategy focused on four distinct areas—hospital visiting, nutrition, commitment reform, and staffing/training—all relevant to the voiceless patients and low-ranking staff members whose interests would not be heard without the Unitarians. The philosophy developed by the Unitarians—respectful, fact-based, and collaborative, while guarding their independence and always in the public interest—drove their approach to each issue.

The Visiting Program

As part of their "close watch" on the system, the Unitarians designed a volunteer service program. The goal was to keep the eye of the outsider on the inside of the institutions, to raise morale and keep the system accountable. Additionally, they sought to demonstrate that laypersons, with training and oversight, could have a therapeutic impact on patients, a concept that the professionals at the institutions had belittled when first proposed.

In January and February 1948, a delegation from First Unitarian Society and Unity Church visited both Hastings and Anoka State Hospitals to gauge the interest of the superintendents in hosting a visiting program. At Hastings, Superintendent Rossen enthusiastically embraced the concept, commenting that "a normal, cheerful lay person, even one without any special knowledge of psychiatry, could be really helpful to a person who was mentally ill, by encouraging the patient to talk, and by listening sympathetically to whatever the patient said."[53] As a result of these planning visits, Foote and Rossen developed a long and deeply respectful relationship. Anoka superintendent Edmund G. Miller, on the other hand, proposed a formidable list of imperative needs, and wanted to use volunteers as extra hands to do the work of staff. The volunteers decided to "limit our job to services of a personal nature to the several hundred patients who have no relatives or friends visiting them." Miller agreed to their plan.

The Women's Alliance of the First Unitarian Society led the planning group to implement the program that included a psychologist, a psychiatrist, and four social workers, all members of the alliance. The Women's Alliance had a long and significant record of involvement. A former minister and a member of FUS, Wendy Jerome, wrote:

> The Women's Alliance engaged in self-education, social service, and political work. Woman suffrage, peace, public education, and reform of government, international relations and services for economically disadvantaged and minorities were among the causes the women supported.[54]

Eva Sardeson Jerome was the inspiring leader. One of the first female graduates of the University of Minnesota in 1899, and from one of the founding FUS families, the politically active Jerome was in her seventies when the project began. She had been a teacher and social worker and civil rights activist throughout her life.[55] Under Jerome's skillful direction, the goal was not just to perform good deeds but also to demonstrate how laypeople, properly trained, can improve patients' lives. They intended to measure and document the impact. There was no need to find outside expertise.

FUS member Charlotte Henry, who oversaw the psychiatric social work program at the Veterans Hospital at Fort Snelling, led a monthly discussion group for orientation, followed later by Janet Wood, another social worker with the Minnesota Psychiatric Institute. These orientation classes provided participants with insight into mental conditions. The aim was "a broader lay knowledge of the problems of mental illness and a highly selected type of volunteer who would seek to establish an individual personal relationship with the patient."[56]

Groups began visiting the two institutions in April 1948. For reasons of proximity, Unity Church adopted Hastings; FUS took Anoka. Unity Church member Phyllis Mickelson, a psychiatric social worker at the Bureau for the Feebleminded and Epileptic in the Division of Public Institutions, led four to five groups a month to Hastings. "Thereafter, for nearly twenty years these women faithfully made monthly trips to Hastings, loading their cars with some of the hundreds of magazines that had been collected at the church, and putting on song fests, bingo and birthday parties."[57] In her journal from the 1950s, Engla Schey, who was working as an attendant at Hastings State Hospital, wrote of the visits from the "grand ladies from Saint Paul." Young volunteers from Tri-U—Unitarian, Universalists at the University—organized sports programs and other festivities at Hastings to supplement the program.

Eva Jerome led the Anoka visiting team, expanding the program over the years to include many different faith-based groups, including Jewish, Catholic, Baptist, Methodist, and Lutheran, offering a wide range of services through the early 1950s.[58] The volunteers, their organizations, and their congregations paid all the costs of the programs.

The leaders used their expertise to develop a systematic study and evaluation of the effectiveness of volunteer services. Ida Davies, Jerome's daughter and a social worker in her own right, compiled the data and experiences into the *Handbook for Volunteers in Mental Hospitals,* which was published by the University of Minnesota Press in 1950.[59] As Eva Jerome wrote:

> The joy of seeing patients respond to unassuming friendship, become kinder to each other, arise for the time being from mental quirks or get release by telling their troubles and perhaps casting these off for an hour of gayety; the satisfaction of finding withdrawn and antagonistic patients growing friendly at last: these are the rewards of faithful visiting. But such experiences do not give the whole measure of the service performed. The fact that citizens are seeing inside a mental hospital strengthens the sense of responsibility of both supervisors and aides, helps to raise standards and morale through the institution.[60]

The Nutrition Committee

Even the casual visitor couldn't miss the unpalatable fare, described as "over-cooked cold masses of unrecognizable food," served to patients.[61] The Unitarian's Committee on Nutrition was concerned with the impact of this type of diet on the physical and mental health of patients and their quality of life. Experts were essential to gather credible and unassailable data on all aspects of food quality, preparation, and service, and to measure the findings against agreed-upon appropriate nutritional standards. But, unlike the visiting program, there was no expertise on the science of nutrition in the Unitarian ranks, and insufficient resources to hire experts for a study on their own. There were, however, nutrition experts in state government, and the Governor's Advisory Council on Mental Health showed some interest. The challenge was to

A typical institution meal was a watery pork stew, potatoes, string beans, and milk. Milk was served in tin bowls, and the only utensil provided to patients was a tablespoon. Photograph by Arthur Hager, *Minneapolis Tribune*. Courtesy of the Minnesota Historical Society.

partner with the state while ensuring its honest acknowledgment of the issues and the scientific integrity of the work.

Trust was essential and had to be earned. In early meetings, the state experts expressed concern that findings of the study could be used to embarrass them. Balancing respect for the professionals within government with the need to solve the problem at hand, the Unitarians agreed only to call public attention to the results of the study in the event that any official agency failed to act, after the facts had been made known to it.[62] Once trust was assured, the parties agreed on the scope of the study: measurement of food values of patients' meals, garbage waste weight, evaluation of hospital cooking methods, and a comparison of these results with the nutritional standards of the Food and Nutrition Board of the National Research Council.

To ensure the integrity of the study, the Unitarians persuaded Dr. Russell Wilder, former chairman and present member of the National Research Council, who was at the time on the Mayo Clinic staff, to voluntarily serve as an adviser.[63] The state agreed that a Board of Health nutritionist would take the lead, in consultation with Dr. Wilder. The Division of Relief of the Minneapolis Public Welfare Department and leading private agencies provided information on how they met the standards of nutrition in their populations.[64] The Unitarians provided funds directly to support Dr. Wilder's travel costs, but did not fund the state directly, thus avoiding the appearance of undue influence on the state's findings.

The Unitarians and the Governor's Advisory Council procured grant funds for a second study to assess the costs to modernize kitchen equipment in the state hospitals.[65] The results—scientific and credible data to support funding for dietary improvements for patients— would be available to all parties, the administration, legislators, and advocates.

These collaborations in data gathering and analysis were constructive. State involvement resulted in widespread support inside government for improvements in food quality, service, and preparation. All agreed to reject the unfair practice of multiple diets, whereby doctors received the best meals, staff less good, and patients the worst of all. When it was time to design and fund new nutrition standards, the Governor's Advisory Council and the state agencies involved in the study carried the issue. The Unitarians, consistent with Crane's assessment, "persuaded other, larger groups to do the job and to take credit for it."[66]

The Commitment Law Reform Committee

The process by which patients were committed to institutions was a critically important aspect of mental hospital reform. Managed by the probate courts, voluntary and involuntary admissions had to be adjudicated "insane." The process criminalized the mentally ill, who were often imprisoned while awaiting adjudication. In Minnesota, there was significant variation from county to county in treatment of the accused, and violations of civil liberties abounded. Engla's own stories tell of individuals spending their lives locked away because their court-appointed guardians would not give required approval of a "parole."

Youngdahl asked his Advisory Council to conduct a review of the commitment laws. Frank Rarig led the effort. To facilitate this key project, they built a collaborative strategy. The Unitarians agreed to finance a study of commitment laws and turn it over to the probate judges and the Minnesota State Bar Association. The Unitarian Conference designed a matching fund arrangement with the State Mental Health Authority, and the Committee appointed a legal advisory group to supervise the research.[67]

There was extensive legal expertise within the Unitarian ranks to provide oversight for a study. University of Minnesota Law School professor Horace Read hired Eugene Heck, a gifted young law student, to research commitment laws under the professor's direction.[68] Heck produced a seventy-seven-page scholarly report that compared Minnesota's commitment laws with more modern laws in other states, as well as the changes these states thought might be desirable.

The Unitarians' Legislative Committee compiled data on how Minnesota counties differed in the use of jails in the commitment of mental patients.[69] The report found that the system in all counties was based on "the outmoded idea that mental illness was a crime to be punished" and that "the actual working out of legal procedures seems grossly unfair." They also concluded that the commitment process criminalizes individuals without "adequate deliberation."[70]

Doctors supported some of the reforms, but lawyers were harder to persuade. Commitment law reform was not part of the reform package in either 1949 or 1951. Nevertheless, the Unitarian lawyers worked for years with the Bar Association and even held sessions with doctors and lawyers together to ascertain where there was common ground.

The Staffing and Training Committee

The last key issue focused on the complicated and controversial issue of personnel. The myriad aspects of this issue included a number of questions, such as: What was the appropriate ratio of employees to patients? What types of personnel were needed—attendants, social workers, occupational therapists, psychiatric nurses? How much treatment versus custodial care was required in a modern hospital system? Could attendants be trained to participate in treatment teams, and if so, what type of training was appropriate? Civil service classifications, union concerns about new classifications, appropriate pay scales, and labor supply issues all presented barriers to recruitment, retention, and training at every level.

The Unitarians knew that increased appropriations alone would not solve these intractable issues. In fact, many of the superintendents had returned money to the state coffers in the past because they could not fill vacant positions that had been authorized and funded. The superintendents and bureaucrats were uniformly pessimistic about solutions.

The Unitarians gamely jumped on the issue and formed the Subcommittee on Training. In February 1948, they held a meeting with four superintendents and the leadership of the DPI to discuss a training plan developed under psychiatric leadership at the VA.[71] Dr. Roger W. Howell of the VA presented the proposal to design a model for an attendant-training course to allow them to develop mental health skills. Training would give attendants the ability to build personal therapeutic relationships with patients, rather than provide only custodial services. The superintendents' views on lowly attendants, attitudes that had frustrated Engla for years, were on full display at the meeting. The superintendents rejected short training courses for attendants, arguing that the urgent demands of daily needs made therapeutic activities impossible. In fact, "impossible" was the answer to most suggestions for the training of "nonprofessional" personnel.

The Unitarians pressed forward. They met with Robert Stover from the State Civil Service and his deputies, the Division of Education in the Minnesota Department of Health, and professors from the Graduate School and the Psychology Department at the University of Minnesota a few weeks later.[72] They gathered data on comparative wage scales, staff ratio recommendations, new classifications and related union issues, and in-service training. Throughout the spring and summer, armed with a long list of challenges, and undeterred by the negativity of the superintendents, they continued to study the issues, knowing that reform proposals would only come from within their ranks.

The Unitarians ran a demonstration project in the summer of 1948. They persuaded the Unitarian Service Committee to sponsor a work camp at Rochester State Hospital. Eight young people from across the country took jobs as attendants at no cost to the hospital, allowing for some personnel to have paid vacations for the first time since the war.[73] Foote called the project "leaven in the life" of staff and patients alike, and said it revealed how idealism and generosity could lead to "many possible changes in approach and services to patients even within the limitations of the old hospital patterns."[74] The campers' reports, written at summer's end, were extremely detailed and insightful.[75]

It is important to note that the Unitarians did not focus on issues of treatment options, or the efficacy of various forms of treatment. They knew that the doctors had the credentials and that they as laypersons could not make a difference. They also knew there were sharp differences among the physicians about the value of lobotomies, for example, or electroshock treatments. Important as those issues were, the Unitarians were determined their energy was best focused where they could make a real difference.

Through these efforts across a range of issues, Unitarians labored to execute according to a gadfly strategy. Many teams invested significant amounts of time and energy on priority issues. Steefel kept the trains running—she organized monthly meetings of the committee as a whole, took notes, invited in experts, organized materials, sent out notices, and held many meetings in her home.

Summer beckoned. In June 1948, Arthur Foote packed up his car and, joined by his wife, children, and the family's boxer dog, set off to Southwest Harbor, Maine. Foote was exhausted from his job as full-time minister and his tireless efforts as the public face of the MUC Committee on Mental Hospitals. He left Steefel, Jacobson, and a growing cast of active Unitarians, to continue to toil on the issues during the long hot political summer of 1948.

NINE

The Long Hot Summer

Luther never assumed he could get elected to anything. He
could have the weakest guy running against him, and he still
felt he had to really put on a terrific effort.

▪ *Bernhard LeVander,* Call Me Pete:
Memoir of a Minnesota Man

On Friday afternoon, June 25, 1948, Luther Youngdahl
slumped in a chair in his suite at the Warwick Hotel in downtown
Philadelphia. He had been up all night and was exhausted. He had
spent the week at the Republican National Convention, working round
the clock for Harold Stassen. Youngdahl disliked party politics—the
intrigue, power plays, endless socializing. He was ready to go home; he
had his own reelection in Minnesota to worry about.

Stassen still dominated Republican politics in Minnesota, although
he had left the governorship during the war. Youngdahl supposed he
owed Harold one. After all, Stassen had personally tapped him to run
for the governorship in 1946. Now, as he was completing a successful
two-year term, Youngdahl often resented the implication that he was
Stassen's man. Youngdahl was his own man. But Stassen had always
wanted to be president, and as early as December 1946, right after
Youngdahl's election, he announced his intent to be a candidate and
opened a Washington, D.C., office. Governor Youngdahl and Senator
Edward Thye, as the highest-ranking Republicans in his home state,
were named honorary cochairs of the Stassen campaign.[1]

Youngdahl had done his part. Since Stassen had almost no support from the national Republican Party, he ran aggressively in the five
states that held primaries.[2] With his unlimited energy, his "modern
Republican" message, and hordes of volunteers called the "Paul Revere
Riders," Stassen threw himself into the game.[3]

Youngdahl made speeches and appearances on Stassen's behalf, and was especially active in the Wisconsin primary, where the Minnesota governor's name was well known. He praised Stassen's experience and credentials and lauded his virtues as superior to any other Republican hopeful.[4]

For a brief time, after his victories in Wisconsin and Nebraska, it appeared that Stassen had a real shot at the presidency. *Time* magazine reported in April: "The prairies are on fire and getting hotter for Stassen all the time."[5] Stassen even led Thomas Dewey briefly in nationwide polls.[6] However, when he stumbled in a debate with Dewey in the Oregon primaries, the power brokers did not align behind him, and he looked very much like an underdog as the Republican convention approached. Nevertheless, Youngdahl was out front in the lead-up to the conclave, stumping for Stassen and managing political reporters on the Tuesday before the convention began.[7]

Youngdahl had run himself ragged, arm twisting and jawboning in the loud, hot Philadelphia Convention Hall. On Wednesday, June 23, seven names had been put in nomination. After Thomas Dewey of New York, Robert Taft of Ohio, and Earl Warren of California, it was Stassen's turn. As historian David Pietrusza described:

> Minnesota congressman Walter H. Judd, speaking, he said, for "the millions of Republicans who are tired of winning in June and losing in November," nominated Harold Stassen. A twenty-five-minute demonstration followed, featuring flags, balloons, Marines carrying a canoe, Sioux Indian chief William Spotted Crow (escorted to the podium by Minnesota governor Luther Youngdahl and a sweat-drenched Joe McCarthy), banners, noise upon noise, and remarkable enthusiasm. The *New York Times* termed the spectacle "unprecedented in the history of political conventions. For sound, for sheer theatre, for variety it has never been matched."[8]

After all the hoopla, the good soldier Youngdahl was beat, but he kept on going. Despite the enthusiasm of his supporters, Stassen's chances were slim. The balloting began on Thursday afternoon, June 24. When it appeared that Dewey would prevail on the third ballot, Stassen, fiercely competitive and no fan of Dewey, was so determined to stop the momentum that he called General Dwight Eisenhower to beg him to enter the race. Eisenhower declined, and Dewey was unanimously nominated.

Stassen angled for the nomination for vice president, despite having vowed in 1947 never to accept a berth on a Dewey-Stassen ticket, thereby gratuitously offending his then opponent. He sent Youngdahl to sit with other surrogates aspiring for the vice presidential nod. At 7:00 a.m. on June 25, after waiting for hours to be summoned, Youngdahl, along with Governor Alfred Driscoll of New Jersey, argued unsuccessfully for Stassen before the unresponsive Dewey team.[9] As a last-ditch and unprecedented effort, Stassen sent Youngdahl to request that he be nominated for vice president from the floor even before Dewey had made his recommendation, as was the custom. The ploy failed. When Dewey announced his choice, Governor Earl Warren of California, the ticket was set and the Stassen effort died.

Youngdahl, the man who hated party politics, was anxious to go home and tend to his own campaign. He thought nostalgically about his 1946 run. It was not a presidential year; the Stassen team had managed the campaign, and all Youngdahl had to do was meet the people and be himself. He enjoyed that role. Two years later, he had to worry about the presidential race and its effect on Minnesota. Not only that, Minnesotans played important roles in all three national conventions. Youngdahl had to keep his eyes open.

The outcome of the Republican convention did little to reduce Youngdahl's worries. Dewey was decidedly unpopular in Minnesota, where enthusiasm for Stassen reigned. After Dewey's nomination, the *Minneapolis Tribune* headline read "GOP Choice Displeases Many."[10] Seventy percent of Republican voters in Minnesota had supported Stassen's candidacy, and the favorite son received a rousing welcome when he returned home.[11] Despite Stassen's call for Republicans to back Dewey in the fall, Youngdahl worried that, with Dewey at the top of the ticket, Minnesota Republicans would not turn out in large numbers in the general election.

Home at last, Youngdahl fretted about the political power of the new Democratic-Farmer-Labor Party, a merger of forces to his left. The good news from Youngdahl's perspective was that President Truman was generally perceived as uninspired and was not particularly popular. Nationally, the Republicans had swept the midterm elections in 1946, and the Democrats lost control of the Congress they had dominated under FDR. Truman's firm stance against Soviet aggression in Europe, and his support of the Marshall Plan, led to attacks from the left, as many feared another war.[12]

In addition, Henry Wallace emerged early as an alternative candidate, causing dissension within the party. Wallace was vice president in Roosevelt's third term (1940–1944), but the president abandoned him in favor of Harry Truman in 1944. FDR gave Wallace the consolation prize of Secretary of Commerce, and, after Roosevelt's death, President Truman kept Wallace on at Commerce. The stay was short. Truman asked for Wallace's resignation in September of 1946 after Wallace delivered a pro-Soviet foreign policy speech.[13] A resentful Wallace believed he would be better than Truman to carry Roosevelt's legacy in the 1948 campaign.

Wallace announced his run for the presidency in late December 1947, calling the Democrats under Truman the party of war and depression.[14] He would mount a two-pronged attack—as an insurgent Democratic candidate and as a third-party candidate under the Progressive Party banner.

In many states a battle had begun within the Democratic Party structure, and Minnesota was no exception. Wallace supporters launched aggressive efforts to capture the fledgling Democratic-Farmer-Labor Party. Former Minnesota governor Elmer Benson, the left-winger whom Stassen defeated in 1938, was a leader among "Wallacites" within the DFL, and later became the national chairman of the Wallace for President Committee.[15]

Minneapolis mayor Hubert Humphrey, who had announced that he was running for the United States Senate, stood on the opposite end of the DFL spectrum. Humphrey was desperately trying to keep the more conservative, anti-Communist members of the old Democratic Party and the liberals from the Farmer-Labor wing united under a single DFL banner. The Wallace attack from the left threatened both Humphrey's Senate ambitions and the Minnesota DFL's effort to gain credibility with the national Democratic Party.[16]

Confrontation came in the spring of 1948 when bitter factional fighting occurred in the April 30 caucuses. The battle was a prelude to the continuing conflict at the state convention in Brainerd in June. Wallace supporters marched out of the DFL convention, set up a rump conclave in Minneapolis, and asserted that they were the true DFL. Legal wrangling, manipulation of party rules, and angry accusations between the factions persisted throughout the summer.

Brainerd grocer Charles Halsted was the endorsed DFL candidate for Minnesota governor in 1948. He had served as the state representative from Crow Wing County from 1936 to 1946. He began his political career as part of the moderate wing of the old Farmer-Labor Party. In 1940, as a New Deal anti-Communist liberal, he publicly left the FL to join the Democratic Party in protest against Benson's election as FL Party chairman in 1940.[17] In 1948, he had joined the new DFL as a moderate ally in the Humphrey camp. From Youngdahl's perspective, Halsted was not a formidable opponent in his own right, but he would benefit from momentum created by Humphrey's candidacy.

After the DFL convention, Halsted came out swinging. He announced that he was "prepared to make the fight of my life against Governor Luther Youngdahl."[18] Youngdahl could deal with campaign rhetoric, but what troubled him most was what appeared to be a DLF effort to co-opt his own signature issue of mental hospital reform.

The Governor's Citizens Mental Health Committee had been formed a few weeks before the DFL convention as a nonpartisan effort to educate the public about the need for mental health reform. Youngdahl had carefully selected his forty-seven-member council, an impressive list that included those affiliated with the DFL.[19] Among the most prominent DFLers was Ione Hunt of Montevideo, who was the DFL Party chair of the convention. Her husband, Douglas Hunt, a probate judge, was also on the Citizens Committee.[20]

On June 15, the *Minneapolis Tribune* reported that "buried deep in the rush of closing the DFL's state convention at Brainerd Sunday was an indorsement of the [mental health] program."[21] Judge Hunt wrote the resolution and was identified as the one who guided it through all the hoops of committee and convention votes of approval. Calling mental health reform a nonpolitical and nonpartisan issue, the resolution "recognizes that mental illness is a major social and medical problem and that handicapped persons can become an even greater problem unless they are rehabilitated and returned to useful place in society."[22]

This endorsement of the signature policy issue of a Republican governor was surprising. The Hunts were passionate supporters of mental health reform. But, however well intentioned their efforts, Youngdahl feared that his issue could be co-opted for DFL partisan ends. Would a vote for the DFL be a vote for mental health reform? Could voters assume that mental health reform was assured if the DFL prevailed in the gubernatorial race? Youngdahl wanted voters to see him as the only path to mental health reform.

On July 12, the attention of the governor and the public turned to the Democratic National Convention opening in Philadelphia. Because Truman was unpopular and the Dewey-Warren ticket considered strong nationally, maneuvering for alternative candidates was hot and heavy. The Wallace supporters had bolted to form the Progressive Party and were not a factor. Humphrey joined others to support an Eisenhower candidacy, but Ike let supporters know, just as he had the Republicans a few weeks earlier, that he would not accept a nomination. When no realistic draftees emerged, Truman was nominated. Humphrey provided the highlight of the convention by positioning himself to second a motion in support of civil rights in the party platform. Humphrey's motion, broadcast to the nation over radio and television, galvanized the conventioneers and the public. The motion prevailed, and Humphrey returned home to a hero's welcome.[23] His momentum raised the DFL's prospects and was a threat to Republicans. Governor Youngdahl was worried.

The Wallace insurgency continued to threaten the DFL momentum in the spring of 1948. As historian Thomas Devine noted, Wallace became a symbol of "liberal idealism, a prophet of a progressive future," the true heir to the Roosevelt legacy.[24] He also attracted many supporters who were associated with the US Communist Party.[25] Minnesotans played a major role in the Progressive Party. Former Minnesota governor Benson, who would emerge as national chairman of the Progressive Party, led the delegation to the July convention.[26] In May Genevieve Steefel became a national cochairwoman in the Women for Wallace organization. She also served as vice-chair of the convention, chair of the Credentials Committee, and introduced the vice presidential candidate there as well.[27]

Steefel's passion and impatience for social change drove her commitment to Wallace. She proclaimed: "I am working for Wallace because I regard him as an individual who is aiming at the same pattern of social reforms to which I have devoted my entire adult life."[28] Also, and importantly, she felt that the Progressive Party welcomed women in leadership roles.[29]

Steefel learned, however, that the Communists in the Progressive Party would not tolerate dissent within the ranks.[30] When she bravely stood up against a platform position that endorsed Soviet foreign policy, she was shouted down, accused of betrayal, and ostracized from the party.[31] After the convention, the Wallace campaign lost steam nationally, and its efforts to disrupt the DFL in Minnesota fell flat.[32] Wallace never repudiated the clear Communist influence, appeared weak and unfocused in public appearances, and was increasingly viewed as quixotic. His showing in the general election and in Minnesota was negligible.[33]

For Steefel, her involvement in the Progressive Party had painful consequences. Because of her support for Wallace, she had burned her bridges with Humphrey and the DFL. She and her husband would be later maligned when anti-Communist fervor grew, despite her clear

Governor Youngdahl, an inveterate campaigner, at the Minnesota State Fair in 1948. At the top of the Republican presidential and vice presidential ticket were Thomas Dewey of New York and Earl Warren of California. Youngdahl had strongly supported Harold Stassen's first run for the presidency that year, but loyally backed the GOP's candidates in the general election. Photograph by Kenneth M. Wright. Courtesy of the Minnesota Historical Society.

position against communism.[34] With her idealism dashed, her pride deeply wounded, and her political ties frayed, Steefel gamely jumped back into action on the mental health project.

Watching the leftist Wallace balloon deflate did not distract Youngdahl for long. He had major challenges from his right flank. The conservative wing of the Republican Party that opposed the reforming instincts of Harold Stassen and his protégés was gunning for a fight. As one rural newspaper editor wrote, "The GOP leadership are today looking for ways to bring the party back . . . clear out the remnants of the Stassen regime and begin anew."[35]

Stafford King filed as a candidate against Youngdahl in the Republican primary slated for mid-September. The press characterized King's entry into the race as a challenge to Republican Party leadership.[36] King, raised near Deer River in Itasca County, was Minnesota state auditor, a position that conferred significant power and influence. He had a loyal following. As party chairman Pete LeVander noted:

> Stafford King was important in the Republican Party for two reasons in my opinion. One was he could always get votes. And number two was that he had a tremendous following among the veterans and the Legion people that just were loyal to Staff. They would do or die for Staff. . . . Staff was colorful; could give the most patriotic speech of any guy I'd ever heard. He could make people cry on patriotism and he could lead a lot of people to believe that he really was a man of substance.[37]

King accused Youngdahl of running a "dictatorship" and seeking centralization of power.[38] The challenger's candidacy was bad news. But soon Youngdahl was hit with a second blow.

The Minnesota legislature at the time had no party designation for candidates running for office. Once elected, State House and Senate members caucused as either conservatives or liberals, roughly but not always equivalent to the official political parties.[39] Many in the conservative caucus were part of the "old guard" as the Stassen wing called them, who edged them out of control of the party machinery.

But the old guard conservatives wielded considerable power in the legislature, and held tight control of the levers of power there. They opposed the growth of government and kept a firm grip on the state treasury. They were not inclined to fund any of Youngdahl's expensive initiatives, including mental health care reform. This was especially true for Claude Allen of St. Paul, the chair of the all-powerful House Appropriations Committee, who ruled "with an iron hand."[40] Allen had already announced his intent to oppose much of the governor's mental health program. Many conservative legislators also flocked to King, believing they had been hurt by the negative publicity in the state hospitals, and that their support for more buildings in 1947 was not appreciated.[41]

In the spring of 1948, the conservatives had a new arrow in their quiver. The 1947 legislature had created the Legislative Research Committee (LRC) with the "power and right to study, consider, accumulate, compile and assemble information on any subject upon which the Legislature may legislate." The material they gathered would "be used by the legislature in its work while in session."[42] The LRC would meet between the biennial sessions of the legislature, employ a research staff, and obtain facts to guide lawmakers in the upcoming session.

Conservative control of the LRC resulted from the selection process. There were eighteen members, divided equally between the House and the Senate. Each body had nine seats on the committee, one for each of the nine US congressional districts. Lawrence Hall, as speaker of the Minnesota House, chose the nine House members; the Senate, in caucuses of fellow members by congressional district, selected theirs. The 1948 committee was packed with conservatives, including Allen.[43] After demands from the liberals, one member from their caucus was added.[44]

During the summer of 1948, the LRC asked its subcommittee on public welfare to conduct a study of the mental hospitals.[45] On August 2 the subcommittee issued its preliminary report to the LRC.[46] Based on visits made by legislators to the institutions in late June and July 1948, the report contradicted virtually all of Youngdahl's conclusions, found in his own visits and the reports of the Unitarians. The legislative investigators found that most of the patients were "custodial" and therefore required little care, the food was palatable, the institutions, while old, were clean, the use of restraints was reasonable, and custodial attendants were adequately paid. The report also disputed the accuracy of the $1.05 per patient per day expenditure, even though it was the DPI's own calculation, arguing that the number doesn't take into account the food production by the institutions' extensive farming operations.

Youngdahl saw the LRC report for what it was—a direct assault from the right on his program. While only a preliminary report, it was announced conveniently only a few weeks before King's primary challenge. Youngdahl had to strike back. He devised a brilliant solution that dealt both with the DFL endorsement issue and the LRC attack.

Youngdahl decided now was the time to mobilize his Governor's Citizens Mental Health Committee. He called its first official meeting in his offices at the Capitol on August 16. Youngdahl had several goals for these "nonpartisan" citizens. First, he wanted to link them to the gubernatorial campaign. This strategy required blurring the lines between partisan electoral politics and a nonpartisan reform effort. The *St. Paul Dispatch* helped the strategy. Its front-page story was ambiguously titled "New Mental Group Backs Youngdahl."[47]

The paper's account of the Citizens Committee meeting with the governor confirmed Youngdahl's strategy. Ione Hunt, the state chair of the DFL, took the lead. At the meeting in the governor's office, she introduced a resolution "encouraging" Youngdahl, "indorsing his work," and pledging the committee's "full support to the program."[48] According to the story, only Judge Hunt knew of his wife's resolution before it was introduced. The paper noted that the governor wanted to avoid any political implications by his presence, so he left the room and the resolution was unanimously adopted.

Youngdahl wanted to be seen as a crusader for issues, not as a Republican. A nonpartisan citizens group, at the behest of a DFL leader, endorsed candidate Youngdahl's mental health program. A vote for Youngdahl was a vote for the issue of mental health, regardless of the voter's party affiliation. The Republican governor was running above partisanship!

Youngdahl's second goal was to reorient the Governor's Citizens Mental Health Committee from a public relations outfit into an advocacy organization. When the governor addressed the assembled group, he told them that their principal task was to "sell the next Legislature" on the need for sufficient appropriations for the mental hospitals. He assured them he was not criticizing anyone and that the legislators had made forward progress in the past. The governor also announced his goal—a four-part program that included "development of a comprehensive system of treatment, establishment of diagnostic facilities and personnel, initiation of a program of training, research and public education, and organization of psychiatric consultation service."[49]

Presumably, the legislative goal was not attainable without Youngdahl as governor.

The third order of business was to elect a small leadership group within the Governor's Citizens Committee that could take action. Youngdahl had prepared a specific task for the group—to respond to the attack from the LRC.

If the forty-seven members of the Governor's Citizens Mental Health Committee were to play a new advocacy role, they needed leaders to speak for the whole. The group elected five individuals to serve as an executive committee. The new chairman was Leslie L. Anderson, a lawyer from Minneapolis with experience in commitment law. The four additional members were Justin Reese, Judge Hunt of Montevideo, Portia Stevens, a social worker from Duluth, and Reverend Arthur Foote.[50] Because Foote was still in Maine for the summer, Jacobson had submitted his name in absentia and served in his stead at the crucial August meeting. He later wrote to Foote, "As I saw it, you were the only person from our group that did have a possibility of being elected to serve on the Executive Committee; consequently I thought it was very important that you act."[51]

During the afternoon session of the new executive committee, Youngdahl asked them to sign a report prepared by Dumas and Reese to rebut the findings of the LRC. The committee signed with Jacobson acting on Foote's behalf.[52]

The rebuttal was written in carefully measured tones. It began by noting that the legislative authors erroneously assumed that the patients were custodial not because they do not require constant attention but rather because "they have had little attention and treatment." The report also lamented that the LRC authors "see no meaning" in the use of restraints, the double standard for food, the "deteriorating idleness," unpaid patient labor, lack of psychiatrists and treatments, underpaid attendants, and other ills. In keeping with a conciliatory and balanced tone, however, the document referred to "honest disagreements" between the Governor's Citizens Committee and the LRC, called the legislators "not unsympathetic" to conditions in the hospitals, praised the generosity of legislators in the past, and looked forward to a further report that addressed what the LRC had been asked to address—the issues of new forms of treatment.[53]

The press coverage was more pointed. The *Minneapolis Tribune* described the Governor's Citizens Mental Health Committee as being "in sharp disagreement" with the LRC, while the *St. Paul Pioneer Press* reported that the executive group "wasted no time Monday in scrapping with the Legislative Research Committee."[54]

On August 18, the *Minneapolis Star* published Steefel's extensive letter to the editor titled "Unitarian Report on Mental Hospitals."[55] She wrote in her capacity as secretary of the MUC Committee on Mental Hospitals. Unlike the careful language in the Governor's Citizens Committee rebuttal, Steefel's letter was exceedingly direct and occasionally caustic. Her razor-sharp analytical skills were on full display. After carefully describing the deliberate process by which the Unitarians undertook their research for its report to the governor the previous March, she proceeded to pose pointed rhetorical questions about the LRC's methodology, implying that they did not rigorously investigate restraint use, food quality, or even the records of their own DPI.

The *Star*'s editors criticized Steefel's tone in a companion editorial on the same page, cautioning that "it would be unfortunate indeed if, just when science and legislators and laymen are learning effective ways to cope with mental illnesses, recriminations are allowed to impede the good work."[56] By contrast, they commented that a "fine note was struck Monday at the first meeting of the citizens' committee, called together by Governor Youngdahl," and concluded, "One of the few things which could interfere is quarreling among the persons who want to help. If ever cooperation and good feeling are needed, this is the place."[57] Perhaps Steefel's incisive response carried with it some residual bitterness from her recent political disappointment; and perhaps the *Star*'s quick rebuke related to her high-profile role in the Wallace campaign just a few weeks before.

Steefel's editorial did spark a positive response from Engla Schey, who wrote to her on the day her editorial appeared. Engla had not been heard from for six months. She explained to Steefel in a letter from Appleton, Wisconsin: "I'm on a six months leave of absence from Rochester. I can't use soap on my hands from too much and constant washing doing isolation (nurses don't do isolation in [Rochester] state hospital. That's for attendants.)." Engla's grueling work and exhaustive schedule kept her from participating in the reform effort. She had been living with her sister in Appleton, and engaged in private duty nursing when she could. Engla's own life was a rebuttal to the LRC's cavalier assessment of pay and working conditions for attendants. She shared her willingness to help, offering to take the legislators back for another visit:

How about me serving as guide to take the subcommittee around on their "recheck"? Should I suggest to them that if they want someone along who knows the tricks of the trade and knows how to get around and get the inside dope, I will volunteer my services while on leave? [58]

There is no evidence Steefel acted on Engla's offer, and it was clear the conservative LRC members did not want the Unitarians' perspective. Engla's need to work to support herself in institutions far from the center of the action in the Twin Cities was a barrier to her and a disappointment. She wrote in her journal:

I thought how wonderful it would be if some mental health agency would just pay me a living wage and expenses with all the literature I needed from NMHF and say to me, "Now go and spread the gospel of better mental health for one year as you see fit and don't worry about where the money is coming from.... But all this was only pipe dreams. No one was going to give me a salary to go out and work for mental health. I would have to exhaust my energy doing routine work on a mental hospital ward indefinitely for my own security—I just wasn't crazy enough yet to let the shore lines of my job go. I was glad that I was still that sane.

Meanwhile, the primary loomed, and Youngdahl did not rest. He continued to campaign hard. One reporter noted, "Don't forget that Youngdahl is letting no grass grow under his feet. He's on the go every day, as he has been almost from the time the legislature finished 15 months ago, traveling the state making speeches and meeting the folks." [59]

Mental health was a key campaign issue. During the lead-up to the primary, King lashed out with seemingly contradictory messages about mental hospitals. While the LRC report proclaimed that the mental hospitals were in fine shape, King charged that Youngdahl had money available to improve the hospitals, but was now making "political capital out of the deplorable conditions in our institutions for the mentally and physically handicapped." [60] Speaking at the Aitkin County fair, the governor "stressed the need for improvement of the state's mental health program and necessity for training of personnel to care properly for patients and a realization that such patients must receive the proper sympathy of being ill, not to be shunned and shamed." [61]

Youngdahl trounced King in the primary on September 14 by an eighteen-point margin. Mental hospitals were the issue in the general election as well. Halsted, the DFL challenger, attacked Youngdahl, asserting that he "has attempted to throw a smoke screen over activities in the hospitals. Conditions are worse than they have been pictured." Halsted traced the blame to the "penny-pinching practices" employed under Stassen, Thye, and Youngdahl.[62] He charged that the Republicans had "wrecked" the mental health program of Democratic governor Floyd B. Olson.[63]

Youngdahl stayed on message. To those who thought the other party might also reform mental health, he insisted, "I think voters need to decide whether these programs should be carried forward and completed by the men who have instituted them and are in sympathy with them."[64] He hammered home the link between his reform program and his reelection.

Six weeks later, on Wednesday, November 2, 1948, Democrat Harry Truman carried Minnesota by seventeen points and DFLer Hubert Humphrey defeated incumbent Republican Joseph Ball by nearly twenty points. In the race for governor, Youngdahl defeated Charles Halsted by eight points.[65] For Youngdahl, the margin of victory in 1948 was significantly less than in 1946. The *Tribune* commented that Youngdahl, "generally regarded as impossible to defeat for a second term, ran into surprisingly stiff opposition from Charles Halsted."[66] How did Youngdahl survive the Democratic tide? As Geri Hoffner wrote the day after the election, "Youngdahl is recognized as a liberal. And his reelection may be recognized [as] an indorsement of his convictions."[67]

Youngdahl was not a party man. In a challenging year for Republicans, he ran and won on his convictions. His next order of business was to deliver what he promised—mental health reform.

TEN

Making History

As we face the new century in Minnesota history we are
confronted with a two-fold task: first to mark out new horizons
in human goals for which we strive. Second, to provide
economic means by which these goals may be achieved.

■ *Governor Luther Youngdahl, 1949 inaugural address*

The balloons had dropped, the confetti had fallen. The celebration ended but there was no time for Youngdahl to savor his victory.
In two short months the legislative session would begin. The session was
only ninety days long. Every minute counted for the sprint to the finish line in April. The governor intended to be ready. In fact, he had done
much of the groundwork already. He focused on two critical tasks—
building public support for mental health reform and designing the legislative blueprint. In both, he relied heavily on his own organizations—
the Governor's Citizens Mental Health Committee and the Governor's
Advisory Council on Mental Health.

The Governor's Citizens Committee, composed of influential people
from many faiths and backgrounds across the state, had filled in for the
absence of support from religious organizations.[1] The committee had
successfully moved from education mode to election mode during the
campaign. As the session approached, it would need to pivot yet again
from an election victory to a lobbying strategy.

The group wasted no time. Within a few days of the election, advocates of reform filled the airwaves. The governor declared November 28–
December 3, 1948, Mental Health Week. Public open house events were
held at the mental hospitals.[2] Youngdahl, along with Citizens Committee chair Leslie L. Anderson, kicked off Mental Health Week with a
radio program on WCCO.[3] The blitz continued with radio shows by the
American Association of University Women and the Junior Chamber of

Commerce.[4] On December 3, WTCN hosted committee leaders Judge Douglas Hunt and his wife, Ione, representing the Minnesota Federation of Women's Clubs.[5] Division of Public Institutions chief Carl Jackson spoke at the Kiwanis Club in St. Paul, and Arthur Foote was featured at a meeting of the Minnesota Association of Social Workers.[6] In the print media, Jack B. MacKay, an Associated Press reporter, wrote a syndicated four-part series on Youngdahl's program that appeared in newspapers across the state.[7] Radio station KFAM-FM ran a series of broadcasts covering a wide range of mental health issues.[8]

The strategy was to excite the public to get involved, and encourage them to start up or join a county-based citizens committee. Martin, Ramsey, and Hennepin Counties had been the first to do so during the fall of 1948.[9] The county committees generated significant public interest in reform and were poised to pressure legislators from their home districts.[10] The statewide Governor's Citizens Mental Health Committee provided information and resources to the local groups, including access to reels of radio broadcasts, lists of speakers, pamphlets, and other materials. Justin Reese, the committee's secretary, deployed his substantial community-organizing skills, visiting towns around the state to build support and encourage the troops. The local committee strategy also opened the door for families of patients to get involved when the reform discussion brought the issue out of the shadows.[11]

MUC Committee on Mental Hospitals members Foote, George Jacobson, and Genevieve Steefel were all leaders in the Governor's Citizens Mental Health Committee. They also participated in their home county groups. In fact, the Hennepin County Citizens Committee used Steefel's home as its headquarters.[12] As Foote reported:

> Members of the [Unitarian] Committee made an uncounted number of speeches in communities all over the State, at Citizens rallies, to Service Clubs and Women's organizations and Churches, etc. describing conditions in the hospitals, outlining the mental health program and urging wide community support for it. They also spoke over the radio and participated in radio panels. They met, also, with small groups of interested individuals to advise on the formation of county mental health groups.[13]

The momentum in the weeks between the election and the opening of the legislative session was palpable, thanks to the indefatigable work of the governor and the Citizens Committee leaders. Foote wrote:

To those who went out to speak to groups everywhere in the state it was evident that radio and newspaper education material was doing its work in effacing the shame and fear so characteristic of popular attitudes toward mental illness. Fewer faces were tense, fewer eyes flooded with tears in the audience which listened. Popular education was at work in the press, over the radio waves and from the speakers' platform to create an atmosphere of expectancy and hope on the basis of thoroughly realistic facts.[14]

Their successes were all the more remarkable given the stigma and shame that had silenced the voices of citizens in the past.

A few days before Christmas, the governor appeared on another radio program along with State Senator Gerald T. Mullin, a lifelong Democrat from North Minneapolis, who, often at odds with the liberal members of his own party, caucused with the conservatives.[15] He was a leader in the Senate, chair of the University Committee, and sat on the important Public Welfare Committee.[16] On the program, he expressed his support for mental health reform, a coup for Youngdahl.[17] Mullin would prove to be a valuable ally.

In addition to building public support, the governor also needed to prepare the blueprint for the mental health reform bill. He formally asked his Advisory Council to draft recommendations for him. Behind closed doors, the council had been meeting weekly since September, sequestered and in strict confidence. To avoid the perception of a conflict between his role as chair of the Unitarian Mental Health Committee and the drafting of legislation of the Governor's Advisory Council on Mental Health, Foote stepped away from his committee chairmanship temporarily. The final product, *Recommendations for Treatment and Administrative Procedures Relating to the Care of the Mentally Ill*, formed the basis of the mental health legislation to follow.[18]

In the interests of time, the council assigned particular members the responsibility of drafting sections of the official recommendations.[19] The council's psychiatrists had keen interest and expertise on issues relevant to their profession. Five of them were affiliated with the University of Minnesota, including Dr. Donald Hastings, chair of the Department of Psychiatry. They drafted the recommendations relating to hospital psychiatrists, including minimum staffing standards, compensation, and university research and residency training programs in the mental hospitals. These provisions supported stronger links between the institutions and the university to introduce medical research and training into every hospital.

Foote and Frank Rarig Jr. played a critical role in the development of the recommendations and the principles underlying them.[20] They were the only nonmedical professionals on the Advisory Council. Consistent with the Unitarians' philosophy, they focused on issues overlooked by the professionals—concerns about the conditions under which the patients lived and issues related to the nonprofessional personnel in the hospitals, primarily the attendants. Without their participation, it is not likely that these issues would have been addressed.

Over the course of their involvement in mental health, the Unitarians grew to understand the serious shortcomings in the care and treatment of individual patients. They developed the concept of fundamental human guarantees that every individual in a mental institution was entitled to receive, including dignity, adequate physical and medical care, proper clothing, personal care items and personal space, up-to-date activities including occupational therapy, and modern therapeutic treatment. The work of the Unitarians' Nutrition Committee and the groups with which it had collaborated formed the core of the recommendation for a single diet standard for patients, employees, and physicians. Rarig and Foote became the conduit whereby these key principles were incorporated into the official recommendations.

Foote and Rarig also drafted the recommendations for all the nonmedical staff. A modern mental health system depended upon "an adequate staff of properly trained and competent personnel as the most important single component of an adequate treatment program for the mentally ill." The recommendations called for changes in civil service classifications, competitive salaries, and better living conditions for the clinical psychologists, occupational therapists, and social workers who would be part of the psychiatric team providing care.

Foote had been assigned responsibility for drawing up the detailed sections on psychiatric aides, the new designation to replace the term *attendant* that was abandoned because of the connotation of low-skill custodial work. Calling these workers "the most important employees in a state mental hospital . . . whose duty is the constant care of the patient," and a key part of the "therapeutic team," the report drew directly from the Unitarians' work on staffing and training issues. There would be higher salaries, a forty-hour week, and opportunities for training and promotion. These provisions were a testament to Engla Schey, the vocal attendant who had exposed the Unitarians to the low pay and limited opportunities for the staff who were closest to the patients. They were also a rebuke to Superintendent Magnus Petersen of Rochester, among others, who condescendingly rejected such proposals during discussions with the Unitarian subcommittee in 1947 and 1948.

A broader system of care, beyond the improved mental hospital, was envisioned. Rarig drafted the sections on outpatient and preventive services in the community, as well as state support for rest homes to move the geriatric population out of mental institutions over time. Alan Challman, who had chaired the Minnesota State Medical Association's shocking revelations of conditions at the Faribault School, ensured specific provisions for significant improvements to conditions at the school. Alexander Dumas, chair of the Governor's Advisory Council on Mental Health, wrote the sections relating to the availability of psychiatrists trained to work with young offenders in the courts and other outpatient settings.

The new system required a new administrative structure in state government. The Advisory Council, in consultation with the DPI and the civil service, developed recommendations for reorganizing, including a new division of mental health and mental hospitals within the DPI with authority over both outpatient and hospital services. Superintendents would no longer have absolute control of all aspects of their institutions. The state would impose greater oversight, centralize some institutional functions, and require a business manager to serve as assistant superintendent in each hospital. The report tweaked the current building program that had been authorized in 1945 and 1947 in order to redirect resources based on changed priorities, and to suggest more funds in the future. The final report was officially transmitted to the governor on January 10, 1949.

The Unitarians were important participants in the state and local citizens committees and on the Governor's Advisory Council during this important period before the legislative session. Their MUC Committee on Mental Hospitals also developed its own legislative strategy. In November 1948, in anticipation of the session, they added the Legislative Strategy Committee to their roster. Rather than use experienced business lobbyists to act on their behalf at the legislature, they decided to speak directly as "the authoritative group working in the field." Having built a reputation for independence based on moral and humanitarian values, the Unitarians were their own best advocates.

Foote had been the primary public face of the MUC Committee on Mental Hospitals throughout 1948, while the work of others was done behind the scenes. As the session approached, however, the committee decided it would be prudent to put forward representatives who spanned the political spectrum. Jacobson was the DFLer, Steefel was to his left, and to his right, Frank Stone, a Republican businessman and member of FUS; Foote was an independent. Steefel accepted the new title of vice-chairman of the committee, a position that reflected her critical contributions to the enterprise. For Steefel, the move up the ladder was about time.

Consistent with their agreed upon values, the Legislative Strategy Committee's goal was to develop and disseminate facts to the legislators and the press, both to inform and to rectify misconceptions or misinformation during the legislative process. The Unitarians knew that factual information, as Foote explained, "must be supplied [to] the legislators and voters if a true picture of the needed legislation were to be brought into the next legislative session." The Unitarians had built a trusted relationship with the press, especially with Geri Hoffner at the *Tribune,* who often sought them out for just such a role.

The opportunity to set the factual record straight arose even before the session began. Foote expressed concern about a "serious omission" in the Advisory Council's work relating to nonmedical personnel. He thought "the psychiatrists simply did not appreciate the realistic conditions that would have to be met if psychiatric social workers, clinical psychologists, occupational therapists, and psychiatric nurses were to be attracted to the new Minnesota program." Psychiatrists paid lip service to the concept of a psychiatric team, but had not focused on how to implement the team concept, leaving the council's recommendations vulnerable to attack.[21] Opponents would argue, as had been done in the past, that persons with the requisite skills were simply not available for employment in the mental hospitals. The vicious circle would continue—there would be no funds appropriated because there were no qualified people to be had, ensuring that, without funds to train or appropriately pay, few qualified applicants would apply. Opponents simply said, "There is little use in voting money for professional personnel that is unobtainable."[22]

Drawing on her ties to the university, Steefel hastily called a meeting of experts to provide accurate data on staffing and recruitment. On December 30, 1948, an all-day conference gathered key university leaders, including John Kidneigh, an FUS member and the director of the School of Social Work, and Starke Hathaway, distinguished professor of psychology. The university's directors of internship training in psychiatric social work, clinical psychology, psychiatric nursing, and occupational therapy also participated.[23] From the state, Dr. Royal Gray, of the DPI's Mental Health Unit, Robert Stover, head of the civil service, and Ralph Rossen, superintendent at Hastings Hospital, lent their expertise. Rossen, unlike many other superintendents, appreciated the importance of nonmedical personnel. Louis Dorweiller, research director of the Legislative Research Committee, Edgar Crane, and Arthur Foote completed the group.

The Unitarians produced a staffing memorandum with the findings of the meeting. The key observations were as follows: (1) Qualified teaching staff was available in sufficient numbers to begin training programs in the institutions; (2) Qualified Minnesota applicants in the fields were being turned away and going out of state because of a lack of internship opportunities in Minnesota; (3) Intern trainees paid tuition and did not cost the hospitals money; and (4) Qualified teaching staff would allow research projects to begin, ensuring more successful treatment and higher cure rates.[24] The staffing memorandum included data-rich appendixes to support the findings. The bottom line was that public investment in training programs would produce sufficient qualified people to meet recommended staffing requirements.

Unitarians distributed copies of the staffing memorandum to the governor, relevant legislators, and the press. Their goal was to put the data on the record to head off opposition based on erroneous or uninformed information from opponents.[25]

In addition, the Unitarians wanted to keep the needs of patients front and center in the public debate. They published a pamphlet titled *An Affirmation of the Fundamental Human Guarantees Which Minnesota Owes to Every Patient in State Mental Hospitals.*[26] These guarantees had been incorporated in the Advisory Council recommendations. The pamphlet was distributed across the state to build public support.[27]

As Foote recalled, one of the Unitarians said, "'It is all right here,' as he read it for the first time, 'everything we are working for.'"[28] The notion that patients had fundamental rights was a breakthrough, and the document was a keen reminder to put the needs of patients first.

■ ■ ■

After a light snowfall during the night, January 6, 1949, dawned bright and clear. The temperature had risen into the midthirties, far above normal. Governor Youngdahl was on his way from his home in Minneapolis to the inaugural ceremonies. As the magnificent capitol dome came into view, rising from the dusting of snow and sparkling against a blue sky, Youngdahl was on top of the world. It was only a year ago, after meeting with Reverend Foote, that he had publicly embraced mental health reform. His "Crusade for Forgotten Souls" had consumed his attention and was the cornerstone of his reelection campaign. He had been buffeted politically from his right and left flanks, but he weathered the challenges and emerged triumphant. Now, his inaugural address would formally launch his legislative effort.

The joint legislative session convened in the elegant House chamber. The sun shone through the ornate glass skylight, dazzling the chamber's soaring, gilded arches, stone pilasters, and grand frescoes. The governor rose and stepped up to the lectern, surveying the packed chamber of legislators, friends and foes alike.

Conservatives controlled both the House and Senate by substantial majorities (the split in the Senate was 57 conservatives, 10 liberals; in the House, 131 conservatives, 45 liberals).[29] The caucus was not a monolith; many on the conservative side identified with Stassen's progressive brand of Republicanism and with Youngdahl's humanitarianism, and a few, such as Senator Mullin, were in the DFL. Old guard Republicans, however, dominated the leadership and wielded substantial power.[30] A former colleague remarked that House majority leader Roy E. Dunn "practically held court in the House. His word was law."[31] Howard Ottinger, chair of the House Committee on Welfare and a member of the House Appropriations Committee, fit the same mold. Claude Allen, chair of the Appropriations Committee, "ruled the committee with an iron hand," holding tight rein on state expenditures.[32] On the Senate side, Donald O. Wright, chair of the Public Welfare Committee, often had the epithets "autocrat" and "dictator" thrown his way.[33] Henry H. Sullivan, who revered seniority, chaired the Senate Finance Committee that oversaw virtually every activity in need of state funds.[34] Youngdahl expected an uphill fight.

This year, 1949, was the centennial; it had been one hundred years since Minnesota became a U.S. territory. Fittingly, the gilded frieze above the dais depicted Lady Minnesota, surrounded by the native peoples and pioneers who built the state. In his heart, Youngdahl knew the people of Minnesota supported his agenda. The people would demand mental health reform. So it was of the people and to the people that Luther Youngdahl spoke:

> The people of our state, in this Centennial year, look back upon a record of achievement. 1849–1949, a century of struggle and growth, a century of toil and sacrifice, a century in which a wilderness has been transformed into a great progressive commonwealth. The Centennial year marks a luminous place along our path; a year dedicated to the people who built Minnesota, to her countless unnamed pioneers who believed enough in her future to be pioneers.[35]

Then Youngdahl turned to the future:

> This next century depends upon the way in which we, the descendants of these great pioneers, build for the future; the way in which we, the children of those sturdy people, maintain the security, the freedom, and the democracy which we have inherited from them.... There must be a place in our scheme of things for those great intangible human values.[36]

Mental health was the first of Governor Youngdahl's stated goals, and the one to which he devoted the lion's share of his remarks.[37] He affirmed the need for change in moral terms, condemning current institutions as "social monstrosities" that are "fundamentally unchanged since the abolition of its moral counterpart, slavery." He then laid out his vision for modern therapeutic hospitals "characterized by research and active training of personnel," linked "with the home and community through clinics and social work services, which would in turn provide early detection, possible non-hospital treatment, post-hospital follow-up care of discharged patients, and consultative and other services to courts, schools, and welfare agencies." Inside the hospitals, trained personnel working as a psychiatric team would improve diets and living conditions for patients, and an upward adjustment in the building program budget would accommodate cost increases (330–36).

In his inaugural comments, Youngdahl argued for a reorganization of the agencies that would oversee the new modern system. He concluded that we are accomplices in the "social crime" of neglecting the mentally ill, noting that there can be no rest until Minnesota holds "the pre-eminent place" among all the states in its mental health system

(330–36). After addressing his other second-term priorities, Youngdahl rejected any hesitation based on costs:

> The pioneers of 100 years ago did not hesitate to pay the price for a strong society. They did not allow their spiritual values to be smothered beneath the false riches of material possessions. May the high idealism, the courage, the selflessness, and the implicit faith in God which characterized the founders of Minnesota, inspire us. In the same spirit of consecration may we also move ahead to our next and even greater century of advancement, building together a nobler Minnesota. (341–42)

Governor Youngdahl took his case for mental health reform directly to a joint session of the state legislature in 1949. Courtesy of the Minnesota Historical Society.

To appreciative applause, the governor mopped his brow, smiled broadly, and stepped down into the chamber. He had done his homework. He was prepared. He was ready to begin.

On January 19, the governor, as required by law, delivered his budget message to a joint session of the legislature and released copies of the detailed budget document.[38] Youngdahl had a hard sell. He began his message with a recitation of the damaging effects of inflation and cost increases since the last biennium that materially reduced the value of the dollar. To hit home, he gave examples of increases in commodities such as gasoline and coal (up 107 percent and 48.5 percent, respectively). He noted, "We are confronted then with the difficult problem of preparing a budget that will meet compelling human needs in a time when prices have risen to new heights, and it is hard to see what the future holds in economic trends."

Next he delivered the impact of his agenda in dollars and cents. Youngdahl's proposed appropriations from the general fund, from which most state departments financed the expansion and improvement of services, were 42 percent higher than the last biennium. Spending for the university, social welfare, veterans' affairs, and penal institutions all grew. The greatest increase—over 100 percent—was for the state mental institutions, with spending rising from $15.27 million to $31 million in the biennium.

Youngdahl argued in defense of his spending proposals: "A large part of the increased cost proposed is for enlargements of personnel and the raising of the quality of help provided for the institutions. As pointed out in my inaugural address, our mental hospitals have only about half the help needed to give the patients proper attention." Of the $15.5 million in higher expenditures, $8.6 million was for salaries, a forty-hour workweek, cost of living increases, added personnel, and civil service reclassification. Another $5.3 million was allocated for current expenses, including food allowances to give patients an adequate diet. There were lesser amounts for repairs, improvements to therapy facilities, the psychiatric training program for attendants and other staff, outpatient clinics, and mental health research. The governor proposed additional taxes on beer, liquor, and tobacco products to cover these new costs.

The budget also addressed the deferred building account issues. Youngdahl reiterated that the 1947 legislature had designated the sites slated to receive support from a $5 million fund set aside for state hospitals in 1945. As a result of inflation, the sums appropriated were barely adequate for half the projects. He requested consideration of a deficiency appropriation to eliminate delay in these deferred projects. He also proposed an additional $19 million for a series of new buildings and capital improvements, over $9 million of which was for state mental institutions.[39] New bonds and mill levies on property taxes would finance these projects.

There was immediate sticker shock following the release of the budget. The *Pioneer Press* noted the "heavy tone of skepticism" from many legislators.[40] The Winona Taxpayers Association was more direct. Concerned with the large expenditures, it urged legislators to "try . . . to do everything possible to keep expenditures within the bounds of reason."[41]

As the session unfolded, the reformers faced risks at every turn. They would have to fight on two fronts—to keep the plan intact in the policy committees and to ensure full appropriations from the House Appropriations and the Senate Finance Committees to fund the plan.

The Unitarians were essential to the strategy. For Youngdahl the reform of mental health care was a moral crusade. As the most visible church group in the movement, the Unitarians spoke on a higher plane, keeping the focus on the needs of patients and those who cared for them. As the "authoritative source," they also provided additional factual information, both proactively and reactively, to refute misconceptions that played into opponents' hands. They worked closely with the press and the local citizens committees to disseminate information. They circulated copies of their original 1947 *Summary of Conditions in the Minnesota State Hospitals for the Mentally Ill,* the staffing memorandum, and the *Affirmation of the Fundamental Human Guarantees* pamphlet to all House and Senate members. The needs of patients and the importance of nonphysician staff were now on the record, making the findings harder to ignore.[42] The press published an editorial praising the analysis in the staffing memorandum.[43]

The governor's "go to the people" strategy placed the conservatives in a bind. The local citizens committees had effectively mobilized support for the reform, making outright opposition increasingly difficult. When Youngdahl presented his mental health program bill to the legislature on February 18, a proposal that closely tracked the recommendations from his Advisory Council, he received pledges of support from

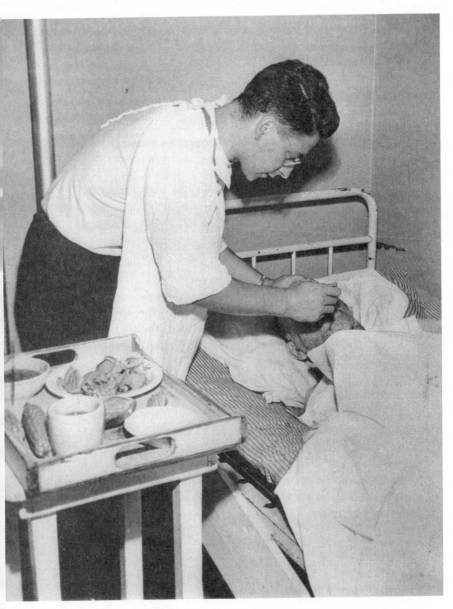

As part of their reform effort, the Minnesota Unitarians organized a summer work program for young people to volunteer at Hastings State Hospital under the auspices of the Unitarian Service Committee. In this photograph, a volunteer feeds an elderly bedridden patient. Author's collection.

the majority leaders in both the House and the Senate.[44] In fact, there was even a tussle over who would get to sponsor the bill.[45] But pledges of support did not mean the bill as written was safe.

Following Youngdahl's presentation of his plan to the legislature, the authors of the bills set to work. The House Appropriations Committee provided the opening public salvo on March 2. In its first hearing on the entire budget, the committee went on the attack. Chairman Claude Allen "appeared unconvinced that the entire mental program could or should be enacted."[46] Legislators questioned the APA standards that justified significantly more and better trained personnel, calling them "a matter of theory, and not experience at all," asked whether treatment should be limited to "curables" to save money, and demanded a concrete comparison with other states, implying that Minnesota was going too far. Earl Berg, the state commissioner of administration, responded decisively: "This is intended to place Minnesota in the lead."[47]

Two days later, a headline in the *Minneapolis Tribune* read, "Pastor Hits Move to Cut Mental Fund."[48] Foote "sharply attacked proposals for 'drastic cuts' in the governor's mental health plan. He took the moral highroad, saying legislators were 'sanctioning the continuance of sub-human treatment of these innocent, sick people.'" He continued: "This and much more I have seen with my own eyes with mounting anger and shame. . . . I know that the majority of these patients receive grossly inadequate care." He called Youngdahl's program "a well-balanced integrated plan to remedy the situation" and said, "the only criticism of the program should be that it does not go far enough."[49] The Unitarians had earned the moral highroad, and they used it to good effect.

On March 3 Youngdahl went on the air to "do some plain talking" about the reception of his proposal in the legislature. Eight stations carried the program statewide. The governor once again presented the need for reform and answered the attacks that had come from the House floor. Soon thereafter, it was reported that the leaders of House and Senate planned to meet with the governor on the form of the mental health bill. It was also noted, however, that despite the pledges of support, "this bill will have no direct effect unless appropriations are voted to make it work."[50]

The governor and the legislators conferred behind closed doors. On March 15 they reached an agreement on the form of the mental health bills that were introduced the same day.[51] The authors made several symbolic changes and some substantive ones. There were two additions to the bill's preamble. First, language was added to give credit to previous conservative-controlled legislatures for mental health improvements, simply a face-saving ploy for the conservatives. Second, they added language to emphasize that appropriations should be "to the fullest extent compatible with the ability of the people of the state of Minnesota to provide funds therefore."[52] The point was clear, putting all on notice that the Appropriations and Finance Committees would have the final say.

Substantively, the bills did not include references to a forty-hour workweek or compliance with APA staffing standards, but proponents knew that fight would play out in the Appropriations and Finance Committees.

The legislators also made changes to the allocation of responsibility among the relevant state departments. The governor's draft included all inpatient and outpatient mental health services under the authority of the new commissioner of mental health. Legislators rejected this concept, restoring to the Department of Social Welfare the authority to oversee outpatient services.[53] The core of the program, however, remained intact. The press once again reminded readers of the "catch"—that the conservative leadership "embraced" the reform, but still had the power to restrict it, or even kill it, during the appropriations process.[54]

The politics were intense. Proponents feared conservatives would give lip service to the bill, then turn around and cripple it with meager appropriations. The Young Republican organization, filled with progressives, and suspecting a conservative ploy, reportedly wondered "whether they or their party can much longer sustain the burden of an intolerant few who obstinately refuse to accept the will of the people, and who are eager and willing to destroy the basic asset of the Republican party—those true liberal principles which first made it great and will do so again."[55]

The minority liberal caucus "insisted they were the first to 'sound the clarion' call" for mental health, and were unhappy at the prospect that the Republican Youngdahl would get all the credit if it passed despite liberal support. Gerry Mullin, an old-time Democrat long at odds with the DFL Party, actively supported the effort and battled alongside Youngdahl "to see that [the bill] isn't killed off or emasculated."[56]

Two days later, on Thursday, March 17, the chair of the House Welfare Committee, Howard Ottinger, and the chair of the Senate Public

Welfare Committee, Donald Wright, announced they would hold a joint hearing on the mental health bill on Monday evening, March 21, in the House chamber. The chairmen announced that "politics will be ruled out" at the hearing, knowing that feelings were running high, especially since the Minnesota Taxpayers Association had just demanded a 75% reduction in the mental health reform budget request.[57] Was the hearing a ploy to showcase opposition to the bill, or was it an effort to placate a mobilized citizenry?

When Steefel got wind of the hearing, she was on the phone immediately. She drafted a letter under Jacobson's signature that she hand-delivered to the Senate committee staff requesting time for the Unitarians to testify. She was frustrated to learn that the statewide Citizens Committee, under Justin Reese, assumed the role of lining up speakers. After dialing Christine Reese, Justin's wife, Steefel secured a slot for three Unitarian speakers.

With little more than a weekend to prepare, Steefel sprang into action. She was at her best in a crisis—efficient, focused, and energized. On Saturday morning, sitting in her little study on West River Road, she produced a four-page memo for the Unitarians' Legislative Strategy Committee.[58] She shared with them what she had learned about the goals of the hearing, what was still in flux, and the challenges that might arise, and suggested how they might divide the three presentations. She enclosed a copy of the Senate bill, announced a preparatory meeting for Monday prior to the hearing, got into her car, and drove the materials to the homes of Jacobson and Foote. There was no time to waste.

Steefel explained that the joint committee would hear both the pros and cons in a single hearing. She feared that the "diversionary" effect of the controversy about departmental control of mental health might distract legislators and bureaucrats from the core issues. She expressed concern about time pressures that might limit the opportunities for proponents to speak, and reminded them that the Unitarian goal was to keep focus on the patients and the staff who cared for them. Foote was to go first. He would speak about the conditions in the institutions and the patients' fundamental guarantees. She noted: "If this is all there is time for, it is the most important and should be given in preference to all the rest."

The second presentation, Steefel continued, would summarize the staffing memorandum, noting that all members had received the document, "but they may not have read it." The final presentation would emphasize the theme that the whole program must be kept intact, "including diet, staffing, quality of staff, activities, social services, recovery and planning for release. Etc." She mentioned the possibility of introducing the "ace card," an appeal for long-term economy through immediate increases in the provision of care. This "trial balloon" referred to a study that she and Ed Crane had just completed (time constraints prevented its presentation during the hearing, however). She noted that Hoffner said the *Minneapolis Tribune* would run a piece on this issue in the Sunday paper on March 27.

Over four hundred people poured into the ornate House chamber on the night of March 21. The size of the crowd at such short notice underscored the organizing power of the local Citizens Committees. There was an air of excitement in the packed chamber. The lead speaker was Dr. Daniel Blaine, national medical director of the APA, who testified about the value of the APA staffing standards. Dr. Ralph Rossen of Hastings said mental institutions "should examine patients, treat them, and send them home again."[59]

A score of other speakers followed, from labor, civic, and social organizations. Leslie Anderson spoke for the Citizens Committee, followed by the Unitarian trio of Foote, Jacobson, and Steefel. Representatives of local Citizens Committees were also heard. Opponents did testify, but the reformers supported by the enthusiastic audience dominated the proceedings.

The story the following day ran prominently in newspapers statewide. Headlines were positive. Hoffner's feature, "Mental Health Bill Gets Boost" in the morning *Minneapolis Tribune,* and "400 Demand Mental Health Aid Program" in the *St. Paul Pioneer Press* spread the word.[60] The pressure was on. Two days later, on March 23, the Senate Public Welfare Committee unanimously recommended passage of the bill without amendments, and it moved for consideration on the Senate floor. The House bill soon followed. The full House unanimously passed the bill on April 9; the Senate followed suit on April 13.[61] Youngdahl signed the mental health bill into law on April 20, 1949. At the signing he said, "Humane provision for the mentally ill is now the law of the state. I join members of the public and relatives of patients in mental hospitals in congratulating the legislature for the unanimous passage of this humane measure."[62]

But victory could not yet be declared. The battle was not yet won.

Legislators had bowed to the pressure to support the bill, but money to pay for it was still necessary to make it work. All eyes turned to the House Appropriations and Senate Finance Committees, both of which took up the matter in early April. Before the big push in the key committees, the Unitarians brought forward the new analysis referred to in Steefel's memo as the "ace in the hole." Drawn from a review of biennial reports, the study demonstrated that expenditures for buildings and services would keep expanding as long as patients only received custodial care. True cost savings would come only after an investment in research, treatment, and cure. As promised, a summary of the study ran in the paper on March 28.[63]

A *Minneapolis Tribune* editorial on April 1 argued that the legislature should split the difference, making "cuts in the interest of economy, for those who think the program moves too fast" but allow for an "adequate" mental health program.[64] The Unitarians knew that splitting the difference would not produce sufficient funds for real change. Their response was imperative.

In a hard-hitting op-ed on April 7, the MUC Committee on Mental Hospitals challenged the "split the difference" conclusion. Using the information from the study, based on a review of the biennial reports of the institutions since 1884, and accounting for changes in the consumer price index, they concluded:

> Stubborn resistance to the use of modern psychiatric treatment for every patient in a state hospital can result only in the continued burden for the taxpayer of a growing backlog of the uncured in more and more buildings, which cost $10,000 per bed to build. . . . If we risk anything more gradual than these minimum modern beginnings we will be back in the same old vicious circle . . . with an ever-increasing patient load and more and more buildings.[65]

Their point, clearly made, was that we can only avoid the "wasteful extravagance" of our current system if we fund the governor's comprehensive plan. The argument turned the debate around—from the high costs of doing something to the higher costs of doing nothing. The theme had resonance and became critical, though not entirely successful, in the appropriations debate to come. Youngdahl turned up the heat on the appropriators. "I feel those people again standing here with me— waiting for their representatives in the Senate and House to vote us the funds to carry out a program under which so many hapless persons will be cured and sent back home to take their deserved places among their fellow human beings."[66]

The Senate Finance Committee met first. Despite the efforts of Senator Mullin, on April 13, the committee approved a 40 percent cut in funds requested for salaries (a $1.6 million reduction) but approved, after much debate, the forty-hour workweek.[67] The House Appropriations came next. Many reformers testified at an April 13 hearing, including Reese, Rarig, and Foote. Chairman Allen asked DPI head Jackson to help the committee set priorities if cuts were to be made. Jackson replied, using the Unitarians' argument that you have to spend money to save money. No cuts. Despite their pleas, the House committee voted to reduce the budget request for employees by 50 percent and upheld a forty-eight-hour workweek. As in the Senate, all other mental health provisions came through unscathed.

The cuts brought sharp protests from proponents, including Unitarian Judge Otis for the Ramsey County Citizens Committee and Foote for the Unitarians, who sent telegrams directed toward leaders Dunn and Allen.[68]

A showdown on the House floor loomed as supporters for a forty-hour workweek vowed a disruptive floor fight. Then, on April 20, in a surprising turnaround, Chairman Allen realized that there were enough members in favor of the forty-hour provision to prevail. He capitulated. The bill passed, 104–17, setting a forty-hour workweek and $27,800,000 in appropriations. At the time, Allen conceded, "This is a generous and sympathetic approach to the problem that we felt we had approached in the past but probably not well enough. We feel it's a good bill."[69] The deadlock was broken with a one-cent tax on cigarettes.[70] Despite a disappointing $2.2 million cut from the $30 million proposed expenditure, the core of the program survived.

Youngdahl went to the people and won. The conservatives swallowed the loss. Allen groused, "This definitely doesn't set a pattern for future legislatures to follow."[71] Why did he give in at the crucial moment? LeVander later recalled:

Well what we did in that instance, was we worked with relatives that were from [Allen's] district. In other words we found out who the relatives were of the mentally ill that lived in his constituency and we got them fired up to put pressure on Claude. And after his

own constituency started in singing a tune to him about their relatives, and just humanitarian conditions that ought obtain for them,
he changed his mind and eventually came around. And so we had to
utilize those kinds of things in order to get the job done.[72]

The *Tribune* opined that "a big group of the conservatives, though they
begrudged giving so much to mental health, kept their opinions private
for fear of being accused of being anti-humanitarian."[73] Public pressure
carried the day.

Less than nine hours after adjournment, Jackson and his key staff
went to work. He told them, "We realize we have a big job ahead of us.
I am, of course, grateful we have had a governor who has championed
this mental health program, and we're grateful to the Legislature and
citizens who supported it."[74] The date for implementation was July 1,
1949.

In June the Minnesota Unitarian Conference convened back at
Camp Ihduhapi where it all began. Foote, on behalf of the MUC Committee on Mental Hospitals, asked for and received the following charge:

> Whereas this conference first authorized formation of its Committee
> on Mental Hospitals in 1946, and
>
> Whereas this committee, having played a leading part in the pas-
> sage of Minnesota's mental health program, has a moral responsibil-
> ity to see that the program is carried on to success, and
>
> Whereas the most difficult part of the program now begins—that
> of translating dollars into new practices and a new spirit of service
> and teamwork, the Conference authorizes the Committee for an-
> other year.[75]

Engla Schey, an attendant at Rochester State Hospital, requested
and received a transfer to Hastings State Hospital as a psychiatric aide
on August 24, 1949.[76]

The bill passed. The real work would now begin.

ELEVEN

The First Step

Money, manpower, and driving enthusiasm have poured into
Minnesota's mental hospitals in the last year. The results are
impressive, even startling. Like a giant Rip Van Winkle, asleep
for years, the state hospital system awoke in July 1949 ...
the state hospitals found a new world, buzzing with ideas
undreamed of a few years ago.

> ■ *Geri Hoffner,* Minneapolis Tribune

On a late August morning in 1949, Engla Schey paid her
cab driver, gathered her belongings, and walked through the tall white
columns into the administration building at Hastings State Hospital.
Hastings was a small river town of six thousand, just twenty miles south
of St. Paul. The hospital had been built the same year as Anoka (1899)
on the cottage model, in wooded rolling hills on the outskirts of town.
Adjacent to administration was a main kitchen and the central dining
hall. Patients lived in one of the nine gabled, red stucco "upper cottages"
on the hillside, or in one of the nine orange brick "lower cottages" set
around a ball field down the hill.[1]

Engla patted the letter in her pocket setting out the official terms
of her new position at Hastings. She had long hoped to transfer from
Rochester, but there had been no new hires until the appropriations
began to flow on July 1. She submitted her application, and here she
was. Engla recalled her trepidation when she arrived at Anoka ten years
earlier in 1939. She had never forgotten her despair over the patients'
living conditions and treatment. After all that water under the bridge,
the National Mental Health Foundation, the Unitarians, and the political battles, Engla thought change might really happen at Hastings.

No longer on the lowest rung on the ladder, Engla was hired as
psychiatric aide II. She would work as part of a new team focused on

recreational therapy. Her salary, while still modest, was higher than ever before. She decided her first purchase would be a typewriter so she could pursue her interest in writing. Then she hoped to save some money for her future. As an added bonus, her new location and a forty-hour week would give her access to Minneapolis and St. Paul on her days off.

But the most compelling reason for Engla to move to Hastings was the enlightened superintendent, Dr. Ralph Rossen. The Rossens were Romanian Jews from Hibbing, a small town on Minnesota's northern Iron Range.[2] Rossen was six feet tall, with coal black hair, and bright blue eyes. His father died while Ralph was still in high school, and his mother moved the family down to Minneapolis so her children could attend the university. Rossen carried mail during vacation and on weekends to pay tuition and help at home, and was a star heavyweight on the university's wrestling team. After a pediatric residency and a fellowship in neuroscience, he became, at age twenty-eight, the superintendent at Hastings in 1938. Gregarious, engaging, and devoted to scientific research, he kept close ties with the university and held a faculty post there.[3]

Dr. Rossen loved life at the state hospital. He lived with his wife and two young daughters in the rambling superintendent's residence, a four-story Tudor-style home with over sixteen rooms. He was a ubiquitous presence, making rounds, often with a daughter in tow, interacting with the patients, curious about ways to make their lives better. His wife's father had offered to set him up in private practice, but he preferred small-town life and loved the institution where he knew all of the patients by name.[4]

On his own, Rossen eliminated restraints at Hastings, claiming they made patients more difficult, not less so, long before Youngdahl's crusade against them. As a result of his humanitarian views, as well as his interest in research and learning, Rossen was "recognized far and wide for his work."[5] In 1942 he had taken leave to serve in the navy, and had returned to Hastings in the spring of 1946. He was glad to be back. Engla, knowing his reputation, was glad to be there too.

Rossen disliked politics. Farmer-Labor governor Elmer Benson had appointed him to the Hastings post in 1938. The following year, Governor Harold Stassen, a Republican, "cleaned house" and Rossen's job was threatened. He managed to survive the cut, but the whole affair put a bad taste in the young doctor's mouth. As reporter Jack Weinberg explained, Rossen was opposed to any talk of mental health care reform until he was sure "the governor was sincere and wasn't using the unfortunates as a campaign issue."[6]

Rossen met Arthur Foote when a group from Unity Church visited Hastings with the proposal to develop a volunteer program. Foote no doubt helped allay the superintendent's fears about political intervention in the hospitals. Rossen subsequently participated in the reform effort, including testimony at legislative hearings.

The Division of Public Institutions chief Carl Jackson led the implementation effort while the search for the mental health commissioner was on. Youngdahl himself called a conference with the leaders of the ten mental hospitals in early May to brief them on the program.[7] By June, Jackson created "teams" made up of superintendents, business managers, and other personnel in the DPI to study clinical procedures, outpatient clinics, research, and training issues.[8] Rossen, with his commitment to research and his close ties to the university, chaired the research committee.[9]

Filling new staff positions was critical. Officials from civil service and the DPI fanned out to colleges around the state in an "intensive campaign" to recruit personnel.[10] Jackson appointed Justin Reese to direct a mental health education and prevention program based in the DPI.[11] In July 1949, Youngdahl, now lauded as a national leader in mental health reform, initiated a comprehensive nationwide study on mental health at the forty-first meeting of the Council of State Governments.[12] Rossen was named the psychiatric consultant on a technical advisory committee.[13]

The governor was a keynote speaker at the Menninger Foundation annual meeting in Topeka in early October. A delegation from Minnesota that included Jackson, Reese, and Foote accompanied him. In his speech, Youngdahl "praised Minnesota citizens for backing the new program, and lauded the legislature for writing a 'mental health bill of rights and backing it fully with money.'"[14]

The local paper in Topeka called Youngdahl the "'fightingest' public official in the growing nationwide cleanup program of the state institutions."[15] A *St. Paul Dispatch* editorial asserted that "Minnesotans, justly proud of the national leadership which the 1949 mental health program involves, will join wholeheartedly in the governor's determination that the ambitious reforms launched become really the ushering in of a new era in public attitudes as to the problem of the mentally ill."[16]

Three weeks later, Governor Youngdahl burned hundreds of strait-jackets and other restraints at Anoka State Hospital. Comparing restraints to witchcraft, he intoned:

> We have no easy job. The roots of demonology are deep. We have burned one evidence of this tonight. We must be on our guard that it does not creep up in other forms—that what the bonfire symbolizes tonight will carry on in public thinking until every last thing is done to make the state hospital truly a house of hope for those most misunderstood of all human beings.[17]

An iconic photograph captured the governor lighting the fire. Mabel Huss, a young nurse at Anoka, recalled watching her patients standing on their beds, looking out the window at the fire, then being told to bring all of them outside for the photo. Huss remembered that the bonfire was confusing to them and her biggest concern was to prevent her charges from getting lost in the crowd as darkness fell.[18]

As the months passed, pressure grew for Youngdahl to fill the position of commissioner of mental health. Youngdahl had had his eye on Ralph Rossen for a long time. The governor wanted an experienced psychiatrist and an outstanding leader committed to mental health reform. He knew Rossen was the whole package. There was just one problem. Rossen didn't want the job.

By December 1949, the national search had not produced a suitable candidate. A frustrated governor finally "drafted" Dr. Rossen. It was reported that

> he [Rossen] has been Gov. Youngdahl's first choice ever since the Legislature last April created the post and set up the huge mental health program for Minnesota. But Dr. Rossen wouldn't listen to any offer, declaring simply "I'm a psychiatrist, not a politician."
>
> When Youngdahl called Dr. Rossen into his office Wednesday [December 14] to tell him he was "it," Dr. Rossen flatly refused to accept. Youngdahl said he was going to make the announcement anyway. Even the governor's soundproof floors couldn't keep the loud give and take discussion from seeping through.[19]

Youngdahl and Rossen struck a bargain. Rossen would assume the post only if he could continue his research work and remain close to patient care. He insisted on three offices: his principal headquarters would

In 1950 Dr. Ralph Rossen was officially appointed commissioner of mental health for the state of Minnesota. Looking over the certificate are Dr. Rossen (left), Governor Youngdahl, Beatrice Rossen (left seated), and Irene Youngdahl. Photograph by the *St. Paul Dispatch/Pioneer Press*. Courtesy of the Minnesota Historical Society.

be at the DPI, but he would also have an office in the Physicians and Surgeons Building in downtown Minneapolis next to an outpatient clinic, and a third at Anoka State Hospital near patients from the "back wards."[20]

The governor presented the commission at a large ceremony and dinner at the university, attended by an overflow crowd of more than a thousand people. Front-page headlines hailed the appointment and coverage of the event in February was extensive. Rossen promised to develop a strategic plan for mental health services in Minnesota. The new commissioner noted that he "needs the help and co-operation of every person in Minnesota if he is to do the big job that confronts him." Rossen estimated that "it will take upwards of ten years to bring about the complete transformation of the situation to the point where Minnesota will really be the nation's leader in the care and treatment of the mentally ill." [21] He saw the reform as a big challenge, but he intended to see it through.

The new commissioner set right to work. To ensure integration of both inpatient and outpatient services and to mitigate interagency squabbles, Youngdahl appointed a committee of all heads of state agencies with mental health authority and named Rossen the chair.[22] In addition to managing the day-to-day oversight of the mental hospitals and the early implementation of the new law, Rossen developed an organizational plan for the new office of commissioner. Rossen's vision was expressed in his book's draft title: *One Mentally Ill Patient: The State Hospital of Tomorrow.* Rossen conceived of the book as

> an attempt to change the way of thinking about state mental hospitals that has heretofore been concerned mainly with per capita costs, the brick and mortar of buildings, and custodial care of large groups of sick people. This book will attempt to show how, through training and education of the layman, the legislator, the educator, and society as a whole, a more efficient use can be made of state mental hospital facilities and staffs in order that their energies may be directed toward the rehabilitation of ONE PATIENT.[23]

Known as "total push," all the energies of a research-based, well-trained psychiatric team would focus on the special needs of each patient. Total push presumed a positive patient environment and services to restore decency and respectability. For each patient, Rossen wrote, we must be sure that "all known research methods in all fields of science have been tried, and if fail, new ones must be added." The custodial ward must become "a clinical investigative center" developing "careful statistical evaluation." This approach, he hoped, would overcome the current "ignorance of psychiatry." [24]

Recognizing that total push had never been attempted in a public hospital because of insufficient personnel, Rossen wanted to gather data to demonstrate the long-term economies of the strategy. In his view, a superintendent's role would be at least half-time clinical, teaching, and research to "maintain proper standards of medical care and knowledge." And, in a tribute to the Unitarian volunteers he had worked with at Hastings, Rossen expressed the thought that "volunteer service is perhaps one of the strongest tools in the progress of any forward-looking state hospital."[25]

Many of the features of total push had been incorporated into the 1949 legislation, including the concept of a psychiatric team, in-service training, and even a small research program. Rossen planned to structure the commissioner's office to facilitate the accomplishment of the vision. He outlined the organizational plan in *The Minnesota Mental Health Program: A Report to Carl J. Jackson*.[26] The commissioner's office was not a central bureaucracy; an assistant superintendent in each institution would oversee administrative and management issues and report directly to the DPI.

The commissioner's office would focus on patients through four major operating divisions: *Hospital Administration*—to assist hospitals to become medically coordinated systems; *Training*—to develop and implement training programs located at various institutions; *Mental Hygiene*—to design well-integrated prevention programs and outpatient and follow-up rehabilitation clinics; and *Research*—to conduct research at all the institutions in order to learn more about the long-term effects of treatments, including prefrontal lobotomies and electro- and insulin shock. The Office of the Commissioner would rely on good consulting staff through the university and the Mayo Clinic, and would work closely with the Governor's Advisory Council on Mental Health.

Rossen's report also contained numerous budgetary requests intended for the 1951 legislative session, including funds to secure additional beds for mentally retarded individuals, a permanent center for emotionally disturbed children, an increase in staffing based on the failure of the 1949 legislature to fully fund the initial request, and research support "within budgetary limitations."[27]

Rossen drew the university's medical leadership into the program, breaking down the separation between hospitals and academics. He touted the "significant and widespread" role the university plays in the state's expanded mental health program.[28] This was a sea change, opening the formerly fortress-like institutions to the newest developments in the field of psychiatry. The link would also open the door to research and training grants from the National Institute of Mental Health.[29]

To relieve overcrowding in the short term, Commissioner Rossen succeeded in persuading the U.S. Congress to allow for the acquisition of a former federal penal institution at Sandstone, Minnesota, on an emergency basis, allowing one hundred patients to move from Rochester and Hastings. The plan was approved, and Dr. Jack Reitmann, who had spent thirty years at Hastings, became superintendent. The Sandstone facility would receive operating income through contingency funds until the legislature could act in 1951.[30]

While there was considerable activity at the state level, did any benefit trickle down to the patients? A steady stream of newspaper articles reported that there were improvements. There were stories on training programs, with "intensive on the ward instruction and training on methods of bathing, feeding and caring" to "activate" previously neglected and deteriorated back-ward patients. Others wrote of collaboration and sharing of best practices across institutions, breaking down the isolation and independence among them.[31]

Press accounts extolled improvement in the food—"with 65 cents a day, dining rooms spruced up, cheerful new dishes ordered and good looking, good tasting food is appearing on menus." The *St. Paul Dispatch* described fresh paint, new sheets, toothpaste and toothbrushes, radios, insulated food carts, and repaired plumbing, as well as added staff at Anoka. To celebrate the end of restraints, blue flags flew outside cottages that had achieved the goal. The press reported that Irwin J. Peterson won the National Mental Health Foundation award for "psychiatric aide of the year" based on his pioneering reactivation program at Moose Lake.[32]

But was the coverage simply public relations and journalistic hype? There were three trusted eyewitness sources as well—Engla Schey, Arthur Foote, and Geri Hoffner—who had their own opinions on the improvements.

Engla did not keep diaries for public consumption or political gain.

Improvement in food provided to patients was one of the reform movement's key areas. Under the new program, meals served at the state hospitals bore little resemblance to the watered-down fare of earlier years. Photograph by Arthur Hager, *Minneapolis Tribune*. Courtesy of the Minnesota Historical Society.

She wrote simply to record her own experiences throughout her career. Entries written during the first week of January in 1952 reflect conditions at Hastings.[33] Change was real:

> Woke about 4 am. Reviewed my 1951 New Years Eve celebration. Quite different from any such previous affairs. Setting: mental hospital auditorium. Patient dance—paper caps on head, gaily colored with tassels, men and women coupling off and talking together under limited and inconspicuous supervision. There were numerous mechanical noisemakers. To top it off, a cool colorful drink and coke. . . . This year I made one single resolution. To make a daily record of the highlights of each day, so here it goes.

Among the activities Engla supervised during the first few weeks of January was taking residents from five cottages to Catholic Mass. The 1949 reform required chaplains for each institution. Engla noted: "The resident chaplain gave a good talk. He had noticed that everyone was getting better. He heard much swearing, quarreling when he came 1½ years ago. Now he seldom heard such things." Engla referred to TV time, weekly movies, a patient singing group accompanied by a volunteer, dances, and coffee parties with chocolate cake. She was given some discretion in her recreation duties, and felt free to bend the rules, noting, "Then I did another unusual thing. I opened the library for a group of working patients to sit around until the show started instead of hanging around with nothing to read."

Recounting an incident during movie night, Engla revealed a significant culture change. Two staff members senior to her insisted that men and women sit on separate sides of the room for the movie. Engla spoke up: "Even tho I was in a lower classification on Recreation I had no idea of submitting to this practice of segregating the sexes in Recreation and I said so loudly and positively, intimating I would go to the highest authority if necessary to hold the ground we have gained in human relationship and objective of a more normal environment for the patient." The next morning, patient Harold M, referring to the seating controversy the night before, remarked to Engla, "'I think Mrs. B should have her rear end paddled. Guess she'd like to go back to the good old conventional days when the women and men both sat on their own side of the church. She ain't going to get away with it. I'll report [it] in.'" Engla admitted, "I giggled inside for now patients have finally gained enough security to question an employee action openly." This was a far cry from the repression of patients and staff she had found at Anoka before the reforms.

Engla's pride and joy at Hastings was *Hospitality*, a monthly newsletter that patients wrote and produced under her supervision.[34] The January 1952 issue acknowledged the many volunteer groups who supported gifts and events over the holiday season. The long list included all manner of faith-based groups—Jewish, Catholic, Unitarian, Presbyterian, Episcopalian, as well as the VFW, Red Cross, and several college student organizations. The newsletter included poems, short stories, and reports of activities such as the patient band and art exhibitions. Engla's diaries contain frequent entries of the trials and

Patients were no longer confined by camisoles or other restraints, and could now even attend hospital dances, sometimes once per week, at some institutions. Photograph by Arthur Hager, *Minneapolis Tribune*. Courtesy of the Minnesota Historical Society.

tribulations of preparation, layout, mimeographing, and distribution. But she and the patient participants loved the conversation, coffee, and camaraderie of the work. Copies even went out to the nonhospital community as well.

Engla described how life had improved for many patients. One patient who had been transferred from Cambridge Hospital bought leather scraps and made them into beautiful belts to sell. Of another transferee from Cambridge, she wrote:

> He was sullen, disturbed when clearing dishes in the cafeteria. Now he had a job in the Lab and enjoyed it. "Just as soon work til 10 pm cause I like it. Don't need to come to shows or dances now, cause I got an interesting job. In Cambridge they made you work and if you didn't do as you were told they could put you in seclusion."

An even greater change was the involvement of psychiatric aides in patient care. Engla participated in decisions regarding the patients' treatment and progress, and was assigned to rounds with one of the doctors on duty and others on the team. One January day, for example, she wrote progress notes on four patients, and raised the issue of appropriate placement in the institution. She met with the team to discuss the care of incontinent patients, commenting on problems with space and toilet facilities. She expressed concern that these patients were not selected for the intensive treatment program. "Why should they be entirely neglected for intense concentration of this [other] group?" she asked.

Previously, as an attendant, she had no access to information about patients' medical or psychiatric conditions, did not participate in decisions about patient care, and would have been reprimanded for questioning a doctor's orders.

But Engla's experience at Hastings was far from perfect. She was frustrated by the constant experiments with new ideas. Hospital leaders would introduce a new plan, only to abandon it for another one. She was skeptical of the skills of some of the college-trained occupational and recreational therapists. Her view was that the ability to connect with patients had little to do with college degrees. Some, she said bitterly, seemed to have degrees in "walking around," with no observable benefit to the patient. She also felt personally "tired and worn down," experienced problems sleeping, and rued that she had "nothing for myself" after giving so much to others' needs. Nevertheless, when she ruminated about Hastings during this period, she observed, "There is so much more kindness [here] than in most mental hospitals."

Reverend Arthur Foote and Josephine Downey, a member of Unity Church, worked incognito as aides at Anoka in December 1949. The goal of their undercover operation was to document the extent of the improvements in the hospital. Downey, a high school teacher, was a 1928 graduate of the University of Minnesota who had served as a cryptographer with the Women's Army Corps during World War II. Apparently at the end of the week, a hospital official came in asking for "the Reverend," ending Foote's anonymity.[35]

The Unitarians recounted their findings on the mental health program in a report issued at the Sixty-Third Minnesota Unitarian Conference in June 1950. Their report was widely covered in the press. It lauded the "marvelous" improvement in morale and praised the

New library building at Hastings State Hospital, 1950s. Funds allocated during the reforms financed the construction of new buildings and renovation of older ones. Engla Schey organized the newsletter written and produced by patients that met in the library space. Copyright University of Minnesota, College of Design.

implementation of a single standard diet despite poor kitchen facilities. It called the nonrestraint goal "very encouraging," praised the real activities program, the completion of new geriatric buildings for senile patients, and the construction of receiving hospitals now under way. The report called the research program "exceptional," and lauded the training programs for doctors and staff. The report also acknowledged, however, that there was work still to be done, including reforming commitment procedures, reducing overcrowding, developing new ways to care for the senile elderly, improving housing for hospital employees, deploying the psychiatric teams more widely, and expanding outpatient clinics.[36]

During this time, *Minneapolis Tribune* reporter Geri Hoffner also provided the public with a firsthand look on the inside. Accompanied once again by photographer Art Hager, she reprised their earlier exposé with a ten-part series titled "Minnesota Bedlam Revisited" that ran in late December 1950 and early January 1951. As compelling and persuasively written as her 1948 exposé, "Bedlam Revisited" told of the many changes she called "impressive, even startling."[37]

Hoffner described improvements in food, recreation, and accommodations, as well as expanded treatment for patients. She observed the vibrant new training plan for staff, raises for workers at all levels, the robust building program, and the assistance of volunteer programs. But she also made clear that the remarkable progress was "uneven and spotty": "Some hospitals are contradictory combinations of the new and the old: new buildings, new workers, old attitudes, old practices." She described hospitals with little medical or psychiatric care, overcrowding, overworked staffs, and many idle patients. The message was consistent with the views of the Unitarians and the state officials— readers should take pride in the accomplishments to date, and understand that much work still needed to be done.

In 1950 Youngdahl prepared for the November election and developed his agenda for the 1951 legislature. He filed for a third term on July 12, 1950. In a brief statement, he said he would continue honesty and humanity in government and that "our new mental health program, our youth conservation program, vigorous law enforcement and other advances will go on."[38]

On July 31, the governor took to the radio to offer a one-year progress report on mental health.[39] Riding on the positive momentum to date, he recounted the program's accomplishments but cautioned,

Occupational and recreational therapy, in the form of parties, dances, crafts, and sports, were a hallmark of the reformed mental health program. The patient pictured here showed her work in an impressive hospital art exhibit. Photograph by Arthur Hager, *Minneapolis Tribune*. Courtesy of the Minnesota Historical Society.

"Such progress as we have made this year is not the final answer, of course, but it is an indication of the work of our employees and a great measure of their ability to correct many remaining deficiencies on schedule during this first step." Youngdahl concluded:

> This is not a small program. And it is not a cheap program. But it is a necessary program. And we have put ourselves in the position where the future success of programs in other states is dependent on the leadership we exert.... I have been humbled by the magnitude of the program and the great distance we have yet to go.... It is for these, the once forgotten, the once lost, and the once misunderstood, that I make this report tonight.[40]

He announced that his number-one issue for the next session was a new institution for "special" children with mental retardation to relieve the severe overcrowding at Faribault.[41] The 1949 legislature had adopted a measure naming Brainerd as a site for a new hospital, but had failed to allocate funds.[42]

While he campaigned, Youngdahl turned once again to the MUC Committee on Mental Hospitals for policy development and support. Foote had signed on for another year as chairman of the committee; Ed Crane took on the secretarial role. Steefel left to lead work on re-settlement of displaced persons, her new interest and passion. She did, however, recruit students from many Minnesota colleges to work in mental hospitals. She also founded the Minnesota Unitarian Service Committee, and tried unsuccessfully to organize a medical research mission to Fergus Falls State Hospital in the spring of 1950.[43]

Youngdahl appointed Foote to chair a group of distinguished physicians, judges, and lawyers, including Unitarian municipal judge James Otis, to review commitment and other legal procedures. The governor empowered them to reconcile conflicting views and "make recommendations for the elimination of any features detrimental to the medical welfare of the mentally ill." The issue proved to be a stubborn one and did not become part of the reform effort. Their work was turned over to the probate judges who had jurisdiction over the commitment process.[44]

Youngdahl also turned to the Governor's Advisory Council on Mental Health to begin work on recommendations for the new legislative session. Frank Rarig Jr. and Foote played an active role in the development of the recommendations, especially because there were so many issues relating to patient care and training that carried over from the previous session. The Advisory Council recommended "additional services and facilities that are required to provide an adequate program of care and treatment in keeping with nationally recognized professional standards." Among them were improvements inside the institutions that included a better activity program, more properly trained and competent personnel, better housing for doctors and staff, and expanded research. There were also recommendations focused on building the comprehensive system of care, among them early discharge supported by well-qualified social work staff, additional outpatient clinics, assistance to counties to develop local institutions for the care of the aged, a permanent center for emotionally disturbed children, and reform of commitment laws.[45]

During the summer of 1950, Rarig helped initiate a new mental health coalition that brought together a number of groups under an umbrella organization called the Minnesota Council for Mental Health. Founders of the council included the MUC Committee on Mental Hospitals, the Minnesota Mental Hygiene Society, and the Association of Parents and Friends of Mentally Retarded Children, which had just been formed by parents.[46] They urged all local mental health committees, state hospital volunteer groups, and other citizens to join. Foote became the first council chairman.[47] Unlike 1948, when the Citizens Mental Health Committee and the MUC Committee on Mental Hospitals took the lead, in 1950 Commissioner Rossen was the key spokesman for the program and its future. The citizen advocates consolidated to make their work more efficient as they assumed a supporting role.

The Minnesota gubernatorial election heated up in the summer of 1950, but the outcome was never seriously in doubt. As he had in his two previous runs, Youngdahl campaigned hard. Under his "humanity" theme, the governor stressed his past achievements in mental health and the work that still needed to be done. Youngdahl also introduced a broad array of new programs, primarily to strengthen the family through reforms in divorce laws, among others. His theme of "honesty in government" encompassed "not only integrity in financial matters, but also a fair and equitable approach to every practical problem relating to our economic resources," which included a constitutional convention, party designation for the legislature, registration of lobbyists, reapportionment, and salary increases for state employees.[48]

During the campaign, DFL efforts to attack Youngdahl's mental health program fell flat. DFL chair Orville Freeman, who was considering a run in the gubernatorial primary, asserted that the Stassen-Thye-Youngdahl administrations permitted state institutions to deteriorate to "shocking conditions" before finally facing the problem. Freeman argued that the Farmer-Labor Party had increased staffing of doctors and nurses before Stassen allowed them to drop. The public, however, was not inclined to link the popular and high-profile advocacy of Youngdahl to any failures in prior Republican administrations.[49]

During the September 1950 primaries, Youngdahl faced three insignificant challengers on the Republican side.[50] On primary day, however, incumbent Youngdahl received more votes than all other candidates combined, including both Republicans and DFLers![51] C. Elmer Anderson, a magazine salesman from Brainerd, who had served two terms as lieutenant governor under Stassen and two terms under Youngdahl, narrowly defeated Ancher Nelsen.[52] Foote rebutted one last-ditch effort to discredit Youngdahl by a disgruntled state employee, who claimed Youngdahl was covering up poor conditions in the hospitals. Foote, speaking as chairman of the Minnesota Council for Mental Health, called the charges "false and politically inspired." He noted: "I speak as a liberal, as one who has voted for a Republican candidate only once in his lifetime. . . . Republicans and Democrats alike share in responsibility for past conditions and in responsibility for their correction." The *Minneapolis Tribune* called the charges made against Governor Youngdahl "beneath contempt."[53]

Youngdahl was reelected to a third term with over 60 percent of the vote.[54] He planned to expand his humanitarian agenda and initiate government reforms. His mental health initiative had garnered national positive attention for the state of Minnesota. How could he miss?

Unfortunately, times had changed in two short years, and there were new and ominous storm clouds on the horizon. America was once again at war when fighting began on the Korean Peninsula. As the Minnesota legislature prepared for its session, stories of battles, the need for defense buildup, conscription, and federal tax hikes to pay for the conflict filled the news. There was rising fear of the communist threat as the Cold War heated up. Of mental health, Hoffner wrote at the time: "How much further progress is made in the next few years, however, depends largely on one overwhelming question: war or peace."[55]

As Youngdahl approached the podium to deliver his third inaugural address on January 3, 1951, he faced a somber audience. Concerning mental health reform, he implored:

> Upon this foundation we must continue to build. It is not enough to hold the line. We must press the attack against the citadels of the asylum-past. The measure of our accomplishment must never be a smug complacency as to the rank we hold in comparison with other states. The only valid satisfaction is to be found in fully meeting the needs of these maligned and forgotten people, whose only hope lies in our compassion and action.

Acknowledging the international challenges, he declaimed:

> The world is in turmoil and crisis. . . . Yet hazards and uncertainties must not sap our courage nor paralyze us into inaction. Any plans we make or any programs we establish which are based on eternal principles of justice and humanity will always prove valid and right as the future unfolds.[56]

The response of legislators to the governor's remarks was guarded. Liberals praised various portions of the address. Karl Rolvaag, the chairman of the DFL Party, called it "a good DFL speech." Conservatives were skeptical. Majority leader Roy Dunn said, "The legislature always desires to keep services for the people at the highest possible level based on the ability of the people to pay for such services." House Appropriations Committee Chair Claude Allen, Youngdahl's powerful nemesis, cautiously remarked, "I reserve all comment until I have heard the governor's budget message." House Speaker John Hartle stated, "Our national defense must come first even if it means we must make many sacrifices on a state and individual level."[57]

In his budget message the following week, the governor proposed total spending of $159 million, a $28 million increase over the previous biennium. Youngdahl considered his budget a "minimum program." For mental hospitals, Youngdahl asked for $43 million, an $8 million increase over the previous biennium. The additional dollars were needed for unfunded commitments made two years ago, for four hundred new employees, to keep up with inflation. He noted, "Every day we have had to adjust our thinking because the price of bed sheets went up or canned tomatoes." He also included a doubling of the mental health research budget, and more funds to cover the costs of Commissioner

Rossen's operations. Youngdahl told the legislature, "We trimmed until it hurts. . . . I could in good grace have suggested a 40 percent increase in mental health personnel."[58]

The governor proposed tax increases on beer and iron ore to pay for his state budget proposals that would exceed anticipated revenues. In the past, Youngdahl had relied on his own "legislative bloc" of progressive Republicans and liberal supporters, along with his go-to-the-people advocates, to overcome the conservatives who dominated the leadership. This time around, however, the liberals rejected the beer tax. Representative George E. Murk announced, "They'll pass a higher beer tax over my dead body," and liberal senator Marvin H. Anderson concurred: "I don't like this business of taxing the poor man's champagne."[59]

The war in Korea was a justification, or possibly an excuse, for "economy-minded" conservatives to flex their budgetary muscles. Dunn said he needed time to analyze the budget "in light of the increased federal spending." And indeed, the headline in the press the next day read, "Truman asks 140 Billions for Defense; Big Tax Hikes." "No new spending except for increased costs and no new state activities," Allen said flatly. Even the governor's old ally, Minneapolis Democrat Gerald Mullin, cautiously reserved judgment. The legislature never seriously considered any tax increase proposals, putting significant pressure to cut items in the governor's budget. It was an uphill fight for every penny.[60]

There were also challenges for the citizen advocates this time around. It was hard to sustain the original fervor. Importantly, too, there were no policy hearings to galvanize public support except for the proposal for a new state hospital for the mentally retarded. With the issues almost exclusively fiscal, the decisions fell directly into the hands of the House Appropriations and Senate Finance Committees.

The Appropriations and Finance Committees controlled the process for determination of budget requests. In meetings between the committee and the state agencies, they reviewed the requests in the biennial reports. These included thousands of specific line items, from repairing gutters at Fergus Falls to moving an icehouse at Rochester, to the larger issues relating to hiring, medical equipment, and research.[61] Public advocates were generally not involved. To make matters worse, the hearings on the Division of Public Institutions budget items began in the first week of January, just days after the session opened, and lasted only a week. No votes were taken on mental hospital budget items for two months.[62] The attention of the public and the press shifted to the many other priorities on the docket, and there was little for mental health advocates to do in the interim.

There was only one policy issue relating to mental health, and it was the highest priority of the governor—what was called the new hospital for retarded citizens. This was not a new issue to the legislators. Faribault, the only existing institution for the mentally deficient, had been dangerously overcrowded for years. The 1945 legislature initiated a site selection committee in 1945; its report was presented to the 1947 legislature, where no action was taken. In 1949 Youngdahl had proposed a new hospital at Brainerd that the legislature authorized, but no funds were appropriated.[63] During the 1951 campaign, he emphasized the urgency of the request given the escalating demand for beds at Faribault.

Bills were introduced in both houses to authorize a $6.5 million facility in Brainerd.[64] Supporters from the new Minnesota Council for Mental Health and interested citizens pressured the legislators to generate popular excitement. The Senate bill passed out of the Public Institutions Committee in mid-March, following pleas from DPI head Jackson and Commissioner Rossen, and landed in Senate Finance. Similarly, the House companion bill went to House Appropriations. The proposal's fate rested in the appropriators' hands once again.

During February and early March, many of Youngdahl's other policy proposals foundered. The legislature defeated party designation and the constitutional convention.[65] The Young Republican League of Hennepin County, composed of Republicans of the Stassen stripe who had wrested party power from the conservatives, passed resolutions in early March "expressing disappointment" over the defeats to date and the "apparent lack of legislative interest" in others. The league urged the governor to carry the fight "to the people" and to abandon any efforts at conciliation with the legislature.[66]

As in the past, Luther Youngdahl sought public support, but this time he had too many different initiatives that diluted the impact of sustained public support. In February the governor took to the radio. He urged "the people to put pressure on their legislators to pass the power-of-arrest and fair employment practices bills. In March he called upon them to lobby for passage of the family court bill.[67] Youngdahl also ratcheted up the pressure and tried to woo the legislators in private arm-twisting conferences, further angering the old timers who resented "interference" with their work. Relations went from bad to worse. Despite these efforts, fair employment practices, the family court bill, registration of lobbyists, and reapportionment all went down to defeat at the hands of conservatives.[68]

In late March, the House Appropriations Committee voted on budget requests for the mental hospitals. The committee disallowed most of the research budget for the mental hospitals and more than half of the new hires, a move that undercut the "total push" treatment concept and the goal to embed research in every hospital. And despite the effects of inflation on buying power, the committee held many budget items flat. The food allowance stayed at sixty-five cents a day, limiting the ability to maintain food quality in the next biennium.

When the bill went to the House floor, the House beat back an amendment to restore the 229 employees disallowed in committee. The House then approved the committee's bill with all the cuts—an appropriation $2.5 million below what Youngdahl had said was the bare minimum needed. After all the appropriations bills were accounted for, the overall budget from the House was $10 million lower than the Senate. Thus, the two bodies deadlocked as the deadline for the session loomed. By mid-April, the press reported that nerves were "frayed" at the tag end of the legislature, and *Tribune* editors urged "tolerance for the dilemmas between human needs and tax increases" in a search for a compromise.[69]

The governor asked the leadership for permission to address a joint session of the deadlocked legislature in hopes of brokering a favorable compromise. He was summarily rebuffed and denied a chance to speak. On the evening of Saturday, April 21, two days before the session was due to end, he went on WCCO radio: his message was direct. He told the people what he had planned to say at the joint session. The broadcast was published in full in the *Minneapolis Tribune* the next day.

The governor made an impassioned case for the new hospital. He opened his talk in classic Youngdahl style: "Shame on us and God help us if we indicate that we love money and comfort more than these sick children,"[70] and concluded similarly: "We are asking you to do justice to our sick children in the name of Him who said, "Inasmuch as ye have done it unto one of the least of these, my brethren—ye have done it unto me."[71]

He expressed his extreme disappointment when he had heard Minnesota lawmakers "have almost killed the appropriations for a building for the mentally deficient children." He quoted letters from desperate parents seeking help, described the severe overcrowding in graphic and compelling terms, and pleaded for appropriations to accommodate 560 new beds.

As the legislature had been known to do, there was a mad rush to finish work before the deadline approached. It failed. Legislators were forced into a one-day, five-hour special session on Tuesday, April 24. Four appropriation bills had failed to reach the governor before the midnight deadline on April 23. In the special session, the House had to "repass" the bills, send them to the Senate, and then to the governor. The legislators had agreed not to reopen any of the bills but to pass them without change.

The governor appeared in both houses shortly before adjournment. He told the Senate jokingly, "Its quite a thrill getting the privilege of addressing the legislature twice in 24 hours," a cutting remark after the denial of his request to address a joint session in the final hours of the deadlock.[72]

Some said that the session was "hardly more than a new and political edition of Murder, Inc."[73] The legislature killed ten of the governor's projects, including the power-of-arrest bill, fair employment practices, the family court bill, constitutional revision, adoption of party designation, and registration of lobbyists. There were a few victories, such as an expanded Youth Conservation Commission, authorization of county convalescent homes, liberalization of workmen's compensation, and a salary increase for state workers, albeit less than the governor requested.[74]

To say that Youngdahl was deeply disappointed would be an understatement. In particular, the results for the mental health program felt like a real rebuff. He had asked for an $8 million increase over the previous biennium, and the final result lopped $1.5 million off the request. The cuts came in key areas of the mental health program—the request for four hundred additional staff was reduced to fewer than two hundred; the salary increase for state employees came in much lower, the research budget was cut in half, and allocated only to the central office, not to individual hospitals. The food allowance was unchanged, and the meager additional dollars for other needs would not keep up with inflation.[75]

The legislature did manage a new appropriation that would have negative consequences in the 1953 session. It approved funds for the

Legislative Research Council "to supply the legislature and the public" with factual information on the mental health program, with additional funds for two staff members to perform the examination.[76] Conservatives armed themselves to attack the mental health program by building the capacity of the LRC under their control.

The most serious blow to Youngdahl, however, was the dismissal of his pleas for a new hospital for "special" children. The need for more space was well known; the legislature had considered the problem since 1945. The answer to his request was added in the special session: "There is hereby appropriated to the Executive Council out of the Minnesota State building fund the sum of $100,000 with which to purchase land and draw plans for a new mental institution."[77] The can was kicked down the road once again. There would be no building to meet the urgent need. Instead, there was another committee, and another review of possible sites. Worse still, the amount appropriated would not even cover the costs of drawing up plans and purchasing land. To save face, Youngdahl implied that something had been done for the "special" children in the session.[78] But he knew, as did the legislators, that the result was paltry and ineffectual.

The governor's disappointment turned quickly into a public clash with House majority leader Dunn. The day after the session adjourned, Youngdahl railed against the legislature in a press conference, and announced that he would "seriously consider" calling the legislature into another special session because of his disapproval of their financing plan—borrowing from state surpluses if necessary to balance the budget—and to reopen his beer and iron ore tax plans. He said the legislature needed to be "more courageous," and accused the conservative leaders of having loaded the conference committees with like-minded members, while overlooking members who did not share their views.[79]

A few days later, in a speech to the Young Republican League, Youngdahl remarked, "When the history of the session is finally completely written, the people will conclude that many of those both within and without the Legislature, who helped shape the course of events, placed greater emphasis on dollars than on lives, on material things, than on things of the spirit."[80] Dunn responded with a radio address of his own. Without naming the governor he charged, "The biggest, most pernicious lobby in St. Paul during the session was the government itself and its agencies. Every time a new appeal was made for public support, more state employees and more people who live off the fat of the government showed up in the legislature."[81]

Commissioner Rossen was also deeply discouraged. A few weeks later, he announced that he would return to Hastings "for the best interest in the program in order to open up the intensive treatment center at Hastings and further develop the program of follow-up care, training of personnel and research." He would continue to function as commissioner but from his base at Hastings.[82] How that could be accomplished was not addressed.

■ ■ ■

By the end of the legislative session in April 1951, Engla had seen enough politics. She focused her attention on the patients with whom she spent her days. Some things were better; some were not. That was life. She would carry on.

Talk was that the legislative rift would not leave lasting scars, and Youngdahl was, as the *St. Cloud Daily Times* wrote, "in the driver's seat. He can be Minnesota's first fourth-term governor by a nod of his head."[83] Surely, the next session would be better.

TWELVE

Lest We Forget

> There were lessons we learned ... that we incorporated in
> policy, performance and in our request to the legislature ...
> a legislature which took first the role of great generosity and
> then of reprisal toward the very child it helped to sire.
>
> ■ *Judge Luther W. Youngdahl, speech at Hastings State Hospital*

In the early summer of 1951, the governor was not himself. His wife, Irene, was worried. Her husband was usually so robust and outgoing, a man always on the move. The legislative session had been devastating. But it was not just the defeat of much of his agenda. Worst of all were the personal insults and disrespect from the legislators. He alternated between feelings of righteous indignation and simmering rage.

Irene insisted that her husband see his doctor at the Mayo Clinic. It was no surprise that his blood pressure was sky-high. The doctor told him he should take it easy. Luther Youngdahl never liked politics. Now all the talk was politics, more and more politics. Would he run for a fourth term in 1952? Would he run against Hubert Humphrey for the U.S. Senate in 1954? There were even a few supporting a Youngdahl for President movement. That didn't sound like taking it easy.

On June 17, 1951, a thousand miles away in Washington, D.C., Senator Humphrey was having his morning coffee. His mind was also on politics. As he perused the *Washington Post,* he noted with keen interest the death of Justice T. Alan Goldsborough, a former Democratic congressman from Maryland whom Franklin Roosevelt had appointed to the U.S. District Court for the District of Columbia in 1939.[1] Rumor had it that Youngdahl could be attracted to a judicial appointment. Humphrey also knew, of course, that Youngdahl was very popular, had had a rough legislative session, and might challenge him for his

Senate seat in 1954. Could this be the federal position that would lure Youngdahl out of Minnesota?

Humphrey wasted no time. He had to act fast. President Truman owed him a favor or two. But this was a big one. Youngdahl was a Republican from Minnesota. The plum seat on the U.S. District Court would have many aspirants clamoring for the post, and Marylanders considered it their seat. He called the White House the following day to discuss his plan with the president.

On July 2, back in Minnesota, Youngdahl was driving home from a meeting with Harold Stassen. Stassen expected him to lead his presidential campaign in the 1952 primary. Youngdahl vividly recalled, and with some distaste, the intensity of the Philadelphia convention in 1948. He did not want to head a presidential campaign, but as his biographer noted, Youngdahl's "refusal to help the man who had given him his opportunity in politics would have looked like political treachery."[2] Youngdahl felt cornered.

When he arrived home, Irene told him Humphrey had called. When Youngdahl returned the call, Humphrey offered him a federal judgeship. After a conversation with his family, Youngdahl arranged a flight to Washington.

The timing was fortuitous. Youngdahl was drawn to a lifetime appointment on the prestigious federal bench. He had relished his time on the Minnesota Supreme Court and, while he also was deeply invested in policy leadership as governor, the job came with stressful and often destructive political conflict.

On July 5, just nineteen days after Justice Goldsborough's death, Senator Humphrey and Governor Youngdahl met with President Truman at the White House. The meeting was so hastily arranged that did it not appear on the president's official calendar. Truman extended the nomination offer with little fanfare or conversation. Youngdahl accepted it on the spot. The White House announced the nomination as Youngdahl and Humphrey emerged from the meeting, followed by an official press conference later that day in Humphrey's Senate office. The news of the appointment took the D.C. Bar Association by surprise; the lawyers were upset that they were not consulted, or even given prior notice.[3]

Youngdahl flew home Friday, July 6, and a gaggle of reporters greeted him at the airport. Minnesotans returned from their Fourth of July celebrations to learn their governor was resigning. Even Lieutenant Governor C. Elmer Anderson, who would assume the top post, had no notice of Youngdahl's decision. Anderson recalled a reporter phoning him at his Brainerd home:

> I received a telephone call from an AP correspondent.... It was about 2 o'clock in the afternoon and he asked me, "Have you heard the news?" I said: "What news?" He said: "You're going to be Governor." I said "what?" He said, "Yes, Luther Youngdahl is going to become a federal judge and he's going to resign as governor." Of course I was, shall we say, shocked, to put it mildly, because I had received no word from no one, and received no forewarning that this was in the making.... As I said at the time, it was like having an atomic bomb burst in your living room. Immediately we were besieged with newsmen, reporters, photographers, wanting to take pictures of course, of the entire family, and that was rather upsetting.[4]

Stassen was furious. It was widely believed that Humphrey facilitated the appointment to sideline the popular Republican governor. Stassen publicly charged that this was "a typical Truman Missouri political trick to help out Humphrey and other Democrats."[5] The *Willmar Journal* editorialized, "In one lightning move President Truman has pulled the rug right out from under the Republican party in Minnesota," and then concluded, "He [Youngdahl] has been too liberal for his own party and this doubtless had something to do with being named by a Democratic president."[6]

No doubt, Stassen would miss having the popular Youngdahl on hand to lead his upcoming primary campaign. But the concern ran deeper. The Stassen Republicans knew from experience that Anderson was not up to the top job. After two terms as lieutenant governor under Stassen in 1938 and 1940, he had been dumped and replaced with Thye in the 1942 campaign. At the time, Stassen was angling to join the service and felt that Anderson was too weak to succeed him as governor during that term. Insiders such as Pete LeVander agreed. Not only would the popular Governor Youngdahl leave the state, but also his successor inspired little confidence in the party.[7] As LeVander later recalled, "This was the end of the kind of strong type leadership that we tried to foster and stood for."[8]

The Republicans were not the only ones worried about the future. Undoubtedly, the advocates for the mental health program were also deeply concerned. The new governor-in-waiting promised there "would be no letup in Governor Youngdahl's law enforcement nor in his mental health and honesty in government program."[9] And, Youngdahl himself rationalized, "programs which have meant so much to our people are now well-established, and with the continuing competent and efficient service by the department heads and those working under them, and the loyal support of the people, our government in Minnesota will continue to improve."[10] After the tumultuous legislative session, it was clear to many that mental health reform was not well established but rather quite vulnerable to attack.

Another blow to the mental health program followed. Dr. Ralph Rossen was also fed up with politics. Youngdahl's departure was the last straw. On August 23, 1951, Rossen announced that he wanted to retire as commissioner and return to Hastings full time as superintendent.[11] Rossen discussed his intention with Anderson. Youngdahl was awaiting confirmation, and it was unclear who would accept his decision. Given the uncertainty, Rossen's resignation was not immediately accepted, although his plan to leave was clear.

Despite his upbeat public comments to the contrary, Youngdahl no doubt worried about the future of the mental health reform movement that he cared about so deeply. He asked his brother the Reverend Reuben Youngdahl, a well-known Lutheran pastor in Minneapolis, to serve as president of the Citizens Mental Health Committee of Minnesota Inc., a new nonprofit organization that replaced the Governor's Citizens Mental Health Committee.[12] The goals of the new organization were based in service, advocacy, recruitment of volunteers, and assistance to individual patients.

As advocates, members planned to fight for legislation to maintain and improve the system as well as inform the public of existing or emerging problems. They distinguished themselves from the Minnesota Mental Hygiene Society, whose membership was primarily physicians dedicated to fields of prevention and education. The two groups did not compete and would continue to work together in the Minnesota Council on Mental Health. Numerous Unitarian activists served on the board of the new Citizens Mental Health Committee, including Arthur Foote, Frank Rarig, and Judge James Otis, along with reporter Geri Hoffner and Leslie Anderson, chair of the original Governor's Citizens Mental Health Committee.

Ironically, just as Youngdahl went off to Washington, *Life* magazine ran a follow-up article on conditions in mental hospitals around the county. The story noted that while about two-thirds of hospitals had made "substantial progress, there are only a handful of shining examples, the few places where great progress has been made."[13] Minnesota was one of those few shining examples. A photo captured Rossen, standing near a new building at Hastings, surrounded by the members of the psychiatric team. The accompanying text explained the concept of "one patient at a time," the intensive patient-focused treatment that characterized the Minnesota reform.

But major changes were on the way, and not necessarily for the better. Anderson became governor on September 27, 1951. He was small, dark-haired, shy, and soft-spoken. He lost his father as a young man, and had to drop out of the University of Minnesota for financial reasons. Congressman Rick Nolan later described him as a "very, very humble man."[14] Anderson had served eleven years as a lieutenant governor under Stassen, Thye, and Youngdahl—all three confident, gregarious,

A sleek new hospital wing was added to the campus at Hastings in the mid-1950s. The hospital's original cottages appear on the hillside in the background of this photograph, taken in 1955. Copyright University of Minnesota, College of Design.

accomplished figures who delegated little to their lieutenant. His primary official duty in that role was to preside over the Senate. During this time, he did not relocate to St. Paul, preferring a quiet life in Brainerd, a small community 140 miles north of the capital.

While Youngdahl awaited official confirmation for his judgeship, Anderson had less than three months to prepare for the job. He set up an office in Brainerd and had department heads visit so that he could become familiar with the operations of state government.[15] The Anderson family reluctantly relocated to St. Paul in the fall.

Anderson's inaugural address in September 1951 was pedestrian, with none of the soaring rhetoric of his predecessor. He recounted his humble beginnings and vowed to continue the work Youngdahl had begun. His first objective was to pursue honesty and efficiency in the government agenda. His second was mental health:

> I want to see a continuation of our humanity in government. I think that, first in this field, we must carry forward and improve the mental health program, which has received such widespread support. Minnesota already has made remarkable progress in this humanitarian effort. . . . I think our legislators and citizens alike will want to see a program which means so much continued and improved.[16]

Despite his words and his undoubtedly good intentions, Governor Anderson was not able to protect Youngdahl's legacy. LeVander's concerns turned out to be valid ones. Anderson was persuaded to make changes to the administration that would dramatically affect the mental health program. In March 1952, he demoted Carl Jackson, Youngdahl's trusted head of the Division of Public Institutions, to warden of the St. Cloud Reformatory for Boys. Jackson privately balked, but to the press, he gamely said, "I view this appointment as a real challenge in the work to be done."[17]

In Jackson's place, Anderson appointed Jarle Lierfallom to head the DPI.[18] Lierfallom was born in Pennington County in 1913 to a penniless itinerant Lutheran preacher. He was a graduate of St. Olaf College, and held a master's degree from the New York School of Social Work and another in public administration from Syracuse University. He had worked his way up through the ranks to become head of the Minnesota Department of Social Welfare before he was plucked to replace Jackson. Anderson had become acquainted with Lierfallom at an interview process with department heads during the summer, and Lierfallom undoubtedly pressed him to make these changes.

In a speech to the new Citizens Committee a few days after Lierfallom's appointment, the governor reiterated that mental health still ranked as the number-one program in the state. He assured them that Lierfallom would carry on the program vigorously. Anderson was pleased that the Citizens group would keep the people committed to mental health: "The fact that you have organized, as you have, shows you realize this, and I am happy that there is a citizens group ready to work for mental health. . . . I will do my best to play my part, and I know you all will do the same."[19] Unfortunately his good intentions were not sufficient.

Lierfallom loved to "administer." He was a fan of organizational charts, hierarchy, and rulebooks. He liked being in charge. He prided himself on his relationship with the governor, bragging in his journal that Anderson appointed L. F. Nichols, Lierfallom's deputy at the Division of Social Welfare, to replace him "on my saying so."[20] Lierfallom's philosophy was to

> keep as many things out of the Governor's worry as possible, and by no means seek to draw the Governor into the trouble; and . . . support the Governor so long as he is honest, and constantly build him up and make his cause prosper . . . and know more about the things you are handling than he does, so that he will seek you rather than you him. (373)

Lierfallom ingratiated himself with the governor, frequently praising him to bolster his confidence: "I told the Governor that the people appreciate very much that they realize that he is not going to take orders from Roy Dunn and others, as so many people had expected he would" (373). The humble man from Brainerd deferred to the confident, officious bureaucrat.

Anderson gave Lierfallom free rein to reorganize the division, and he wasted no time. Lierfallom found the independence of the commissioner of the mental health office from his own direct control "intolerable." The legislation that created the commissioner role consolidated a wide range of mental health functions to facilitate coordination across a continuum of care. That design infuriated Lierfallom. "I had told the Governor that the proper subordinate relationship of the

Commissioner of Mental Health was so important, that in my opinion if (candidate) cannot fit himself into that type of picture we should not take him. . . . I made it very clear that I would not permit this to happen" (368).

Moreover, Lierfallom had little respect for doctors who held administrative positions. Administration was his bailiwick. He even criticized one commissioner candidate as having a "prima donna—Jehovah attitude." After visiting Hastings, where Rossen was superintendent, he fumed: "The arrogance of these medical people, in particular the psychiatric people, on matters of administration just floors me. . . . The stupidity that come out in observations . . . the inanities of petty and obvious observations released in a pontifical and profound style" (391). As one of his key goals in 1949, Youngdahl had insisted that the mental health program have a doctor at the helm. Clearly, Lierfallom was not on board, believing instead that "if you get a mental health commis-

Jarle Lierfallom, circa 1954, served as commissioner of public welfare under Youngdahl's successor C. Elmer Anderson. Courtesy of the Minnesota Historical Society.

sioner he will be tempted to run off with the whole thing into a corner, like a dog takes a bone" (394). Lierfallom was not about to let that happen.

In April, just weeks after his appointment to the DPI, Lierfallom announced a broad reorganization of the division, designed "to simplify and make more efficient operations." He created three functional division-level jobs to oversee operations across the institutions: a business manager to set standards; a director of correctional rehabilitation to plan and direct rehabilitation, recreation, and leisure programs; and a third post to plan programs for the mentally deficient and handle social work issues. Within the reorganization, the mental health commissioner, while still holding the title, would be reduced to a line officer in charge of developing and directing medical policies for all institutions, including prisons, reform schools, and mental hospitals, while still overseeing the mental institutions. Lierfallom made sure the next commissioner would have no independent authority.

The following month, Anderson formally accepted Rossen's resignation.[21] Lierfallom disliked Rossen and believed he undercut his authority, was disloyal, childish, and deprecated Lierfallom's efforts (390). He would allow a subordinate operating committee, which included Rossen, to run the mental health system only until a new commissioner was found. Rossen, recently acclaimed as the one man who could lead the reform, and feted by more than a thousand people at the university just two years before, would see his office dismantled—his vision for mental health fundamentally threatened.

The reform advocates met with Governor Anderson to try to explain why some of his decisions were damaging to the state's mental health goals. The governor listened but did not change course. Lierfallom noted ruefully in his diary that "Reverend Foote has gone to the Governor with the rumors that we are destroying the Mental Health program" (394). Lierfallom resented such interference that, from his perspective, would publicize any internal problems or thwart his administrative imperative. He was committed to setting the governor straight.

Lierfallom also undermined the volunteers who had served patients in state hospitals so faithfully and effectively. He created an office to oversee volunteer work and removed that role from the Citizens Committee. In his diary, he noted, "They [volunteers from the Citizens Committee] would be a considerable nuisance walking in and out of hospitals." The takeover of the volunteer effort would, in his words, "take the sting out of the program that they had in mind to claim credit for, which should really be done by us" (402).

As 1952 wore on, the concerns of mental health advocates grew. Accustomed to access to and support from Youngdahl, they could not get through to the new governor or to Lierfallom. The Citizens Committee took to the media to express their concerns. Reuben Youngdahl charged that the Minnesota legislature was "gambling with human lives" by failing to provide adequate safety protection.[22] Foote spoke out on the failure of the legislature to appropriate sufficient funds for "an adequate diet" for mental patients.[23] After a business manager for the state tried to refute Foote's claims, Ed Crane, as spokesman for the Citizens Committee, contradicted the state official.[24] On August 11, Lierfallom wrote in his daily journal:

> During the week of my vacation there has been a lot of publicity about the mental health program put out by Foote, Crane, and company. We have to try to stop this, lest mental health become a political football. Either some of the local men are stirring the pot and causing trouble in the absence of Youngdahl and Foote, or they are allowing the pot to be stirred, thinking that they are doing the program good, or for political purposes but they are doing a lot of harm. (405)

How far the reformers had fallen—from trusted allies of the governor, consulted, included, and welcomed, to troublemakers "stirring the pot"!

Word of the threats to the mental health system had spread to Luther Youngdahl in Washington, D.C., and he demanded an explanation. Youngdahl called the governor, who was not available. The next day, August 12, Lierfallom, not Anderson, returned the call, a serious breach of political etiquette. Lierfallom's version of the conversation revealed his arrogance and disrespect:

> A long call to Luther Youngdahl, who told me that many rumors were continuing to come to him about how the mental health program is falling apart, indicating that he believed we were sabotaging the program, refusing to accept the fact that we are trying to build the program, utterly unaware of the administrative mess the program is in, and from my knowledge of the past, unable to be talked to at all

in this connection, totally unaware that I had been breaking my neck trying to get legislative groups to keep from blasting the program as a criticism for him. (405)

Lierfallom was offended by Youngdahl's angry reaction. Youngdahl, he concluded, walked out "on his own mess" and then abused the man who was cleaning it up. Such behavior, he asserted, "is most unbecoming" (405).

During that challenging week, the DFL candidate for governor, the young, up-and-coming Orville Freeman, seized the mental health issue. He called for a vast improvement in the mental hospitals that were falling below the standards set by the reform. Anderson responded that his position and Freeman's were similar, and should not be part of the political debate.[25]

While Lierfallom struggled to manage concerns from Youngdahl and pressure from the DFL, another threat emerged. The Legislative Research Council was poised to level sharp criticism against the mental hospital system, challenging Lierfallom's control over the message. Louis C. Dorweiler, director of research at the LRC, headed the investigation. A former House member who had served on the Appropriations Committee, Dorweiler knew the old guard expected him to expose all the flaws in the mental health program in preparation for attacks in the 1953 legislative session.[26] Lierfallom worried that any negative disclosures would affect the reputation of his division and play into the hands of the reformers. But Dorweiler, he feared, wanted to report all failures of the mental hospital system in order to get personal credit for his investigation (367–68).

Tension between the LRC and Lierfallom continued to simmer into the fall. "We are increasingly concerned," Lierfallom wrote, "with the Dorweiler committee's report which we feel will completely undermine public confidence in the program and have been discussing with . . . the Governor how to effectively counter this development" (438). Lierfallom, fearing the fallout from leaks, called Reuben Youngdahl to let him know what might be coming. The stand-in for his brother as head of the Citizens Committee, Youngdahl was, according to Lierfallom, "apoplectic" and "very critical of the Governor and us for allowing this situation to develop" (368). The reformers, who knew the power of economy-minded Appropriations chair Claude Allen, feared a bloodletting in the 1953 session and anticipated that the governor and his sidekick Lierfallom would be unwilling or unable to mount a successful defense.

In the fall of 1952, the biennial process to develop the budget request began. The governor directed department heads to prepare their budgets to submit to his office for review. The governor, no doubt having been lobbied by both Youngdahls and the Citizens Committee, the Council on Mental Health, and others, told Lierfallom he wanted no cuts in the mental health program. Economy and efficiency, he said, should be focused on organization of the office and clerical work and routine, not saving money on patient care.

Despite the governor's directive, in the hands of Lierfallom, economy and efficiency meant cuts into the core of the program. In his sessions with each institution under his authority, Lierfallom's goal, in his words, was to "shake down" requests for new staff positions, which made up the largest portion of the institutions' increases over the prior biennium and were essential to the total push concept. Lierfallom crowed privately that he had "shaken" 750 positions down to 358 (370). While Luther Youngdahl's budget strategy had been to open with high numbers and fight hard for them, knowing the legislature would try to whittle them down, Anderson's budget request would start low and, with the hostile conservative legislature, end up even lower.

The 1952 election was a strong one for the Republicans. Eisenhower was at the top of the ticket; Senator Thye was popular. As LeVander commented, "C. Elmer was able to get elected, it was only because, in my opinion, Ike Eisenhower was running for the United States Presidency, Ed Thye was running for re-election, both of whom carried Minnesota by huge votes and swept C. Elmer along in."[27] The LRC report became public in early December and represented a frontal attack on the mental health program.[28] It was purported to be a "deliberate objective" study to present the facts "clearly and unprejudicially." Given that the report characterized Governor Youngdahl's burning of restraints in 1949 to symbolize the end of a repressive system as an "illegal destruction of state property," there was no doubt about the LRC's intent.[29] Their report did not acknowledge the terrible conditions that led to reform or the reforms' successes in improving them. Nor was there any mention of comprehensive treatment goals or the national recognition for Minnesota's program.

What followed were 180 pages attacking business and personnel

practices, flawed record keeping, misuse of training funds, and wasteful and extravagant spending. The details were excruciating and petty;
the report accused the hospitals, for example, of buying beef when
cheaper cuts of pork would do. Improvement of unpalatable diets had
been an important pillar of the 1949 reform. Now, even though they
were staying within the minimal daily budget of sixty-five cents per
patient, the institutions took heat for serving decent food. Other recommendations presaged policy changes favored by the conservatives,
including assessing families for costs of care and greater scrutiny of
voluntary patients, as well as those involuntarily committed, to be sure
they were really mentally ill.

In the wake of the damning report, Lierfallom did damage control.
To the press he praised the progress in the mental health reform as "astounding." He welcomed the LRC report, saying it was "excellent" and
"will be valuable to us and will serve as a checklist of administrative
matters requiring attention."[30] Privately, he agreed with all the calls for
administrative changes (437–38).

The governor's official response was equally mild. He said Lierfallom
and others had made progress, and so much had already been accomplished, but it took time to reorganize. "I am deeply interested in the
mental health program and want to do all I can to further it. I will
have some definite measures to recommend in my inaugural message
to continue and advance the program."[31] To the public, the administration supported the mental health program; the advocates were not
so sure.

Governor Anderson's 1953 inaugural address reflected the influence of the DPI director. He cited improvements in food, personnel, and
care, and stressed the need for research, training, and more doctors.
He then praised the DPI, the administrative changes it had made to
date, and what was to come. He said there were "in action and in blue
print stage a considerable number of sound, forward looking plans and
projects to improve the mental health program," and noted that "while
these services should accent humanitarianism in the strongest possible way, they should also be professionally up to date and efficiently
administered in every sense. This has been and is the purpose of the
extensive reorganization taking place in the division of public institutions."[32] Packaged as sound improvements to the program, Minnesota's
acclaimed mental health reforms would be undermined in the name of
efficiency.

The following week, the governor presented his budget message. He proposed a modest increase in the mental hospitals budget of $3.8 million, including a slight increase in food allowances, funds for fire safety improvements, and the addition of two hundred personnel slots, less than a third of what the hospitals had initially requested. His proposals to pay for his total budget—taxing beer and mining companies—were as likely to be nonstarters in 1953 as they had been in 1951. Big fights over spending loomed once again.[33]

Both the Minnesota Mental Hygiene Society and the Citizens Committee mounted a publicity campaign that questioned the LRC report and budget proposals and the process by which they were developed.[34] The criticisms fell on deaf ears.

Lierfallom, like Jackson before him, faced eight tough days of hearings before the Appropriations and Finance Committees. Allen, who had tangled with the governor on other issues, grilled the chagrined Lierfallom aggressively (461). The process frustrated and angered the embattled DPI head, who was simultaneously dealing with a scandal at the Stillwater prison that required an enormous amount of his time and attention.[35]

When the Institutions Appropriations bill emerged from the committees, the House and Senate had drawn battle lines. The Senate cut $4 million from the governor's recommendations; the House cut $6 million, causing the mild-mannered Anderson to accuse the House of "inhumanity and ill-advised economy."[36] In the conference to reconcile the differences, the Senate made far greater concessions than the House, and the result was over $5 million cut from the governor's initial request.[37] The bill allowed for only one hundred new positions, perpetuating the understaffing that had resulted from reduced allotments in 1951.

Less money was not the only blow, however. Several policy bills hit the mental health program hard. The attitude, reflecting the LRC report, seemed to be that many mental hospital patients and their families were "freeloaders," loafing around at public expense. A new law held that responsible relatives could be assessed for costs if they were able, and all inmates would be screened more thoroughly as to need for continued treatment.[38] There were a few small victories—such as flexibility in funds for personnel and fire safety measures for the hospital at Cambridge.[39]

The most devastating blow was organizational change. The office of the commissioner of mental health was abolished, replaced by a medical officer who reported to the director, not the governor. The director, not the governor, would have a newly formed medical policy committee to advise him. The legislature also consolidated the DPI and the Division of Social Welfare to create the new Division of Public Welfare (DPW).[40] A week after the session ended, the governor appointed Lierfallom to run the expanded agency.

Relations with physicians within and outside the mental hospital system deteriorated rapidly. In July Lierfallom wrote privately that he faced a "revolt" by University of Minnesota psychiatrists who felt good doctors could not be attracted to the current program, particularly with the medical director now a mere line administrator (402–4). In September 1953 the Governor's Advisory Council on Mental Health resigned "en masse" after claims the mental health program had bogged down. Anderson, who had rarely called upon them, said he would be "retaining them on a stand-by basis" until a medical policy committee was named, which did not occur until May 1954. Dr. Donald Hastings of the university agreed to head the new policy group that served Lierfallom, commissioner of the new Division of Public Welfare.[41]

In March 1954 Dr. Dale Cameron, a well-qualified psychiatrist from Washington, D.C., became the new DPW medical director. The press reported that the position had "general stewardship over the ill in all the state institutions and the medical care of old age assistance recipients, the crippled and the blind."[42] Cameron had a very different portfolio from that of the commissioner of mental health.

The vision of the reformers for a true system—run by a physician and focused on each patient as a unique human being; a vision driven by research and supported by a caring team providing intensive services across a continuum of care—had been stopped at the first step.

■ ■ ■

Friday, April 23, 1954, dawned bright and clear in the little river town of Hastings. Spring was in the air. Superintendent Rossen had set aside the day to honor the many volunteers who had served the patients of Hastings State Hospital so faithfully since 1947. In return, the honorees from the Volunteer Council decided to present a gift to the hospital on the occasion. Judge Youngdahl, home from Washington, D.C., was there to address the gathering.

The assembled audience included Rossen, the hospital staff, patients, and volunteers, many of them from Unity Church. No doubt, Engla Schey was also there. At the gathering, the volunteers unveiled a six-foot-high photograph of Youngdahl. On the inscription attached to the photograph were words from the former governor's inaugural address of 1949: On one side, "The time must end when the mentally ill can be considered 'out of sight—out of mind'"; on the other, "Our human goal should be to make our state the first in the nation to reach the standards of decency." Superintendent Rossen accepted the gift on the hospital's behalf.

A silence fell as Youngdahl stepped to the podium. The judge surveyed the audience with visible emotion and spoke from his heart. He recounted the conditions at Hastings when a young Dr. Rossen arrived in 1938, his refusal to accept the status quo, and his effort to replace incarceration with humane treatment. He spoke of the great inspiration Rossen provided to all who knew him. With a jarring reference to present-day Minnesota, he said, "Just as the state program then to-be drew upon the lessons of Hastings, so do other states in the country today—*if not our own*—draw upon Hastings for those same lessons."[43]

Youngdahl reminded listeners that "in every one of the many controversies in which he [Rossen] was involved and, for all I know, the many future ones in which he will be involved—the issue was the patient and only the patient. He fought against politics. He fought against apathy. And he fought against everything and everybody that would impede the organic growth of an asylum to its present—and future—status as a hospital."

Youngdahl rejected "those who seek to destroy the program by limiting its spiritual drive, by decrying it for 'emotionalism.'" He recognized and assured the crowd that appropriations were important and were still tragically inadequate. But it was the "program content guided by the Advisory Council, and the mobilization of the public from the Citizens Mental Health Committee that were incorporated into policy, performance and in our requests to the legislature." He continued that it was "a legislature which took first the role of great generosity and then of reprisal toward the very child it helped to sire."

He emphasized that only a first step had been taken toward a modern program. "We must tell the lessons of this first step, or what we spent will have been wasted and in that mound of waste will lie the shattered hopes of our patients and their families." Remember, he said passionately, that our goal remains: "For each patient a specific program geared to his needs and to his own individual problems and improved status."

Youngdahl refused to concede that the program had slipped. But he did believe that "lessons learned from the first step—the only step to date—of the program are in danger of being forgotten; that there may be even a grave lack of follow through of that magna charta of the patients—the Mental Health Policy Act."[44] He continued by enumerating a litany of uncompleted tasks: a lack of social supports and a skeleton crew to help patients function on the outside, failure to deal with a shortage of doctors, among many others. "We must end an environment where employees operate under pressures, apprehension of criticism, constant scrutiny and lack of meaningful support. Our own patients and their families are the unwitting victims of our failures, controversies and restrictions. What is needed is a meeting of minds—a meeting that can cast aside old controversies and scores and settle down to the only thing that matters: how can we help the patient."

The story of mental health reform in Minnesota appeared to have ended at the first step. The intrepid attendant Engla Schey had fought a one-woman battle for humane treatment since 1939. Bolstered by the work of conscientious objectors and national attention on mental health after World War II, Engla had helped persuade the Minnesota Unitarian Conference to study the issue. Arthur Foote and the Unitarian Committee on Mental Hospitals undertook the job and, determined to educate the public on the problems in the system, offered solutions. Foote's fortuitous meeting with Youngdahl had persuaded the governor to lead the crusade. Geri Hoffner's powerful reporting, along with the tireless work of the Unitarians and the mobilization of a Citizens Committee, inspired a legislative victory and catapulted Youngdahl into a position of national leadership. Ralph Rossen as commissioner of mental health moved the bureaucracy on a path to compassionate treatment of patients as individuals.

Minnesotans told of the terrible conditions in the institutions, mobilized the state, rejected the stigma, changed the laws, implemented the reforms, and ultimately fought the losing battle of 1953. They moved on.

■ ■ ■

Luther Youngdahl earned renown as a federal judge during the height of Joe McCarthy's anti-Communist activities in the 1950s. Judge Youngdahl found unconstitutional critical parts of the case against Owen Lattimore, a Johns Hopkins professor and key target of McCarthy. He received many honorary degrees and awards, most notably the Swedish government's Royal Order of the Polar Star. Youngdahl died in June 1978. His brother Reuben, pastor of Mount Olivet Lutheran Church in Minneapolis, died in 1968.

C. Elmer Anderson was defeated in his bid for a second term. Orville Freeman of the DFL succeeded him as governor. Anderson later became mayor of Nisswa (1960–62) and of Brainerd (1976–86). Following his defeat in 1986, he retired to private life to pursue "theatrical interests." He died in January 1998 at age eighty-five.

Jarle Lierfallom was asked to resign from the DPW upon the election of Orville Freeman in 1954. He spent a year (1954–55) as executive director of the Republican Party, then owned and ran two nursing homes in St. Paul (1956–67). Governor Harold LeVander appointed him to be commissioner of conservation (1967–71), in which post Lierfallom proceeded to reorganize that department. He died in January 1997 following an eleven-year battle with Alzheimer's disease.

In May 1954 Ralph Rossen suffered a heart attack. He left Hastings State Hospital in the fall of 1954 to become director of the I. E. Phillips Psychobiological Research Center, which had been funded by a gift to Mount Sinai Hospital. He made substantial contributions to medicine through his research activities. Dr. Rossen died on June 26, 1974, at age sixty-five. North Memorial Hospital in Robbinsdale, Minnesota, honors his memory with the annual Ralph Rossen Award for Excellence in Nursing.

Arthur Foote served as pastor of Unity Church in St. Paul until 1970. He remained active in mental health organizations even as the Unitarian Committee moved on to other issues. He served on the advisory board of Parents and Friends of Mentally Retarded Children, the precursor to ARC, and was recognized in 1958 for his work with the Citizens Mental Health Committee and the Minnesota Mental Health Association. He was periodically asked to serve on mental health commissions, the last when Governor Elmer L. Andersen created a Minnesota Mental Health Survey Committee in 1961, on which Foote served as vice-chairman alongside his respected friend Dr. Ralph

Rossen. Foote retired to Maine in 1970 and became a potter. He died in December 1999 at age eighty-eight.

Genevieve Steefel resigned from membership at Unity Church in 1950 and joined the First Unitarian Society of Minneapolis, where she was listed among the Women of Distinction. At FUS, she organized and chaired the Minnesota Chapter of the Unitarian Service Committee, and chaired the Committee on Displaced Persons. Steefel withdrew from partisan politics, and faced some challenges during the McCarthy era for her work for Henry Wallace. She later led the Radcliffe College fund-raising drive in the 1960s. She died in October 1971 at age seventy-two.

Eva Jerome continued to manage the visiting program at Anoka State Hospital into the early 1950s. She was engaged in numerous organizations related to peace, civil rights, civil liberties, and international relations. She was an active member of First Unitarian Society of Minneapolis until her death in 1966 at age ninety-one. Her daughter, Ida Jerome Davies, published the *Handbook for Volunteers in Mental Hospitals* with the University of Minnesota Press in 1950. In the 1950s she helped psychiatric patients live in the community, and supervised student social work interns at Hennepin County Mental Health Center. Davies was also an assistant clinical instructor in the School of Social Work at the University of Minnesota, and worked with at-risk youth in her retirement. She died at age ninety-six.

Geri Hoffner (Joseph) won six American Newspaper Guild awards for her work at the *Minneapolis Tribune*. She was chosen by Sigma Delta Chi, an all-male fraternity, to receive an award for distinguished journalism for her 1949 series on mental hospitals. When the fraternity learned she was a female, she was given the award anyway, one of many "firsts" for her. Hoffner stayed involved in mental health by serving as president of the National Association of Mental Health. She was active in Democratic politics, serving as ambassador to the Netherlands under President Jimmy Carter, and on the Humphrey Institute Board at the University of Minnesota. She married Burton Joseph in 1953 and lives in Mendota Heights, Minnesota.

Engla Schey worked at Hastings State Hospital until the early 1960s. She experienced firsthand the decline of public interest in mental hospital improvement, noting in her later diaries how the "bughouse" mentality of the 1930s and 40s was returning. She continued to fight against bureaucracy in all its forms, experienced periods of bitterness and depression, but always found solace in her relationships with the patients she cared for.

After Engla retired, she lived in a series of apartments in Minneapolis, and remained an active member of FUS. She and her cousin Emma were close friends. In the late 1950s, Engla and her sister Josie had a nostalgic visit to her childhood home in Spruce Valley, where she recalled some of her happier days of childhood with old friends. She traveled with her sister in the 1960s to visit their brother, Ole, and his family in San Diego. She remained opinionated and outspoken on political issues, and became active in the peace movement. Engla died in a nursing home in St. Paul in 1980 at age eighty-four. She wanted no fuss and no funeral.

■ ■ ■

On a quiet Sunday afternoon, a family sat in the shade near a small lake. Young John played in the grass nearby, watching the boats on the water. The three grown-ups, his parents and his grandfather, spoke softly in Norwegian. His mother held his sleeping baby brother in her arms. His grandfather's large home, a castle, it seemed to the young boy, stood tall in the distance. His grandfather was very old, and this would be the last time he would see him. After thirty years "seeking his salvation among strangers," Anders Schey died in January 1955. He was eighty-nine years old. His daughter Engla's love for her dad started it all.

In his speech at Hastings State Hospital in 1954, former governor Luther Youngdahl warned that the lessons of the first step of mental health reform were at risk of being forgotten. His concern was justified. Minnesota had quickly lost its leadership role. Even as early as 1956, Minnesota ranked fifth among ten midwestern states for per diem expenditures for the mentally ill, and third for the developmentally and intellectually disabled.[1] Was the Crusade for Forgotten Souls an essentially forgettable moment in Minnesota history, a well-meaning but failed attempt at reform? On the contrary, the crusade left a powerful legacy from which a number of lessons emerge.

The first lesson was foundational for Minnesota and the nation. The crusade gave voice to the voiceless and inspired mental health organizations to keep that voice alive.

When Engla shouted from the rooftops, unheeded until the Unitarians listened, when the governor embraced the facts they presented, when word spread from the pages of the *Minneapolis Tribune* and other newspapers, and the airwaves echoed with the impassioned pleas of the governor, a door opened. No longer silenced by shame, families, parents, neighbors, friends, and fellow citizens raised their voices too. From across the state, local citizens spread the word for change. Although there was growing awareness of the issue across the country, Minnesota was the first to initiate a successful statewide reform, and, thanks to the policy work of the Unitarians, the new law addressed the rights of patients to dignity and a comprehensive system of care.

The Crusaders formed the precursors to today's advocacy organizations. In December 1946 a small group of concerned parents of retarded children met in a living room in Minneapolis. In 1948 they created the Association of the Mentally Retarded. Reuben Lindh, one of the founders, also served on the Governor's Citizens Mental Health Committee. In Minneapolis in 1950, along with others from around the country, the National Association of Parents and Friends of Mentally Retarded Children was born. Governor Youngdahl spoke at their first meeting, and Arthur Foote and Leslie Anderson served on the board in the early 1950s. The fledgling organization is now the ARC, the leading advocacy group for the intellectually disabled in the country.[2]

The citizens organizations driving the reforms collaborated in August 1950 to form the Minnesota Council on Mental Health. Two years later, the Citizens Committee merged with the Minnesota Mental Hygiene Society to create the Mental Health Association of Minnesota, a group still active today.[3] Additional organizations followed, including the National Alliance for Mental Illness (NAMI), a powerhouse in both Minnesota and the national arena. The heirs to the early Crusaders, building on the foundation laid in the 1940s, continue to raise their voices. Many of those voices are the intellectually disabled and those suffering from mental illnesses speaking for themselves.

The legacy of the Crusade for Forgotten Souls is a vision that remains aspirational to this day: care for the mentally ill and developmentally disabled is a right best assured by a comprehensive system of professional care services that can deliver on that right.

Thus did the crusade embody a powerful moral imperative as expressed by the Unitarians: "an affirmation of the fundamental human guarantees which Minnesota owes to every patient in state mental hospitals." Those who were incarcerated in dilapidated institutions, crowded in schools that did not teach, in hospitals that did not provide care, were human beings. They were individuals entitled to dignity, respect, compassion, and care. They had souls.

The fundamental human guarantees included the right to physical and mental care, humane and courteous treatment, activities, protection of rights in commitment procedures, and care grounded in research by well-trained experts. When the Unitarians said, "We invite your help in securing these rights for Minnesota's mental patients," the public accepted the invitation. The governor embraced the guarantees, his Advisory Council included them in their legislative recommendations, and they were ultimately enshrined in law.

The crusade defined a modern mental health system though which to deliver care. In the words of Dr. Ralph Rossen, Minnesota's first and only commissioner of mental health, the new system would guarantee "for each patient a specific program geared to his needs and to his own individual problems and improved status."[4]

The system would offer a continuum of care, from community prevention and education to intensive care in the hospitals, transition to outpatient clinics and halfway houses, as well as county-based nursing homes and other facilities appropriate to the elderly. In every setting, trained professionals and staff, informed by continuous research, would provide the best care to patients. The new Office of the Commissioner of Mental Health had direct authority across the continuum to ensure coordination in the implementation of the vision.

When Rossen accepted his commission from Youngdahl, he said it would take at least ten years to accomplish the transformation. He got just two. Tightfisted conservatives in the legislature, aided by bureaucrats who valued form over reform, and a weak new governor abandoned the march forward. The crusade was disrupted, but its vision remained.

■ ■ ■

For most of the 1950s and 1960s, the lessons of the crusade seemed forgotten. State hospital populations fell, and discharged patients relied on an inadequate patchwork of community clinics. Successive governors commissioned surveys and formed task forces, calling for studies, reports, evaluation, and recommendations. State support was unreliable. When times were good, there was more state funding; when times were bad, there was less.[5]

A new generation of reformers in Minnesota built on the legacy of the 1949 crusade. In 1972, a plaintiff named Richard Welsch sued the state of Minnesota on behalf of his daughter Patty, who, as a child, had been labeled "mentally retarded with autism." He challenged the living conditions and "habilitation" services in the institutions that housed people like Patty.[6] Thanks to the tenacity of legal aid attorneys, and after years of litigation, the court found that the Due Process Clause of the U.S. Constitution *entitled* individuals like Patty to humane psychological and physical living conditions, including the least restrictive living environment possible, and with proper staffing and care. The moral force in 1949 became a constitutional right. But implementation of that right was more challenging. A consent decree in 1980 imposed a court-appointed monitor to ensure consistent state compliance.

Almost fifty years after the postwar crusade, however, the fundamental right to comprehensive mental health care in the United States still has not yet been achieved. Nonetheless, major achievements in access to care have occurred. During the crusade in Minnesota, the state government was solely responsible for the costs of care, stretching the capacity of state budgets and commitment of state leaders. When the U.S. Congress took on financing access to health care for defined populations, opportunities arose. In 1965 Congress enacted Medicare (for the elderly) and Medicaid (for low-income people) for those who were left out of the private insurance markets. Individuals who qualify under these programs are entitled to covered benefits.

In the 1970s advocates for the developmentally disabled worked to ensure that these individuals qualified under Medicaid and Medicare.[7] Once someone is qualified, advocates sought alternatives to the huge impersonal institutions, and the new dollars flowed to small group homes and other preferred settings. Qualified disabled individuals also included a large segment of the severe and persistently mentally ill. Medicaid covered some mental health services for its low-income, nondisabled population as well. The program also offered coverage to low-income individuals for nursing home care, which provides a safety net for the poor elderly in appropriate settings.[8]

In general, publicly and privately funded health plans distinguished between physical and mental health, burdening the latter with higher copays and other restrictions, or excluding mental health altogether. Minnesota's U.S. senator Paul Wellstone highlighted the discrimination against mental health in American's private and public health insurance plans, and worked with colleagues to address the disparities in coverage from 1995 until his death in 2002. Another Minnesotan, U.S. representative Jim Ramstad, picked up the effort and finally succeeded with the passage of the Mental Health Parity and Addiction Equity Act of 2008. The law removed many barriers to coverage in public and private plans, though implementation was painfully slow.

The Affordable Care Act (ACA) of 2010, also known as Obamacare, was one of the largest expansions of mental health and substance abuse disorder coverage in a generation. The ACA deemed mental health an "essential health benefit" required in all public and private plans. Under the ACA, Medicare beneficiaries have lower copays and access to important psychiatric medications. Medicaid beneficiaries also have expanded benefits, although patients trying to access these new public-sector benefits have encountered a shortage of mental health professionals, especially for Medicaid beneficiaries given the program's low reimbursement rates.[9]

The benefits of the ACA are under threat. In 2017, a new president and Congress threaten expanded access to mental health by advocating repeal of the ACA. Loss of the ACA's "essential health benefit" will jeopardize mental health care for all Americans. The threat does not stop with the ACA. In the summer and fall of 2017, the Trump administration and Congress proposed significant cuts to the traditional Medicaid program passed in 1965 that force states to cut millions from the Medicaid rolls and reduce benefits. Medicare cuts have also been discussed, affecting access to nursing homes and disability benefits as well.

Assuming federal funding continues in the future, states will be primarily responsible for their systems of care. Insurance coverage is worth little without the ability to find appropriate care, and states have overall responsibility for the design of the system. Mental health care in Minnesota has been described as "a product of well-intentioned efforts to add programs, improve coverage for services and contain costs." But fragmentation and complexity are barriers to quality care.[10] As Sue Abderholden, executive director of the National Alliance on Mental Illness (NAMI) Minnesota, said, "The system isn't broken; we just haven't built it."[11]

There has been a significant effort over the past fifteen years to overcome these barriers to care. In 2003, the Minnesota Mental Health Action Group (MMHAG) joined a coalition of the private sector—advocates, providers, hospitals, and health plans—and the public sector—the Minnesota Departments of Human Services and Health. This public-private partnership worked collaboratively for several years, and became a model of a nonpartisan long-range effort. In 2005, MMHAG produced a comprehensive action plan, *Road Map for Mental Health System Reform in Minnesota.* They agreed upon a vision, a set of guiding principles, and desired outcomes, such as better coordination, innovative workforce solutions, and earlier identification of problems.[12] The Minnesota Unitarian Committee on Mental Hospitals would have been proud.

In 2007, the Governor's Mental Health initiative, developed by this public-private partnership, and supported by Governor Tim Pawlenty and a bipartisan legislative majority, was passed into law.[13] It was the first major investment in mental health in Minnesota, and brought a comprehensive mental health benefit to many previously excluded individuals.

Despite these steps forward, Minnesota received a dismal grade of C from NAMI's 2009 state report card, though many states were rated far worse. The report cited Minnesota's urgent needs for a strengthened workforce, housing and employment programs, and attention to the increasing criminalization of mental illness. It also noted, however, that MMHAG's *Road Map* was a foundation for progress. According to NAMI's report, "The state's challenge now is to build momentum to meet the needs of its citizens living with mental illness."[14]

Minnesota has built on that momentum. In 2015 the state approved $46 million in new funding for state mental health initiatives, including unmet needs such as crisis training programs.[15] NAMI's 2015 annual report singled out Minnesota, New York, and Virginia as the states with the strongest commitment to improving mental health through legislation.[16] In 2016 the Minnesota legislature granted $48 million more in new funding, defying the national trend.[17]

In April 2016 Governor Mark Dayton, recognizing that 200,000 adults and 75,000 children live with mental illness in the state, issued Executive Order 16–02, establishing a task force, composed of public- and private-sector representatives to make comprehensive recommendations for improvements in the continuum of care.[18] That group's final report once again articulates a vision and set of principles for a mental health system, calling for "a person- and family-centered system that offers timely, culturally responsive community based services."

These efforts echo those of the Crusade for Forgotten Souls— fundamental guarantee to comprehensive systems of care. The 2016 task force recommendations include calls for eliminating gaps in the system, developing the workforce, strengthening promotion and prevention—all goals articulated seventy years earlier.[19]

While recognizing some clear strengths in Minnesota's mental health services, the system is not yet good enough. News reports documenting the failures of the system are often in the headlines. Recent descriptions of current conditions at St. Peter Security Hospital could have been written in 1948, causing one to ask, "What year is this, anyway?" Proposed funds to address St. Peter's problems, though widely supported, were overlooked in the 2016 session.[20] Federal regulators threatened to withhold millions of dollars in federal funding to Anoka-Metro Regional Treatment Center because of "decades of neglect" that put patients at risk. Anoka will be under federal oversight until 2018, and a consultant will look into problems with staff training, inadequate treatment plans for complex patients, and the use of restraints.[21] Youngdahl burned restraints at Anoka in 1949. Now they are back. Lamenting the gaps in the state's mental health safety net has led to laments from state legislators on both sides of the aisle. Republican state representative Nick Zerwas noted "complete and utter dysfunction" in a "broken down" system. Democratic state senator Tony Lourey noted, "We can't just simply wait for the crisis and respond any longer. That's never going to work for us."[22]

It is clear that as a nation, and as a state, we have not fully achieved the crusade's vision of the right to care in a comprehensive system that delivers on that right. And the accomplishments that have been made to date are at risk. There is much work to do.

As the fight for a just and comprehensive mental health care system advances, and policy making responds to evolving needs, a number of important considerations should be kept in mind.

First, effective political leadership is essential to success. In the 1940s Governor Youngdahl embraced the cause and led the charge for mental health reform. He encountered legislative resistance, and when he left the state in 1951, the momentum was lost. In the partisan environment of today, political, bipartisan leadership is essential.

Second, even with strong political leadership, the policy process is fickle. Long-term goals are vulnerable in the short-term reality of two-year or four-year terms, partisan divides, competing political demands, and limited budgets. New administrations bring new priorities. There are many interests vying for the limited funds available.

Third, we must not forget the trusted voices of citizen advocates. The Unitarians were laypersons with no self-interest in the outcome of their crusade. They took no outside money and demanded no credit or glory. Their goal, first and foremost, was to be the purveyors of reliable facts to support good policy and to counteract erroneous information. The governor, the public, and many legislators trusted them. While the Unitarians were not immune to forces trying to discredit them, they brought dignity, respect, and integrity to the process.

Fourth, the Crusade for Forgotten Souls reminds us of a time when the press played an important and constructive role in shaping public discourse. Journalists told the human interest story in words and pictures, accurately reported the facts, and kept the public informed as this important debate unfolded. As Geri Joseph recalls, in her days as an investigative reporter, there was always a "healthy tension between the politicians and the press," but there was also mutual respect between them.[23] What happens when politically motivated forces undermine the press by claiming their own truths?

The model of citizen advocates and a free and fair press is hard to find in our current hyperpartisan, cash-infused, cutthroat political environment. Health care has become a battle of ideologies, with huge industries—insurance, pharmaceuticals, hospitals, professional organizations, and big business—all working to protect their own interests, and often drowning out the voices of citizen advocates. Public policy making must be, in the end, for the people and by the people. Perhaps the recent collaborative efforts such as the governor's task force, which included those living with mental illness, their family members, and public interest advocates sitting alongside providers of care and public officials, is a start.

The crusaders learned a painful lesson in 1951 and 1953, when the legislature began to dismantle the program they had worked so hard to create. But they left a legacy—a vision of the right to treatment in a comprehensive and responsive system of care. The best way for us to honor that legacy is to heed Governor Youngdahl's passionate call: "Protection of the patient depends on our eternal vigilance."

SIGNIFICANT ORGANIZATIONS

Minnesota Unitarian Conference (MUC). Founded in 1887, has the purpose of fostering religion through the organization and support of liberal churches in Minnesota and the promotion of educational and any other activities to that end.

National Committee for Mental Hygiene (1909). Formed by former mental patient Clifford Beers with a focus on education, prevention, and improvement of mental health services.

Minnesota Mental Hygiene Society (1939). A state affiliate of the National Committee on Mental Hygiene formed by Minnesota psychiatrists, social workers, and state hospital superintendents to educate the public, prevent mental illness, and improve services to the mentally ill.

National Mental Health Foundation (NMHF) (1946). Conceived by conscientious objectors who served in mental institutions during World War II; formally established as a national organization in 1946.

MUC Committee on Mental Hospitals (1946). The Minnesota Unitarian Conference formed this committee to first investigate and then actively engage in an effort to reform mental hospitals in Minnesota.

Governor's Advisory Council on Mental Health (1947). Panel of nine members (seven psychiatrists and two laypersons) chosen by Governor Luther Youngdahl to advise him on mental health issues.

Governor's Citizens Mental Health Committee (1948). Forty-seven member committee from diverse religious, civic, and labor organizations to promote mental health reform.

County-based Citizens Committees (1948–49). Grassroots groups established in many Minnesota counties to educate, promote, and lobby for mental health reform. The state Citizens Committee provided advocacy materials and speakers for local committees.

Citizens Committee on Mental Health of Minnesota, Inc. (1951). Replaced the Governor's Citizens Committee as a nonprofit organization following Youngdahl's departure from office in the summer of 1951. Its focus was advocacy for individual patients needing mental health services or assistance and support of the mental health reform efforts in the 1950s.

Mental Health Association of Minnesota (1953). An organization resulting from the merger of the Minnesota Mental Hygiene Society and the Citizens Committee on Mental Health of Minnesota, Inc.

The **State Division of Public Institutions** had jurisdiction over a wide range of public institutions in Minnesota, including mental institutions, prisons, state reformatories, and the State School at Faribault. The DPI was one of three divisions (the other divisions were Social Welfare and Employment and Security) in the state's Department of Social Security. The Mental Health Unit in the DPI oversaw the seven mental institutions and the State School at Faribault. The DPI and the Division of Social Welfare were merged in 1953 to become the Division of Public Welfare.

The **Legislative Research Committee (LRC)** was a joint committee of the state legislature. The LRC determined and directed the study of problems expected to come before the legislature. Its research department staff designed, directed, and disseminated the studies in advance of legislative action.

The **Office of the Commissioner of Mental Health** was authorized by the 1949 legislature to oversee a wide range of mental health programs and institutions. The office was abolished by the legislature in 1953.

The **Minnesota State Medical Society** was an organization of practicing physicians in the state of Minnesota; it was governed by a council of members.

NOTES

Preface

1. Jill Lepore, *Book of Ages: The Life and Opinions of Jane Franklin* (New York: Vintage Books, 2013), 21.

2. Robert Esbjornson, *A Christian in Politics: Luther W. Youngdahl* (Minneapolis: T. S. Dennison, 1955), 174.

3. Minnesota Session Laws 2010, Resolution 4, House File 1680, https://www.revisor.mn.gov.

4. James Atlas, "Headed for the Graveyard of Books," *New York Times Book Review,* February 12, 2017, 20.

Introduction

1. Albert Deutsch, *The Mentally Ill in America: A History of Their Care and Treatment from Colonial Times* (New York: Columbia University Press, 1949), 55–65.

2. Ibid.

3. David Gollaher, *A Voice for the Mad: The Life of Dorothea Dix* (New York: Free Press, 1995). For the Unitarian focus, see Barbara Meyers, "The Spirit of Dorothea Dix: Unitarians, Universalists and the Mentally Ill," *UU History,* part II (Spring 2002). http://www.sksm.edu/research/papers/mentallyill.pdf.

4. Gollaher, *Voice for the Mad,* 128.

5. Gerald N. Grob, *Mental Illness in American Society, 1875–1940* (Princeton, N.J.: Princeton University Press, 1983), 4.

6. David J. Rothman, *Conscience and Convenience: The Asylum and Its Alternatives in Progressive America* (New York: Walter D. Gruyter, 2002), ix.

7. William D. Erickson, "Something Must Be Done for Them: Establishing Minnesota's First Hospital for the Insane," *Minnesota History* 53, no. 2 (1992): 42–55. See also William D. Erickson, *This Great Charity: Minnesota's First Mental Hospital at St. Peter, Minn., 1866–1991.* https://www.archive.org/details/ThisGreatCharity.

8. Michael Resman, *Asylums, Treatment Centers and Genetic Jails: A History of Minnesota's State Hospitals* (St. Cloud, Minn.: North Star Press of St. Cloud, 2013).

9. Grob, *Mental Illness,* 61. See also Nancy Tomes, *The Art of Asylum-Keeping: Thomas Story Kirkbride and the Origins of American Psychiatry* (Philadelphia: University of Pennsylvania Press, 1994).

10. Grob, *Mental Illness,* 70–75.

11. United States Public Health Service, "A Survey of the State Hospitals in Minnesota," section 1 (unpublished report, Washington, D.C., 1940), 3. Further citations by page number in this introduction are in parentheses. References in subsequent chapters are to USPHS, "Survey."

12. Dave Niles, "Sunset on the Sentinels" (unpublished report, 2006, Anoka County Historical Society).

13. Ibid., 71. See also Carla Yanni, *The Architecture of Madness: Insane Asylums in the United States* (Minneapolis: University of Minnesota Press, 2007).

14. *The Anoka (Minn.) Herald,* April 7, 1937.

15. Niles, "Sunset," 77.

16. Mechanical restraints referred to physical items of the type described. Chemical restraints referred to the use of powerful drugs, such as sodium amytal, that rendered patients in prolonged sleep.

17. Niles, "Sunset," 120.

18. Chap. 431, General Laws of 1939, set forth in Biennial Reports of DPI—State of Minnesota (Stillwater, Minn.: Prison Printing Department).

19. Erickson, "Something Must Be Done," 55.

20. Alfred Q. Maisel, "Bedlam 1946: Most U.S. Mental Hospitals Are a Shame and a Disgrace," *Life,* May 6, 1946, 102–18.

21. Lawrence Boardman, "No Snake Pits in Minnesota Asylums," *St. Paul Pioneer Press Magazine,* October 27, 1946.

22. The group used the name MUC Mental Institutions Committee in early documents, but later changed the name to MUC Committee on Mental Hospitals to emphasize the goal of treatment rather than warehousing in institutions and to reflect the belief that, with reform, the institutions would become real hospitals. To avoid confusion, MUC Committee on Mental Hospitals will be used throughout. Quotations have not been altered.

23. Final Report, Governor's Task Force on Mental Health, November 15, 2016. https://mn.gov/dhs/mental-health/tf/report.

24. National Alliance on Mental Illness, *State Mental Health Legislation: Trends, Themes, and Effective Practices.* http://www.nami.org/statereport.

25. *Minneapolis Star Tribune,* September 8, 2013; May 23, 2014; November 2, 2015.

26. Chris Serres, "Minnesota's Second-Largest Psychiatric Hospital Reaches Deal to Keep Federal Funding, Improve Care." http://www.startribune.com/chris-serres/10645926, April 26, 2016.

27. Andy Mannix, "Bottleneck Traps Patients, Costs State Millions," *Minneapolis Star Tribune,* October 15, 2017.

1. Voices of Forgotten Souls

Engla Schey's journals are in a private family collection. Engla's extant journals span a period of over six years. Some are handwritten in ledger notebooks, and in later years, she typed sheets she placed in three-ring binders. Not all entries are dated or paginated. The entries, not intended for publication, are recorded as written here. Engla uses terminology that has gone out of fashion or is now considered pejorative. Specifically, she refers to one of the patients as "colored." The term is included as written for historical accuracy and in no way reflects a negative opinion of the individual to whom she refers.

1. There is an extensive literature on the history of mental health in America. The best includes Deutsch, *The Mentally Ill in America*; Gerald N. Grob, *The Mad among Us: A History of the Care of America's Mentally Ill* (New York: The Free Press, 1994); Grob, *Mental Illness in American Society*; Rothman, *Conscience and Convenience*; and Erving Goffman, *Asylums* (New York: Doubleday, 1961).

2. Grob, *The Mad among Us*, 124.

3. Rothman, *Conscience and Convenience*, 349. Justin G. Reese, *An Analysis of the Minnesota State Mental Hospitals*, prepared for the Division of Public Institutions, Mental Health Survey, Statistical Series No. 1 (April 1949), 21.

4. Edward Shorter and David Healy, *Shock Therapy: A History of Electroconvulsive Treatment in Mental Illness* (New Brunswick, N.J.: Rutgers University Press, 2007); Jack El-Hai, *The Lobotomist* (Hoboken, N.J.: John Wiley and Sons, 2007); Jack D. Pressman, *The Last Resort: Psychosurgery and the Limits of Medicine* (Cambridge: Cambridge University Press, 1998).

5. Reese, *An Analysis of the Minnesota State Mental Hospitals*, Chart E.

6. Grob, *The Mad among Us*, 125.

7. Jeffrey A. Liberman, MD, *Shrinks: The Untold Story of Psychiatry* (New York: Little, Brown, 2015), 36. Five Minnesota mental hospitals treated patients with malarial injections; one used other febrile agents.

8. Reese, *An Analysis of the Minnesota State Mental Hospitals*, Chart C.

9. Douglas P. Hunt, judge of probate, Chippewa County, to Governor Luther Youngdahl, March 3, 1947, Luther W. Youngdahl Papers, Minnesota Historical Society.

10. Reese, *An Analysis of the Minnesota State Mental Hospitals*, Chart C.

11. Rothman, *Conscience and Convenience*, 374–75.

12. Reese, *An Analysis of the Minnesota State Mental Hospitals*, 12.

13. USPHS, "Survey," 56–58. Lucy Freeman, "Law Held to Abet Many Mental Ills," *New York Times*, August 4, 1951; Geri Hoffner, "New Setup Urged in State to Commit Mental Cases," *Minneapolis Tribune*, December 1, 1948.

14. USPHS, "Survey," 88–101.

15. Mrs. Valerie Boe to Luther W. Youngdahl, March 12, 1947, Luther W. Youngdahl Papers, Minnesota Historical Society.

16. Engla Schey to Dr. Alexander Dumas, Minnesota, December 7, 1948, State Archives, Division of Public Institutions, Minnesota Historical Society. Dr. Dumas was a psychiatrist and an adviser to Governor Luther Youngdahl.

17. Faribault State School resident to Governor Youngdahl, October 19, 1947, Luther W. Youngdahl Papers, Minnesota Historical Society.

2. Finding Engla Schey

Information on the lives of the Schey family pioneers comes from multiple sources, including interviews with descendants, census data, birth and death records, town records, local newspaper entries, centennial publications, and memoirs from individuals in the community. Like the journals, Schey's autobiographical essays are undated.

1. Loiell Dyrud, Peter Solem, Alfred Solem, and Rebecca Solem, eds., "Excel Township: A Story of the First Hundred Years," *Thief River Falls Times Print,* 2009, 4.

2. Warren Upham, *Minnesota Geographic Names: Their Origin and Historic Significance* (St. Paul: Minnesota Historical Society Press, 1920), 329. The town was named after Folden, a seaport in northern Norway.

3. Joy K. Lintelman, *I Go to America: Swedish American Women and the Life of Mina Anderson* (St. Paul: Minnesota Historical Society Press, 2011).

4. Rudolph J. Vecoli, "Immigrants and the Twin Cities: Melting Pot or Mosaic?," in *Swedes in the Twin Cities: Immigrant Life and Minnesota's Urban Frontier,* ed. Philip J. Anderson and Dag Blanck (St. Paul: Minnesota Historical Society Press, 2001), 21.

5. Many of the Norwegian names were anglicized when they arrived in America. Often census records or land records use anglicized names, but the usage is inconsistent. I have put the anglicized version in parentheses here, but use the anglicized version thereafter.

6. Theodore Blegen, *Minnesota: History of the State* (Minneapolis: University of Minnesota Press, 1951); John R. Tunheim, *A Scandinavian Saga: Pioneering in New Folden Township, Marshall County, Minnesota 1882–1905* (John R. Tunheim, 1984). (The township kept the name as two words, but the town itself chose to spell the name as one word, Newfolden; Tunheim, 8.) Under the federal Homestead Act of 1862, citizens, or aliens intending to become citizens, who were over twenty-one or head of a family were allowed to file a claim on 160 acres of the public domain. Before title could be secured, a claimant had to "prove up his claim" by residing on the land for five years, improving and cultivating some portion of it, and becoming naturalized. The Treaty of 1863 transferred eight million acres of land in northwestern Minnesota from the Ojibwe peoples to the United States. The government did not survey the land until the 1870s, after which it was released for settlement.

7. Lintelman, *I Go to America,* 80. Following family is called chain migration, where personal connections influenced both the decision to emigrate and the emigrant's destination.

8. *Centennial Spruce Valley Township: 1888–1988;* Martha Kleppe and Elizabeth Kleppe Haugen, *Down Memory's Lane* (Newfolden, Minn.: privately printed, January 1, 1974).

9. Surnames were not commonly used in rural Scandinavia in the late 1880s, and immigrants had to adjust to the American convention when they arrived. Many used the Norwegian name of their father ending in "son"—Hanson, Larson, Anderson, and so on. Others chose the names of family farms or villages, church parishes or landmarks, such as Lokebo.

10. Odd S. Lovoll, "Norwegian Immigration and Women," in *Norwegian American Women: Migration, Communities, and Identities,* ed. Betty A. Bergland and Lori Ann Lahlum (St. Paul: Minnesota Historical Society Press, 2011), 60.

11. Lintelman, *I Go to America*, 92–134.

12. *Population of Counties by Decennial Census 1900–1990* (U.S. Census Bureau). Like many rural counties in Minnesota, Marshall has experienced population declines since 1920.

13. Tunheim, *Scandinavian Saga*, 74–160.

14. Ibid., 135–36.

15. Eugene Fevold, "Norwegian Immigrant and His Church," *Norwegian American History Association* 23 (May 1966), 3.

16. Tunheim, *Scandinavian Saga*, 120–33.

17. "Helene Schey Laid to Rest in Minneapolis," *Middle River (Minn.) Record*, March 27, 1957. Although the Scheys were not among the founding families of the Mission Church, Helene remained close to its longtime minister Myhrer, who came from Newfolden to preside over her funeral in Minneapolis many years later.

18. *Centennial Spruce Valley*, 11.

19. Stephen was born in 1880, Oliver in 1885, followed by Jennie in 1890 and Emma in 1891. Another son born in 1882 died in infancy.

20. *Statistical Record*, Rochester State Hospital, Case 12117—Annie Schey. Minnesota State Archives in the Minnesota Historical Society, 51. Fergus Falls State Hospital was the closest mental institution to Marshall County, a long distance of 153 miles from Argyle to the south. Hereafter cited as *Statistical Record*.

21. "Death Scans List of Our Pioneers," *Warren (Minn.) Sheaf*, February 8, 1912.

22. *Statistical Record*, 51. The records indicate that Anna Schey resided at the Southside Sanitarium for thirteen weeks and the Minnesota Sanitorium for ten weeks in 1917. These private facilities were costly and often unwilling to accommodate challenging cases.

23. Ibid.

24. "Death Scans List of Our Pioneers."

25. For a brief history of the institution, see http://www.oakgrovelutheran.com.

26. Telephone conversation with secretary, Oak Grove School, March 19, 2015. The records of Engla Schey confirm she attended Oak Grove from 1912 to 1913 and that she studied religious subjects—Old Testament and catechism—along with academic ones—geography, arithmetic, rhetoric, and American history.

27. Clarence A. Glasrud, *The Moorhead Normal School* (Moorhead, Minn.: Moorhead State University, 1987), 176–77. It was not until 1928 that Moorhead developed a four-year curriculum for high school graduates.

28. *Bulletin of the State Normal School*, Moorhead, Minn., 1913, Minnesota State University Moorhead Archives. A fire in the administration building in 1930 destroyed student records, so no additional information is extant. The *Bulletin* for the years 1913–15 lists Engla as a first-year student both years. It is likely she did not complete the first-year requirements or had to repeat courses.

29. Glasrud, *Moorhead Normal School*, 59.

30. *Bulletin of the State Normal School*, 1, 11.

31. Susan Mitchem, national archivist, Salvation Army National Archives, e-mail message to author, October 16, 2013. The records include Engla's titles,

assignments, and locations from 1915 to her resignation in 1929. Hereafter cited as SA Archives.

32. Edward H. McKinley, *Marching to Glory: The History of the Salvation Army in the United States, 1880–1922*, 2nd ed. (Grand Rapids, Mich.: Eerdmans, 1995), 132.

33. Anne Gillespie Lewis, *Swedes in Minnesota* (St. Paul: Minnesota Historical Society Press, 2004), 40–41.

34. McKinley, *Marching to Glory*, 115.

35. SA Archives. Engla's work with the SA took her throughout the Upper Midwest, including Red Wing, Minnesota; Janesville, Green Bay, and Appleton, Wisconsin; several towns in Michigan; and Mitchell, South Dakota.

36. *Appleton (Wis.) Post-Crescent*, February 19, 1921. After five years of exemplary service, individuals are eligible to be promoted to rank of captain. uss.salvationarmy.org.

37. *Appleton (Wis.) Post-Crescent*, June 8, 1921.

38. SA Archives.

39. Blegen, *Minnesota*, 480.

40. Ole served in World War II, married, and lived in California with his wife and two sons. He was a successful engineer and professor of mathematics and statistics at San Diego State University.

41. *Report to the Governor for the Biennium Ending in June 30, 1926* (Stillwater, Minn.: Prison Printing Department, 1926).

42. Fergus Falls State Hospital Records, Andrew Schey, obtained from the state of Minnesota. Anders's name is anglicized to Andrew in the records. Hereafter cited as Fergus Falls Records.

43. Ibid.

44. *History of the Provident Company in St. Louis.* http://www.ProvidentStL.org.

45. This is the only one of the five existing autobiographical essays that is written under a pseudonym, and no names are used. They are "the daughter" and "the father," but all the facts fit Engla's own experience.

3. Engla Crashes the Gates

1. Niles, "Sunset," 116–17, quoting Margaret Hickey, "No Strait Jackets Now, Mental Hospital Reforms," *Ladies' Home Journal*, May 1951. This description is based on the comments of a volunteer at Anoka State Hospital in 1946. See also Margaret A. Stanchfield, "History of Anoka State Hospital" (master's thesis, University of Minnesota, 1948), Minnesota Historical Society.

2. Engla Schey to Alexander Dumas, MD, December 7, 1948.

3. Ibid. Walter P. Gardner was superintendent at Anoka from February 1938 to November 1943. He served previously as a physician at Hastings State Hospital for three years and assistant superintendent for two years at Fergus Falls State Hospital. After he left Anoka, he entered private practice as a physician for "nervous disorders" in St. Paul. Niles, "Sunset," 201, citing the *19th Biennial Report of the State Board of Control for the Period Ending June 30, 1938*.

4. Schey to Dumas.

5. Niles, "Sunset," 99. Pay scale differentials for comparison: Dr. Gardner, $291 per month; Esther Nelson, $80; Engla and other attendants, $45.

6. Schey to Dumas.

7. Ibid.

8. Niles, "Sunset," 120.

9. USPHS, "Survey," 56–58.

10. Niles, "Sunset," 121.

11. USPHS, "Survey," 121. See also Dr. Markle Karlen, interview transcript, April 4, 2014, Anoka Oral History Project, Anoka County Historical Society.

12. Dr. Royal Gray to Carl Swanson, August 8, 1946, State Archives, Department of Public Institutions, Minnesota Historical Society.

13. USPHS, "Survey," 67.

14. Niles, "Sunset," 116–17.

15. FA (Florence Arndt) to Dr. Royal C. Gray, August 28, 1945, State Archives, Department of Public Institutions, Minnesota Historical Society. FA reports to Gray concerning Engla's desire for a transfer and includes her qualifications. The letter begins, "Engla Schey, Attendant I at Anoka State Hospital, was in the office today. She wants advice from you in regard to a change in position."

16. Jennie lived for some time in Chicago during her nursing career, and returned to Minneapolis for the rest of her career. Emma taught elementary school in Minneapolis until her retirement.

17. Archives, First Unitarian Church, Minneapolis. Emma joined FUS in 1937–8 and Engla became a member in January 1943. She continued as an active member until 1972, though while she worked at Rochester and Hastings, she was listed as an out-of-town member on the membership rolls.

18. Elinor Sommers Otto, *The Story of Unity Church, 1872–1972* (St. Paul, Minn.: Unity Church of St. Paul, 1972).

19. Ibid., 35. See also Mark W. Harris, *Unitarian-Universalist Origins: Our Historic Faith* (Boston: Unitarian-Universalist Association, 1998). There were also Universalist congregations in Minnesota. Universalism was more evangelical than Unitarianism, but the groups had much in common. Unitarians and Universalists officially merged in 1961.

20. Colette A. Hyman, "Culture as Strategy: Popular Front Politics and the Minneapolis Theater Union, 1935–1939," *Minnesota History* 52, no. 8 (1991): 297.

21. Wendy Jerome, "The First Unitarian Society of Minneapolis: Its First 125 Years" (unpublished manuscript, undated). The support of the FUS Women's Alliance for Margaret Sanger and birth control led to the founding of Planned Parenthood. FUS activists included Maud Stockwell and Clara Ueland, well-known crusaders for women's rights.

22. Alan Seaburg, "John Hassler Dietrich," *Dictionary of Unitarian and Universalist Biography,* an online resource of the Unitarian Universalist History and Heritage Society, http://www.uudb.org/articles/johnhasslerdietrich.html.

23. Jim Grebe, "Raymond Bragg," *Dictionary of Unitarian and Universalist Biography,* http://www.uudb.org/articles/raymondbragg.html.

24. Hyman, "Culture as Strategy," 297.

25. Grebe, "Raymond Bragg."

26. Archives of the First Unitarian Society, Minneapolis.

27. Records of Rochester State Hospital, State Archives, Minnesota Historical Society. On the line for designating religion on the employee card at Rochester State Hospital, Engla wrote "Humanist."

28. Schey to Dumas.

29. Ibid.

30. Niles, "Sunset," 99.

31. Dr. Markle Karlen, interview.

32. Shirley Lynch, retired employee at Anoka State Hospital, interview with the author, March 2015.

33. USPHS, "Survey," 67. Of Anoka the surveyors wrote, "Male tuberculosis patients are poorly cared for and overtaxed employees take few precautions against infection."

34. Schey, letter, "Everybody's Ideas," *Minneapolis Tribune*, August 13, 1945.

35. Schey to Dumas.

36. FA to Gray.

37. Schey to Dumas.

38. Ibid.

4. Spreading the Gospel

1. Resman, *Asylums, Treatment Centers and Genetic Jails.*

2. Ibid., 13–17.

3. Rochester State Hospital, "Centennial Audio Visual Program," text of presentation, April 23, 1979, 2, Rochester State Hospital Collection, Olmsted County Historical Society.

4. Magus C. Petersen, medical superintendent, "History of the Rochester State Hospital, 1879–1951" (unpublished manuscript), Rochester State Hospital Collection, Olmsted County Historical Society.

5. Ibid.

6. USPHS, "Survey," 14, 18, 31.

7. FA (Florence Arndt) to Royal Gray, memorandum re: Engla Schey, September 24, 1946, State Archives, Department of Public Institutions, Minnesota Historical Society.

8. "Dr. Petersen, 83, Dies: Ex-State Hospital Supt.," *Rochester (Minn.) Post-Bulletin*, May 17, 1976.

9. *Rochester Centennial*, 19. The DPI's 1944 *Biennial Report* singled out Rochester: "The existing condition of buildings at the Rochester State Hospital is, in our opinion, such as to require almost complete replacement" (84). The money, however, was not allotted for any of the hospitals pending another evaluation, and was put off until the next legislative session in 1947.

10. Liberman, *Shrinks,* 40.

11. Dorothy M. Bernstein, MD, "The University Sets the Education Standard,"

in *Minnesota Psychiatry Evolves from the Past to the Present and Beyond,* ed. Dorothy M. Bernstein, MD (Minneapolis: Psychiatric Publishing Press, 1989), 84.

12. Liberman, *Shrinks,* 246.

13. Ibid.

14. Ibid., 15.

15. Deutsch, *The Mentally Ill in America,* 301–30.

16. Rothman, *Conscience and Convenience,* 312–23.

17. Bernstein, "The University Sets the Education Standard," 85. Bernstein noted that "the term 'psychopathic hospital' was in widespread use at the time. It indicated a site to observe, examine, treat or temporarily retain patients showing evidence of mental disturbance."

18. Mental Health Association of Minnesota (MHAM), *The History of MHAM: Celebrating 70 Years of Mental Health Advocacy and Education in Minnesota* (2009), https://mentalhealthmn.org.

19. Maurice J. Martin, MD, *The View of the First 50 Years: Mayo Clinic; Psychiatry and Psychology* (Rochester, Minn.: Mayo Foundation for Medical Education and Research, 1997), 5.

20. Ibid.

21. Division of Public Institutions, State of Minnesota, *Tenth Biennial Report for the Period Ending June 30, 1944* (Stillwater, Minn.: Prison Printing Department, 1944), 58.

22. Ibid., 84.

23. Division of Public Institutions, State of Minnesota, *Eleventh Biennial Report for the Period Ending June 30, 1946* (Stillwater, Minn.: Prison Printing Department, 1946), 83. By comparison, Anoka did not acquire an electroshock device until 1946.

24. Resman, *Asylums,* 151–53. Resman reports that in 1952, shock patients at Rochester received an average of forty shock treatments each. Patients at Willmar were given an average of ten shocks during a single convulsion.

25. El-Hai, *Lobotomist,* 1–2. This is the definitive biography of Dr. Walter Freeman and his quest to expand the use of lobotomies.

26. Ibid., 181.

27. DPI, *Tenth Biennial Report,* 58.

28. DPI, *Eleventh Biennial Report,* 84.

29. Resman, *Asylums,* 154–55.

30. El-Hai, *Lobotomist,* 181. Petersen remained close to Freeman, even as the procedure fell out of favor. In a letter to Freeman in 1956, he expressed disdain for the medical board's concern about performing too many lobotomies: "That appeared to me slightly illogical. If the operation was good for five individuals there was no reason why there might not be ten who might benefit from it."

31. Pressman, *Last Resort.* Pressman's work leans toward the view that it was the desperation of physicians to help suffering patients that led to the use of psychosurgery. David Rothman's work is less forgiving, emphasizing the use of lobotomy as a means of control and punishment.

32. Renato M. E. Sabbatini, "The History of Shock Therapy in Psychiatry," *Brain & Mind: Electronic Magazine on Neuroscience*, no. 4, www.cerebromente.org.br, quoting David Rothman at the National Institutes of Health, Consensus Development Conference: Electroconvulsive Therapy, June 10–12, 1985.

33. *St. Cloud (Minn.) Times*, July 27, 1939. Dr. Orr died in September 1945, so this interview may have taken place before Engla left Anoka to go to Rochester.

34. Steven J. Taylor, *Acts of Conscience: World War II, Mental Institutions and Religious Objectors* (Syracuse, N.Y.: Syracuse University Press, 2009), 289–90.

35. Selective Training and Service Act of 1940, Section 5[g], reprinted in Mumford Q. Sibley and Philip E. Jacob, *Conscription of Conscience: The American State and the Conscientious Objector, 1940–1947* (Ithaca, N.Y.: Cornell University Press, 1952), 487.

36. Taylor, *Acts of Conscience*, 22.

37. Alex Sareyan, *The Turning Point: How Men of Conscience Brought about Major Change in the Care of America's Mentally Ill* (Washington, D.C.: American Psychiatric Press, 1994), 14.

38. Todd Tucker, *The Great Starvation Experiment: The Heroic Men Who Starved So That Millions Could Live* (New York: Free Press, 2006). The University of Minnesota participated in the Office of the Surgeon General's "human guinea pig experiments" to study rehabilitation from a semistarvation diet under the research direction of Dr. Ancel Keys.

39. Sareyan, *Turning Point*, 64. *Bughouse* was a pejorative term used to describe mental institutions. The bughouse drifters were men considered uneducated and brutal who moved from one institution to another; they were often let go for harsh practices only to be hired in a new place.

40. Ibid.

41. Taylor, *Acts of Conscience*, 244–47.

42. Ibid., 272. The foursome had diverse backgrounds. Harold Barton was a Baptist from Oregon with a B.A. from the University of Oregon and had done graduate work in mine engineering; Leonard Edelstein was Jewish, from Germantown, Pennsylvania; Willard Hetzel, was an Ohio Methodist with a law degree from the University of Michigan; and Philip Steer, also Methodist, was from Chester, Pennsylvania. All four had worked at Byberry under the direction of the American Friends Service Committee.

43. Sareyan, *Turning Point*, 141–45.

44. Albert Q. Maisel, "Bedlam 1946: Most U.S. Mental Hospitals Are a Shame and a Disgrace," *Life*, May 6, 1946, 102–18.

45. Ibid., 103.

46. Ibid., 102.

47. Taylor, *Acts of Conscience*, 296–97. Albert Deutsch, a journalist and social historian, wrote articles in *PM* and *Reader's Digest*, and a book, *The Shame of the States*. Local newspaper stories appeared widely, including in the *Cleveland Daily Press*, the *Chicago Daily News*, the *Daily Oklahoman*, and the *San Francisco News*. Mary Jane Ward's novel *The Snake Pit* was later made into a movie with Olivia de Havilland starring as a delusional woman in the mental hospital.

48. National Mental Health Program, *News-Views,* series 3, no. 1, December 11, 1946, 2, State Archives, Department of Public Institutions, Minnesota Historical Society. Hereafter NMHP, *News-Views.*

49. Alice B. McGinty, "Bedlams's Answer," *Forum,* August 1946, 124–28.

50. Taylor, *Acts of Conscience,* 136, 282.

51. University of Chicago Roundtable, transcript of "Our State Mental Hospitals: What Can We Do to Improve Them," September 21, 1947, 707th Broadcast in Cooperation with the National Broadcasting Company. The "Tenth Man" refers to the fact that one in ten will require treatment for a mental illness during his lifetime.

52. Quoted in NMHF, *News-Views,* 1.

53. President Harry S. Truman to Honorable Owen J. Roberts, July 26, 1946, reprinted in Sareyan, *Turning Point,* 147.

54. Ibid.

55. While Engla makes reference to stories she has written and the flyleaf of one of her journals includes notations of rejections from magazines, there is no evidence that any of her stories were published.

56. Constance Coiner, *Better Red: The Writing and Resistance of Tillie Olson and Meridel Le Sueur* (New York: Oxford University Press, 1995), 82–83.

57. Hyman, "Culture as Strategy," 297.

5. The Modest Visionary

1. Program, 58th Minnesota Unitarian Conference, Unity Church, October 22, 1945, Unity Church-Unitarian Collection, Minnesota Historical Society.

2. *Unitarian Statistical Record, 1890–1947* (Boston: American Unitarian Association, 1949), 2–3. National membership dropped from a high of 70,542 in 1906, to 60,152 in 1926, to 59,228 in 1936, rebounding in 1946 and 1947.

3. Otto, *Story of Unity Church, 1875–1975,* 68.

4. Edgar Crane, "How to Turn a State Upside Down," *Christian Register,* June 1951, 15–18, 16.

5. Otto, *Story of Unity Church,* 73. Jerome, "The First Unitarian Society of Minneapolis: Its First 125 Years." In 1938 FUS membership was 546; in 1945 it had dropped to 453.

6. The Unitarian Society of Duluth, which had flourished in the late nineteenth century, was down to thirty adult members and considering closing its doors (http://www.uuduluth.org). The Nora Unitarian Church in Hanska, formed by liberal Norwegians under the leadership of Kristofer Jansson, had also sharply declined in this period (http://www.norauuchurch.org), as had another small Norwegian effort in Underwood in northern Ottertail County (http://www.ucofu .org). The church in Willmar, kept alive with AUA funds, had rejected a merger with four Presbyterian churches, but their minister was so unpopular that he conducted only a few services during his years there (http://www.uuchurchofwillmar .org). A handful of individuals from these struggling churches participated in MUC programs during this period.

7. Otto, *Story of Unity Church,* 53–68. Frederick May Eliot had a long tenure in

St. Paul, from 1917 to 1937. He left reluctantly to lead the AUA during this difficult period.

8. Carol R. Morris, "It Was Noontime Here . . . : Frederick May Eliot and the Unitarian Renaissance 1934–1961," in *A Stream of Light*, 2nd ed., ed. Conrad Wright (Boston: Skinner House Books, 1989), 141.

9. Winfred Overholser, *Dynamics of Unitarian Advance* (Boston: American Unitarian Association, January 1946). The statement was included in the Unity Church bulletin of June 1946 along with a reminder of the upcoming MUC meeting in October. For a profile of Overholser, see Edric Lescouflair, "Winfred Overholser: Psychiatrist, 1892–1964," http://www.Harvardsquarelibrary.org /biographies/Winfred-overholser.

10. Otto, *Story of Unity Church*, 26 note 38.

11. Hyman, "Culture as Strategy," 294–306, 297.

12. Stefan Jonasson, "The Story of Unity Church" (lecture, February 2014, posted to YouTube Video, March 7, 2014).

13. Otto, *Story of Unity Church*, 75–76.

14. Program, 59th Annual Minnesota Unitarian Conference 1946.

15. In the fall of 1946, Edward J. Thye, the outgoing governor, would quash information on the conditions at Faribault. See chapter 7 for a discussion of the Faribault controversy and its aftermath.

16. https://www.uusc.org. The Unitarian Service Committee was founded in May 1940 to assist European refugees in escaping from Nazi persecution.

17. Wright, *Stream of Light*, 26–27.

18. David Bumbaugh, *Unitarian Universalism: A Narrative History* (Chicago: Meadville Lombard Press, 2000), 99.

19. Charles C. Forman, "Elected Now by Time," in Wright, *Stream of Light*, 24.

20. Ibid., 29 note 29.

21. Gollaher, *A Voice for the Mad*.

22. Mary Wilder Tileston, ed., *Caleb and Mary Wilder Foote: Reminiscences and Letters* (Boston: Houghton Mifflin, 1918), 291–356. The volume also includes an autobiography Caleb Foote wrote for his children. Mary and Caleb Foote were the parents of Henry Wilder Foote I.

23. Correspondence between Henry Wilder Foote and Dorothea Dix, who was advising the government on military hospitals at the time, documents the contributions. Letters from Dorothea Dix to Henry Wilder Foote, dated 1862–63, Foote Family Collection, Andover-Harvard Theological Library.

24. Charles H. Lyttle, *Freedom Moves West: A History of the Western Unitarian Conference 1852–1952* (Boston: Beacon Press, 1952).

25. David B. Parke, "A Wave at Crest: Administrative Reform and Depression, 1898–1934," in Wright, *Stream of Light*, 98. By 1900 Unitarianism remained predominantly New England–based: of the 457 Unitarian churches in America, 301 were in New England and 60 were within ten miles of the Massachusetts State House.

26. Arthur's older brother, Henry Wilder Foote III, became a journalist after

his graduation from Harvard. His younger brother, Caleb IV, after his antiwar activism, became a law professor. There were two sisters, Agnes and Elizabeth.

27. Dean A. C. Hanford to Henry Wilder Foote, August 10, 1929, Foote Family Collection, Andover-Harvard Theological Library. Grades for his freshman year indicate he was a C student, in good standing but ranking (Rank List) V. Transcript dated June 30, 1930.

28. Harvard College, *25th Anniversary Report, 1958.* Reprinted in "Arthur Foote II: The Celebration of Life 1911–1999, " Notable American Unitarians, with permission from the Trustees of Harvard College. http://www.harvardsquarelibrary.org. Arthur confirmed: "I was not at all sure that the ministry would prove 'my dish.' More than one college mate took me aside to assure me that with my stammer it was bound to be a mistake. I guess only cussedness kept me from agreeing."

29. Lyttle, *Freedom Moves West,* 228–29. Meadville had been founded in 1844 in Pennsylvania and had served for years as an outpost for Unitarian education in the "west." The school affiliated with the University of Chicago and moved there in 1926.

30. Harvard College, *25th Anniversary Report, 1958.*

31. http://www.kings-chapel.org.

32. Order of Service for the Ordination of Arthur Foote, 2nd, in King's Chapel Boston, At 5:00 o'clock Sunday September Twentieth 1936, Archives of the Unitarian Universalist Society, Sacramento, California.

33. David Robinson, *The Unitarians and the Universalists* (West Port, Conn.: Greenwood, 1985), 239–40. Reverend Foote was followed by his cousin the Reverend Samuel A. Eliot, the son of Harvard president Charles Eliot and grandson of Boston merchant and politician Samuel A. Eliot. Eliot led the American Unitarian Association (AUA) and was minister at Boston's Arlington Street Church, another historic Boston congregation. Reverend Lewis Cornish, Arthur's uncle, succeeded Eliot at the AUA.

34. Nicholas E. Tawa, *Arthur Foote: A Musician in the Frame of Time and Place,* Composers of North America, no. 22 (Lanham, Md.: Scarecrow Press, 1997).

35. Arthur Foote to Henry and Eleanor Foote, his parents, June 15, 1939. In author's possession.

36. Gerald Rose, "The March Inland: The Stockton Cannery Strike of 1937," *Southern California Quarterly* 54, no. 1 (Fall 1972): 67–82.

37. First Unitarian Universalist Church of Stockton, http://www.stocktonuu .org.

38. Arthur Foote, "A History of the Unitarian Church of Stockton, California" (unpublished manuscript, March 1945), Archives of the First Unitarian Universalist Church of Stockton.

39. Rodney Cobb and Irma West, *In Good Times and in Bad: The Story of Sacramento's Unitarians, 1868–1984; A Compilation of Two Authorized Histories of the Unitarian Universalist Society of Sacramento,* ed. Doris Simonis, Jeff Voeller, and Kathryn Young (Sacramento, 2008).

40. First Unitarian Society of Sacramento to Hugh Orr, April 16, 1935, Archives of the First Unitarian Universalist Society of Sacramento.

41. Cobb and West, *Good Times and Bad*, 40–51.

42. Ibid.

43. Ibid.

44. Arthur Foote to B. W. Begeer, January 4, 1937, Archives of the First Unitarian Universalist Society of Sacramento.

45. B. W. Beeger to Arthur Foote, February 29, 1938, Archives of the First Unitarian Universalist Society of Sacramento.

46. Harvard College, *25th Anniversary Report, 1958*.

47. Steven M. Arvella, *Sacramento: Indomitable City* (Charleston, S.C.: Arcadia Publishing Company, 2003), 51.

48. Stockton Assembly Center, Stockton California, http://www.japanese-american-internment-camps.mooseroots.com.

49. "College Draft Evader to Jail," *San Mateo (Calif.) Times*, August 2, 1943.

50. Caleb Foote, *Outcasts! The Story of America's Treatment of Her Japanese-American Minority* (New York: Fellowship of Reconciliation, 1943). http://www.outofthedesert.yale.edu. The pamphlet included photographs by Dorothea Lange.

51. *San Bernardino County (Calif.) Sun*, April 13, 1944.

52. Ethan Foote, son of Caleb Foote, interview with the author, Santa Rosa, Calif., May 18, 2015.

53. Special Bulletin, January 1945, Unity Church, St. Paul, Unity Church-Unitarian Collection, Minnesota Historical Society. The bulletin describes the process of selection and lists the five members of the selection committee.

54. Frederick May Eliot to Arthur Foote, March 13, 1945.

55. Celiac disease, or gluten-sensitive enteropathy, is an autoimmune disorder that prevents absorption of nutrients and damages the small intestine.

56. *St. Paul Pioneer Press*, April 15, 1945.

57. Pauline F. Eichten and Ellen B. Green, *Sacred Spaces* (St. Paul: Unity Church-Unitarian, 2005).

58. Foote to Mrs. Thomsen, May, 10,1945 (no first name on letter). Archives of the First Unitarian Universalist Society of Sacramento.

59. Program of the 59th Annual Minnesota Unitarian Conference, October 17–19, 1946, Unity Church-Unitarian Collection, Minnesota Historical Society.

60. Ibid.

61. Lawrence Boardman, "No Snake Pits in Minnesota Asylums," *St. Paul Pioneer Press Magazine*, October 27, 1946.

62. Arthur Foote, *Minnesota Unitarian Conference Committee on Mental Hospitals 1946–1949*, 1. Unity Church-Unitarian Collection, Minnesota Historical Society. Hereafter Foote, *MUC Report 1946–1949*.

63. *A Report to the 1948 Minnesota Unitarian Conference on the Work of the Committee on State Hospitals for the Mentally Ill 1946–1948*, Unity Church-Unitarian Collection, Minnesota Historical Society.

64. Foote, *MUC Report 1946–1949*, 1.

6. The Arduous Climb

1. http://www.ias.umn.edu. Constructed in 1936, the Continuing Education Center was designed to draw community professionals wishing to keep current in their fields.

2. Notes of the December 17, 1946, meeting, Lewis Russell Collection, Minnesota Historical Society. J. S. Jones, a university regent, was executive secretary for the Farm Bureau. Luverne Noon was a newly elected state legislator from Hennepin County who served only one term in the legislature. Neither of these two played any further role in the mental hospital reform.

3. Steefel's biographical data comes from the Radcliffe College Archives, Radcliffe Institute, Schlesinger Library, Harvard University, Cambridge, Mass.

4. Membership book, Unity Church-Unitarian, St. Paul, Minnesota.

5. Unity Church-Unitarian Collection, Minnesota Historical Society.

6. Radcliffe Development Fund form, stamp-dated 1959, Genevieve Fallon Steefel, class of 1923, Radcliffe College Archives, Schlesinger Library, Harvard University.

7. Professor Carl Steefel, interview with the author, November 6, 2013, Berkeley, California.

8. Transcript of Genevieve Rose Fallon, Medford High School, 1918, Radcliffe College Archives, Schlesinger Library, Harvard University. Principal J. D. Howlett wrote these comments on her transcript by hand.

9. Radcliffe College Archives, Schlesinger Library, Harvard University.

10. Henry Coyle, Theodore Mayhew, and Frank S. Hickey, *Our Church, Her Children and Institutions*, vol. 2 (Boston: Angel Guardian Press, 1908), 204. The address was a facility run by the Grey Nuns (Sisters of Charity of Montreal) in Boston. Residents had to pay a modest fee for the transitional accommodation that "offers board in a house presenting the comforts of a refined home at a moderate charge to respectable working women and young girls, whatever their employment."

11. Lewis Russell Collection, Minnesota Historical Society.

12. Jack Shaffer, *History of the Cooperative Movement* (Lanham, Md.: Scarecrow Press, 1999); Steven J. Keillor, *Cooperative Commonwealth: Co-ops in Rural Minnesota, 1859–1939* (St. Paul: Minnesota History Press, 2000).

13. George W. Jacobson, "The Story of One Health Cooperative in the Making," reprinted from Consumers' Cooperative, Lewis Russell Collection, Minnesota Historical Society. Dorothy Jacobson was a professor of economics and the author of *Our Interests as Consumers* (New York: Harper, 1941); and was later staff to Governor Orville Freeman. Group Health survives today as Health Partners, a large health care provider and health insurance company in Minnesota.

14. http://www.wilder.org. The name was later changed to the Wilder Foundation; Rarig served as the foundation's president for thirty years (1941–71). Margaret Rarig, interview with the author, Mendota Heights, Minnesota, September 10, 2014.

15. Corruption at the Board of Control led to the reorganization of state departments under Governor Harold Stassen in 1939. See discussion in chapter 4.

16. Ibid.

17. Dr. Ruhberg does not appear on any of the later documents as an active participant in the committee work.

18. There are eight letters over the period of 1947–48 from Engla to Steefel in Steefel's papers at the Minnesota Historical Society. Engla responded to the first by saying Steefel should not feel obligated to reply, as she was busy, so the exchange was one-sided.

19. Arthur Foote, *Minnesota Unitarian Conference Committee on Mental Hospitals, 1946–1949,* 2. Hereafter cited as Foote, *MUC Report, 1946–1949.*

20. Minutes of meeting called for discussion of the care of the mentally ill, Continuation Study Center, University of Minnesota, December 17, 1946, Lewis Russell Collection, Minnesota Historical Society.

21. The content of the United States Public Health Survey is discussed at length in chapters 2–3.

22. Minutes of the December 17, 1946, meeting.

23. Ibid.

24. Liberman, *Shrinks,* 200.

25. http://www.va.gov.

26. https://www.nih.gov.

27. Ellen Herman, *The Romance of American Psychology* (Berkeley: University of California Press, 1995), 245.

28. Bernstein, "The University Sets the Education Standard," 84.

29. Ibid.

30. Ibid., 89–90. In 1946 the Mayo Clinic hired Dr. Francis Braceland, who headed the neuropsychiatry branch of the navy in World War II. He was a friend of Dr. Hastings.

31. Minutes of the December 17, 1948, meeting.

32. *A Report to the 1948 Minnesota Unitarian Conference on the Work of the Committee on State Hospitals for the Mentally Ill, 1946–1948,* Unity Church-Unitarian Collection, Minnesota Historical Society, 1–2. Hereafter cited as *1948 Unitarian Conference Report.*

33. Dumas, a veteran of World War I, was professionally committed to veterans' mental health and author of *A Psychiatric Primer for the Veteran's Friends and Family* (Minneapolis: University of Minnesota Press, 1945).

34. Mental Health Association of Minnesota, *The History of MHAM,* https://www.mentalhealthmn.org.

35. *1948 Unitarian Conference Report,* 2. The Mental Hygiene Society later was challenged by the differing views among its members as the reform effort evolved.

36. Minutes of the December 17, 1946, meeting.

37. Foote, *MUC Report 1946–1949,* 3.

38. Mark Shepard and Patrick McCormack, "Regular Sessions of the Minnesota Legislature," House Research Short Subjects, updated July 10, 2010, https://www.house.leg.state.mn.us. A "legislative day" was "any 24 hour period when the legislature was called to order." The legislative session was limited to 90 days. In 1962 a constitutional amendment raised the limit from 90 to 120. The 1947

session opened on January 7 and adjourned on April 24, https://www.leg.state .mn.us.

39. Elsa Krauch was the author of *A Mind Restored: The Story of Jim Curran* (New York: Putnam & Sons, 1937). The book recounts one person's experiences in a state mental hospital and two private hospitals.

40. Minutes of the December 26, 1946, meeting, Genevieve Fallon Steefel Papers, Minnesota Historical Society.

41. Engla Schey to Genevieve Steefel, January 6, 1947, Genevieve Fallon Steefel Papers, Minnesota Historical Society. Engla included information on how the institutions manipulated the civil service classifications to discriminate against attendants by giving higher attendant classifications to student nurses, thus capping any possibility of promotion for attendants.

42. Minutes of the January 2, 1947, committee meeting, Genevieve Fallon Steefel Papers, Minnesota Historical Society.

43. *Minneapolis Star and Journal*, January 13, 1947.

44. Genevieve Steefel to George Jacobson, January 17, 1947, Lewis Russell Collection, Minnesota Historical Society.

45. Steefel to Jacobson, January 27, 1947, Lewis Russell Collection, Minnesota Historical Society.

46. Foote, *MUC Report, 1946–1949*, 1.

47. Ibid.

48. Engla Schey to Genevieve Steefel, March 20, 1947, Genevieve Fallon Steefel Papers, Minnesota Historical Society.

49. Ibid.

50. Minutes of the April 2, 1947, meeting, Lewis Russell Collection, Minnesota Historical Society.

51. Genevieve Steefel to Arthur Foote, May 6, 1947, Genevieve Fallon Steefel Papers, Minnesota Historical Society. Frank Rarig Jr. was on the board of the Mental Hygiene Society as well, but his membership preceded the Unitarian involvement, and he did not have a position of leadership in the MUC Committee on Mental Hospitals.

52. Stories in the media reported on the legislative consideration of budget requests, for example, "Housing Problem of State Mental Patients Acute," *St. Cloud (Minn.) Times*, March 6, 1947.

53. Lawrence Boardman, "State Mental Hospital Crowded Like a Slave Ship," *St. Paul Pioneer Press*, March 9, 1947.

54. Foote, *MUC Report, 1946–1949*, 3.

55. Ibid.

56. Foote, *1948 Unitarian Conference Report*, 2.

57. Ibid., 3.

58. Much of the work was later incorporated into a report to the governor in the spring of 1948. See the discussion in chapter 8.

59. The September 1947 resolution used the name Minnesota Unitarian Conference Committee on Mental Institutions, which later was changed to MUC Committee on Mental Hospitals to reflect an emphasis on treatment rather than

warehousing patients in institutions. The latter name is used throughout this book.

7. Where There Is Smoke

1. Bernhard LeVander, Call Me Pete: Memoir of a Minnesota Man, ed. Grant Dawson (Reno, Nev.: Dawson Creative Ltd. Effort, 2006). The book is in two parts, LeVander's memoir, and a separately paginated transcript of a tape-recorded interview of Bernhard LeVander by the Minnesota Historical Society, August 22 and September 4 and 18, 1974. Hereafter cited as LeVander, *Memoir,* or LeVander, interview. Bernhard "Pete" LeVander was the younger brother of Harold LeVander, who was governor of Minnesota from 1967 to 1971.

2. G. Theodore Mitau, *Politics in Minnesota,* 2nd ed., rev. (Minneapolis: University of Minnesota Press, 1970). See also Richard D. McKinzie, oral history interview with Harold Stassen, June 26, 1973, Harry S. Truman Library, https://www.trumanlibrary.org.

3. LeVander, interview, 14.

4. Theodore Blegen, *Minnesota: A History of the State* (Minneapolis: University of Minnesota Press, 1951). Elmer Benson went on to run unsuccessfully against Henrik Shipstead in 1940, and in 1948 became a leader in the Progressive Party in Minnesota. See Elmer A. Benson, "Politics in My Lifetime," *Minnesota History* 47, no. 4 (1980): 154–60.

5. Esbjornson, *Christian in Politics,* 128–30.

6. Ibid. Minnesota governors served two-year terms until 1958, when the Minnesota Constitution was amended to set the term at four years. Stassen defeated Hjalmar Petersen in 1940 by 52 percent to 36 percent and in 1942 by 51.6 percent to 37.7 percent, http://www.sos.state.mn.us.

7. "Stassen Trend to Be Decided in Vote Today," *News-Herald* (Franklin, Pa.), July 8, 1946.

8. LeVander, interview, 15–16.

9. Ibid., 14.

10. Ibid., 16–17.

11. "Stassen Trend."

12. Esbjornson, *Christian in Politics,* 95.

13. LeVander, interview, 17.

14. Blegen, *History of Minnesota,* 536–38. Petersen, a Danish newspaper editor from the town of Askov, was lieutenant governor under Floyd B. Olson of the Farmer-Labor Party. After Olson died on the eve of the 1936 election, Petersen served out the remaining months of the term. The fiery Petersen fought and lost a brutal primary battle with Elmer Benson. Petersen ran unsuccessfully against Stassen in 1940 and 1942.

15. Resman, *Asylums,* 4–6. See also Division of Public Institutions, State of Minnesota, *State Hospitals and Facilities for the Mentally Deficient and Epileptic: Biennial Report for the Period Ending June 30, 1948* (Stillwater, Minn.: Prison Printing Department), 3.

16. "Swanson Renamed Head of State Institutions," *Winona (Minn.) Republican-Herald,* March 15, 1947.

17. *Veterans' News* (St. Paul), June 19, 1946.

18. *St. Paul Dispatch,* June 28, 1946.

19. Edward J. Thye, text of KSTP radio address, June 29, 1946, Governor Edward J. Thye Papers, Minnesota Historical Society.

20. www.editions.lib.umn.edu. Thye bested Shipstead, 57 percent to 38 percent; Youngdahl beat Petersen, 64 percent to 33 percent.

21. Esbjornson, *Christian in Politics,* 138.

22. Carl H. Swanson to Governor Edward J. Thye, August 2, 1946, Governor Edward J. Thye Papers, Minnesota Historical Society.

23. Ibid.

24. R. R. Rosell to Edward J. Thye, October 4, 1946. The special committee included Dr. Challman, who was also on the Minnesota Mental Hygiene Society board. Governor Edward J. Thye Papers, Minnesota Historical Society.

25. Harold Barker was a member of the Minnesota House of Representatives. He lost to Luther Youngdahl, 59 percent to 39 percent. Thye defeated his opponent, Theodore Jorgensen, by a similar margin.

26. *Report of the Grand Jury General Term, District Court Fifth Judicial District, State of Minnesota, County of Rice, November 1946,* 2. There was widespread coverage of the news. See "Grand Jury Clears Faribault School," *St. Paul Pioneer Press,* November 16, 1946.

27. Jack Coughlin to Carl Swanson, November 15, 1946. Governor Edward J. Thye Papers, Minnesota Historical Society.

28. Carl J. Swanson to E. J. Engberg, November 16, 1946, State Archives, Division of Public Institutions, Minnesota Historical Society.

29. Engla Schey to Hjalmar Petersen, February 19, 1946, Hjalmar Petersen Papers, Minnesota Historical Society.

30. Ibid.

31. Inaugural address of Governor Luther W. Youngdahl, delivered at a joint session of the Minnesota legislature, Wednesday, January 8, 1947; Esbjornson, *Christian in Politics,* 326. Esbjornson includes the full address in the appendix, 319–28.

32. Jack Mackay, "$109,007,690 Budget Submitted by Youngdahl," *Winona (Minn.) Republican-Herald,* January 15, 1947.

33. Youngdahl, inaugural address, Esbjornson, *Christian in Politics,* 327.

34. Esbjornson, *Christian in Politics,* 297.

35. Ibid., 140.

36. Ibid., 146. The legislation defined gambling devices to mean slot machines, roulette wheels, punchboards, numbers jars, and pinball machines that return coins or tokens redeemable in cash or goods. Bingo games when played to raise money for churches or charities were not prohibited.

37. "Faribault May Not Be Host to Legion Conclave," *Winona (Minn.) Republican-Herald,* January 25, 1945: "The American Legion post at Faribault expressed its

doubt that it could finance the state convention the following summer without the help of income from slot machines."

38. LeVander, interview, 52. He later commented: Youngdahl "didn't have a particularly strong party background and wasn't really too understanding of what partisan organizational problems were."

39. Esbjornson, *Christian in Politics,* 149.

40. Ibid., 90–93.

41. http://www.ali.org. The American Law Institute was established in 1923 as a leading independent organization to produce scholarly work, including model laws that states could adopt.

42. Richard C. Warmann, "Criminal Law—Minnesota Youth Conservation Act—Validity under Constitution," *Washington University Law Review,* no. 1 (January 1950): 143–46; Maynard E. Pirsig, "Procedural Aspects of the Youth Conservation Act," *Minnesota Law Review* 32, no. 1 (1948): 471.

43. Esbjornson, *Christian in Politics,* 299, Graph A, which shows the extent of church support for Youngdahl's initiatives. Genevieve Steefel to Arthur Foote, May 6, 1947, Genevieve Fallon Steefel Papers, Minnesota Historical Society.

44. "Senate Committee Approves Youth Conservation Program," *Winona (Minn.) Herald-Republican,* April 1, 1947.

45. There was also an eight-year building program specifically for Rochester State Hospital, estimated to cost approximately $5 million more. The Rochester funding was to be obtained through a complicated future taxing scheme. It is unclear whether any funds actually reached Rochester under this arrangement before the 1949 legislative reform bill.

46. All state institutions reported their activities and made requests in biennial reports to the governor. The governor's staff would review the requests, and then propose funding levels; the legislature could accept or amend the proposals.

47. Transcript, "Public Institutions in Minnesota after the 1947 Legislative Session," interview, Mr. Carl Swanson, May 21, 1947, KSTP at Radio City. http://www.mn.gov/mndcc/past/pdf/40s/47/47-RIP-CHS.pdf.

48. Alexander Dumas to Luther Youngdahl, March 7, 1947, Luther W. Youngdahl Papers, Minnesota Historical Society.

49. Alexander Dumas to Luther Youngdahl, March 12, 1947. Luther W. Youngdahl Papers, Minnesota Historical Society.

50. "A Report by the Special Committee Appointed by the Council of the Minnesota State Medical Association at the Request of Governor Edward J. Thye," April 16, 1947, http://www.mn.gov/mnddc/past/pdf/40s/47/47-RSS-MSM.pdf.

51. Ibid. The committee did a thorough job. It held a series of preparatory meetings, studied the charges made during the campaign, interviewed present and former employees, held meetings at the school, including a lengthy interview with the superintendent, toured the facility, and then made an unannounced inspection.

52. Ibid.

53. This conclusion is based on the fact that there was no mention of the investigation or the findings in the *Minneapolis Tribune,* the *Minneapolis Star,* or the

St. Cloud Times. Since Thye had requested the report from a nongovernmental entity, there may not have been a requirement or an expectation to make it public. Youngdahl named four of the medical association's investigators to his new Governor's Advisory Council; perhaps they all agreed to work to fix the problems without embarrassing the governor with a damaging disclosure.

54. "Governor Names State Health Aids," *Minneapolis Star,* June 5, 1947. The nine-member panel included Drs. Dumas, Braceland, Heersema, Challman, Gardner, Hammes, Chowan, and Hastings, and Frank Rarig from Wilder Charities.

55. Royal C. Gray to Luther Youngdahl, June 10, 1947, http://www.mn.gov /mnddc/past/pdf/40s/47/47-RSS-MSM/pdf.

56. Ibid.

57. Frank M. Rarig Jr. to E. J. Engberg, September 18, 1947, http://www.mn.gov /mnddc/past/pdf/40s.

58. http://www.asylumprojects.org/index.php?title=Willmar_State_Hospital.

59. Stanley B. Lindley to Carl H. Swanson, November 1, 1947. A copy was sent to Governor Youngdahl. Luther W. Youngdahl Papers, Minnesota Historical Society.

60. Frank Rosemeier to Luther Youngdahl, September 3, 1947. As Youngdahl was once a municipal judge, he may have paid special attention. The language of the communications does not indicate that the two knew each other. Virginia, Minnesota, is a small town in St. Louis County, two hundred miles north of St. Paul. This letter, and the subsequent letters exchanged among the relevant parties, are in the Luther W. Youngdahl Papers, Minnesota Historical Society.

61. Rhoda G. Lewin, "Geri M. Joseph," *Jewish Women: A Comprehensive Historical Encyclopedia,* http://jwa.org/encyclopedia/author/lewin-rhoda. Hoffner married Burton Joseph in 1953. She went on to leadership positions in the Democratic Party, continued freelance reporting, and served as ambassador to the Netherlands in the Carter administration.

62. *The Gopher,* University of Minnesota yearbook, 1945, 173, 269.

63. Geri Joseph, interview with the author, June 3, 2014, Minneapolis, Minn.

64. Geri Joseph, interview with the author, June 14, 2016, Mendota Heights, Minn.

65. Ibid.

8. Political Dynamite

1. *St. Paul Pioneer Press,* November 8, 1947, 1.

2. William E. Leonard, *The Saturday Lunch Club of Minneapolis: A Brief History* (Minneapolis: Art Services Press, 1927). See Carl H. Chrislock, *The Progressive Era in Minnesota, 1899–1918* (St. Paul: Minnesota Historical Society Press, 1971).

3. Margaret Allison, "Pastor Calls Mental Hospitals 'Horrible,'" *Minneapolis Sunday Tribune,* November 9, 1947.

4. The actual title was "Bedlam 1946: Most U.S. Mental Hospitals Are a Shame and a Disgrace," *Life* magazine, May 8, 1946.

5. Arthur Foote, "The Care of the Mentally Ill in Minnesota," speech text in the possession of the author.

6. Ibid. Foote's comment about commitment papers signed without examination quoted in Allison, "Pastor Calls," 10.

7. Ibid. Capitalization in original text.

8. Allison, "Pastor Calls," 10.

9. Foote, *MUC Report 1946–1949,* 4.

10. Edgar Crane, "How to Turn a State Upside Down: Minnesota Unitarians Lead Successful Struggle to Clean-up Mental Hospitals," *Christian Unitarian Register,* June 1951, 15–18.

11. Foote, *MUC Report 1946–1949,* 4.

12. Ibid., 4–5.

13. Ibid.

14. George W. Jacobson, president, Minnesota Unitarian Conference, to Raymond B. Bragg, executive director, Unitarian Service Committee, November 17, 1947, Lewis Russell Collection, Minnesota Historical Society.

15. Bragg to Jacobson, November, 24, 1947, 2, Lewis Russell Collection, Minnesota Historical Society.

16. Foote, *MUC Report 1946–1949,* 5.

17. Justin Reese to Genevieve Steefel, November 10, 1947. Steefel participated in the hiring process and was hoping to attract Reese to Minnesota. Indeed, in a letter to her, Reese confided that the work of the Unitarians in Minnesota motivated him to consider the post. Genevieve Fallon Steefel Papers, Minnesota Historical Society.

18. Justin Reese to Dr. Allan Challman, president, Minnesota Mental Hygiene Society, November 11, 1947. Reese attached his biography, which contained no mention of the Civilian Public Service (CPS). Reese entered CPS in June 1941 and left in April 1944. He served in the unit at Cleveland State Hospital that initiated a statewide exposé of conditions there. See http://www.civilianpublicservice.org/camps/69/1. Reese's role is also described in Taylor, *Acts of Conscience.*

19. Opinion/editorial, "Conscientious Objectors," *Minneapolis Star Tribune,* October 8, 1946.

20. Arthur Foote to Herbert Stats, November 15, 1946, Unity Church-Unitarian Collection, Minnesota Historical Society. Stats, a member of Unity Church, provided temporary housing. With a husband-wife team, the Reeses could observe both men's and women's wards that were strictly segregated by sex.

21. Foote, *MUC Report 1946–1949,* 5.

22. Ibid., 6.

23. Engla Schey to Genevieve Steefel, March 18, 1948. Genevieve Fallon Steefel Papers, Minnesota Historical Society.

24. Ibid.

25. Carl H. Swanson to Luther W. Youngdahl, December 4, 1947, Luther W. Youngdahl Papers, Minnesota Historical Society.

26. "Jackson to Head State Institutions," *St. Cloud (Minn.) Times,* December 29, 1947.

27. "Youngdahl to Push Mental Health Program," *Minneapolis Star,* December 23, 1947.

28. Foote, *MUC Report 1946–1949,* 6.

29. Ibid.

30. *A Summary of Conditions in Minnesota State Hospitals for the Mentally Ill,* a report to Governor Luther W. Youngdahl by the Minnesota Unitarian Conference Committee on Institutions for the Mentally Ill, Reverend Arthur Foote, chairman, Mrs. Lawrence D. Steefel, secretary, March 15, 1948, Luther W. Youngdahl Papers, Minnesota Historical Society. The report is also available at http://www.mn.gov /mnddc/past/pdf/40s.

31. Ibid. The copy of the report in the Luther W. Youngdahl Papers at the Minnesota Historical Society has the handwritten comments of Carl Jackson on the cover page.

32. *St. Paul Pioneer Press,* March 21, 1948; *Minneapolis Tribune,* March 21, 1948. Youngdahl's press release, Sunday, March 21, 1948, provided materials for the story. http://www.mn.gov/mnddc/past/pdf/40s.

33. Youngdahl referred to the MUC Committee on Mental Hospitals as the Committee on Mental Institutions for the Mentally Ill of the Unitarian Conference Committee, a variation on its title.

34. *St. Paul Dispatch,* March 22, 1948.

35. *Minneapolis Star,* April 25, 1948. The official report was quite similar to the draft submitted earlier. The changes comported with Jackson's concern that individual hospitals not be named.

36. Minutes of meeting with Dr. Magnus Peterson, Mental Hospital Committee, May 12, 1948, Genevieve Fallon Steefel Papers, Minnesota Historical Society.

37. Ibid.

38. Governor Luther W. Youngdahl—statement on State Mental Hospitals, 9:30 p.m., Wednesday, May 5, over WCCO; at 10:30 over KDAL. http://www.mn .gov/mnddc/past/pdf/40s.

39. Matthew 25:40, King James version.

40. Interview with Geri Joseph, February 6, 2017. Geri Joseph still remembered the quarters as "bare and stark" sixty-nine years after the visits.

41. Hoffner, "Bedlam," *Minneapolis Tribune,* May 25, 1948, 1, 18.

42. Magnus C. Petersen, MD, letter to the editor, "'Minnesota Bedlam,' a Garbled Series," *Minneapolis Tribune,* May 25, 1948.

43. Hoffner, "Bedlam: Patients Need Sympathy," *Minneapolis Tribune,* May 25, 1948, 18.

44. "Mental Health Unit Appointed," *Minneapolis Tribune,* May 27, 1948.

45. The American Association of University Women was supportive, especially when Genevieve Steefel was president of the Minnesota chapter in 1947. The Federation of Women's Clubs came on board as well.

46. Minutes of the MUC Committee on Mental Hospitals, October 1948.

47. *A Report to the 1948 Minnesota Unitarian Conference on the Work of the Committee on State Hospitals for the Mentally Ill, 1946–1948,* 1–2, Unity Church-Unitarian Collection, Minnesota Historical Society. Rabbi Albert Minda, senior rabbi at Temple Israel in Minneapolis, Reverend E. S. Hjortland of Central Lutheran Church (ELC), Rev. Howard J. Conn, Plymouth Congregational Church, and the Rt. Reverend James H. Moynihan, former president of the University of St. Thomas and priest at Incarnation parish. Arthur Foote, served as treasurer of

the organization and, as he noted, "was instrumental in assisting with the meager financial support provided during its first year."

48. Citizens Mental Health Committee of Hennepin County, *How to Mobilize Your Organization behind the Mental Health Drive* (undated document). Over time, many county groups organized citizens committees that were affiliated with the governor's statewide committee. The office address listed on this document was Steefel's home address.

49. Foote, *MUC Report 1946–1949,* 7.

50. Ibid.

51. Crane, "How to Turn a State," 16.

52. Ibid.

53. *Mental Hospital Project in the Minneapolis Unitarian Church,* December 1948, 1. First Unitarian Society Archives, Minneapolis, Minnesota.

54. Jerome, "The First Unitarian Society of Minneapolis." See also Janet Salisbury, *The Women's Alliance of the First Unitarian Society of Minneapolis: A Centennial History* (First Unitarian Society of Minneapolis, 1981); Barbara Stuhler, *Gentle Warriors: Clara Ueland and the Minnesota Struggle for Woman Suffrage* (St. Paul: Minnesota Historical Society, 1995). Wendy Jerome is the granddaughter of Eva Sardeson Jerome.

55. See Charles W. and Eva S. Jerome and Family Papers, Minnesota Historical Society.

56. *Mental Hospital Project,* 3.

57. Otto, *Story of Unity Church,* 85.

58. In 1950 Mrs. Jerome reported that one hundred volunteers, staff members of mental hospitals, and professional leaders in the psychiatric field participated in a short course for volunteers at the Continuation Study Center at the university. A May 1952 volunteer schedule for Anoka State Hospital in the FUS archives included Catholic, Presbyterian, Baptist, and Methodist church groups, a Jewish group, and the Salvation Army. Activities included dancing, community singing, music and treats, mending, weaving, sewing, typing, walks, monthly birthday parties, and assistance with meals.

59. Ida Jerome Davies, *Handbook for Volunteers in Mental Hospitals* (Minneapolis: University of Minnesota Press, 1950).

60. Eva Jerome, *Annual Report of the Mental Hospital Committee of the First Unitarian Society,* April 15, 1952, 2. First Unitarian Society Archives, Minneapolis, Minnesota.

61. Foote, *MUC Report 1946–1949,* 10.

62. Minutes of the Nutrition Committee of the Committee on Mental Hospitals, June 23, 1948, Genevieve Fallon Steefel Papers, Minnesota Historical Society.

63. Ibid.

64. Minutes of the Nutrition Committee, August 16, 1948, 2, Genevieve Fallon Steefel Papers, Minnesota Historical Society.

65. Ibid.

66. Crane, "How to Turn a State," 16.

67. Foote, *MUC Report 1946–1949,* 10–11.

68. Professor Read developed one of the first courses on legislation in the nation; he also served as vice-chair of the Legislative Committee of the Minnesota State Bar Association.

69. *Preliminary Report: The Use of Jails in the Commitment of Mental Patients,* material compiled by Ed Crane, secretary, Unitarian Conference Committee on State Hospitals for the Mentally Ill, 1949. Genevieve Fallon Steefel Papers, Minnesota Historical Society.

70. Ibid., 1.

71. Minutes of the Sub-committee on Training of the Minnesota Unitarian Conference Committee on Mental Institutions, February 5, 1948, Genevieve Fallon Steefel Papers, Minnesota Historical Society.

72. Minutes of the Sub-committee on Training of the Minnesota Unitarian Conference Committee on Mental Institutions, March 4, 1948, Genevieve Fallon Steefel Papers, Minnesota Historical Society.

73. *Rochester (Minn.) Post Bulletin,* July 24, 1948.

74. Foote, *MUC Report 1946–1949,* 9.

75. American Unitarian Association Collection, Andover-Harvard Theological Library, Cambridge, Mass.

9. The Long Hot Summer

1. Alec Kirby, "A Major Contender: Harold Stassen and the Politics of American Presidential Nominations," *Minnesota History* 55, no. 4 (Winter 1996–97): 150–65, at 153.

2. Ibid. Primaries were a way to break party control and permit the popular selection of delegates. States had experimented with primaries during the Progressive Era, but many states had abandoned the primary process by 1948.

3. David Pietrusza, *1948: Harry Truman's Improbable Victory and the Year That Transformed America* (New York: Union Square Press, 2011), 133–34.

4. "Governor Youngdahl's Speech at Stout Institute" (undated document), Luther W. Youngdahl Papers, Minnesota Historical Society. See also Undated Master Sheet of radio broadcast to Northern Wisconsin and Minnesota, 4. Luther W. Youngdahl Papers, Minnesota Historical Society.

5. Kirby, "A Major Contender," 158, citing *Time* magazine, April 19, 1948, 20, and April 26, 1948, 23.

6. Pietrusza, *1948,* 140.

7. "Youngdahl Steps to Forefront to Urge Stassen Nomination," *Minneapolis Tribune,* June 22, 1948.

8. Pietrusza, *1948,* 190. The Joe McCarthy referred to was the Wisconsin senator who became notorious after alleging Communist infiltration of the State Department.

9. Ibid., 190–92.

10. *Minneapolis Tribune,* June 25, 1948.

11. *Sunday Minneapolis Tribune,* June 20, 1948; "Cheers Ready for Stassen: Hero's Welcome Planned for Tonight," *Minneapolis Tribune,* June 30, 1948.

12. Pietrusza, *1948,* 99.

13. Jacqueline Castledine, *Cold War Progressives: Women's Interracial Organizing for Peace and Freedom* (Urbana: University of Illinois Press, 2012), 15.

14. Pietrusza, *1948*, 99.

15. Thomas W. Devine, *Henry Wallace's 1948 Presidential Campaign and the Future of Postwar Liberalism* (Chapel Hill: University of North Carolina Press, 2013), 79.

16. John Earl Haynes, *Dubious Alliance: The Making of Minnesota's DFL Party* (Minneapolis: University of Minnesota Press, 1984), 151.

17. Ibid., 36, 76.

18. M. W. Halloran, "DFL Rivals Unite for State Contests," *Minneapolis Tribune*, June 14, 1948.

19. Barbara Stuhler and Gretchen Kreuter, eds., *Women of Minnesota: Selected Biographical Essays*, rev. ed. (St. Paul: Minnesota Historical Society Press, 1998), 352–53. Dorothy Jacobson worked closely with state party chair Orville Freeman, then as his full-time aide while he was governor (1955–61).

20. "Ione Hunt," obituary, *St. Paul Pioneer Press*, March 10, 2005. Ione Hunt was the "Grand Dame and icon of Minnesota's DFL party," and first chair of the new DFL party in 1948. She had a distinguished career in Democratic politics for decades.

21. Wallace Mitchell, "DFL Backs Mental Aid: Youngdahl Plan Indorsed at Parley," *Minneapolis Tribune*, June 15, 1948. The convention at the time was to spell *indorsement* with an *i; endorsement* is now the preferred form.

22. Ibid. It is important to note that the resolution clearly included mentally handicapped individuals at the Faribault School in the reform effort.

23. The civil rights issue angered southern Democrats, who formed their own States' Rights Democratic Party (known as the "Dixiecrats"). There was extensive coverage of Humphrey in the hometown papers. The *Minneapolis Tribune* published the full text of his address on July 15, 1948, on the front page of the paper under the headline "Mayor Triumphs on Civil Rights Issue." His triumphal return rated the headline "2,000 Cheer for Mayor," *Sunday Minneapolis Tribune*, July 18, 1948.

24. Devine, *Henry Wallace*, 18.

25. Ibid., 43–44. While the extent of Communist influence on Wallace has been debated, it was clear that Communists and Communist sympathizers played an influential role.

26. Haynes, *Dubious Alliance*, 19, 176.

27. "Mrs. Steefel Named Wallace Drive Aid," *Minneapolis Star*, May 3, 1948; *Minneapolis Tribune*, July 25, 1948. The other cochair was Eleanor Gimbel of New York, widow of the heir to the Gimbels department store fortune.

28. "Mrs. Steefel Raps Hero Cult," *Minneapolis Tribune*, July 25, 1948.

29. Castledine, *Cold War Progressives*, 6; "Mrs. Steefel Raps Hero Cult." Women comprised 25 percent of the platform committee, half of all the state party directors, and almost half of the nearly three thousand delegates. When her daughter, Nina, asked, "Why can't you be like other mothers who don't think about politics,"

Steefel had answered, "Many of us, mothers or not, do think about politics, education, ways of life—which is as it should be."

30. "New Party Women Quizzed," *Minneapolis Star*, July 23, 1948. Steefel told the press, "Personally, I would never cater to a communist nor would I persecute him."

31. "Soviet Slap Rejected: Progressives Shun Anti-Russ Move," *Minneapolis Tribune*, June 26, 1948; *Minneapolis Tribune*, July 26, 1948. Benson became chairman of Wallace for President by acclamation. The state committee did not include Steefel.

32. Haynes, *Dubious Alliance*, 208–10. Orville Olson ran against Halsted and Youngdahl, and Benson ran against Humphrey and Republican incumbent Joseph Ball for US Senate, but dropped out in September. M. W. Halloran, "Benson Jilts Senate Bid," *Minneapolis Tribune*, September 12, 1948.

33. Norman Sherman, *From Nowhere to Somewhere: My Political Journey* (Minneapolis: First Avenue Editions, 2016); Pietrusza, *1948*, 151.

34. Hyman Berman, professor emeritus, University of Minnesota, interview with the author, Minneapolis, Minnesota, June 18, 2014. Berman was a colleague of Lawrence Steefel in the History Department at the university.

35. Hjalmar Bjornson, "Bring Back Party Label for State Legislators," *Minneapolis Tribune*, November 24, 1948. Bjornson is quoting Sidney E. Kienitz, editor of the *Good Thunder (Minn.) Herald*.

36. "Stafford King's Entry against Youngdahl for the Republican Nomination Challenge to Party Leadership," *Minneapolis Tribune*, September 13, 1948.

37. LeVander, *Call Me Pete*, 46–47.

38. L. D. Parlin, "King Raps Youngdahl Drive Tactics," *Minneapolis Sunday Tribune*, August 15, 1948, 10; *Minneapolis Tribune*, September 13, 1948.

39. http://www.leg.state.mn. In 1973 the law changed to allow party designation, effective in 1974 for the House and 1976 for the Senate.

40. LeVander, interview, 20–21.

41. Gene Newhall, "Mental Need Report Group Raps Critics," *Minneapolis Star*, August 5, 1948.

42. 1947 MN Stat. 3.31.

43. "House 'Bloc' Named to Research Council," *Minneapolis Star*, April 24, 1948. Lawrence Hall, from Stearns County, was affiliated with the Democrats but caucused as a conservative. His successor as speaker during the 1949 session was John Hartle, who was on the LRC's Public Welfare Subcommittee. Hartle had expressed doubts about the mental hospital reform on the basis of its costs.

44. Ibid. The new member, Ed Chilgren from Koochiching County in northern Minnesota, caucused with the liberals.

45. "Mental Probe Report Spurs Action Plans," *Minneapolis Star*, April 27, 1948. The official charge was to study "new medical and confinement practices for the treatment of mentally ill and mentally incompetent people." The subcommittee members were all conservatives and included the chair of the Senate Public Welfare Committee, Donald O. Wright from Hennepin County, and the chair of the

House Welfare Committee, Howard Ottinger; both committees had jurisdiction over the mental health legislation.

46. *Report of the Sub-committee on Public Welfare to the Legislative Research Committee*, Appendix M, August 2, 1948, Luther W. Youngdahl Papers, Minnesota Historical Society.

47. *St. Paul Dispatch*, August 16, 1948.

48. "Mental Group Backs Youngdahl: DFL Chairwoman Indorses Aim of Governor," *St. Paul Dispatch*, August 16, 1948, 1.

49. Ibid.

50. Foote, *MUC Report 1946–1949*, 7. Justin Reese later left the employ of the Mental Hygiene Society and became the secretary of the Governor's Citizens Committee on Mental Health. The exact date of his departure from the Mental Hygiene Society is not clear. He may have served in both capacities until the fall of 1948.

51. George Jacobson to Arthur Foote, August 19, 1948, Lewis Russell Collection, Minnesota Historical Society.

52. Alexander Dumas and Justin G. Reese, *An Analysis of the Mental Hospital Report of the Legislative Research Committee*, August 16, 1948, Lewis Russell Collection, Minnesota Historical Society.

53. Ibid.

54. Geri Hoffner, "State Unit's Mental Care Study Scored: Citizen Group Denies 10,500 Patients Get Proper Treatment," *Minneapolis Tribune*, August 17, 1948; Jack Weinberg, "Mental Health Unit Raps LRC Report on Institutions," *St. Paul Pioneer Press*, August 17, 1948.

55. Genevieve F. Steefel, editorial, "Unitarian Report on Mental Hospitals," *Minneapolis Star*, August 18, 1948.

56. Editorial, "Time for Co-operation," *Minneapolis Star*, August 18, 1948.

57. Ibid.

58. Engla Schey to Genevieve Steefel, August 19, 1948, Genevieve Fallon Steefel Papers, Minnesota Historical Society. The isolation wards included patients with communicable diseases such as tuberculosis. To prevent infection, attendants washed with strong lye-based soap. Engla's hands were so raw she couldn't work, necessitating a leave of absence.

59. "Thye Backs Youngdahl over Stafford King," *Minneapolis Tribune*, August 22, 1948.

60. "King Denies Charges of Liquor Backing," *Minneapolis Star*, September 13, 1948.

61. Wallace Mitchell, "Youngdahl Flays Slots," *Minneapolis Tribune*, August 19, 1948.

62. "Political Notes," *Minneapolis Star*, August 20, 1948.

63. "Mental Health Plan Wrecked, Halsted Charges," *Minneapolis Star*, September 13, 1948. These statements were made in a speech aired over the radio. In an interesting twist, Ione Hunt introduced Halsted at the program.

64. *Minneapolis Sunday Tribune*, September 13, 1948.

65. http://www.sos.state.mn.us/home/index.asp? (Truman, 57.1 percent to

Dewey's 39.89 percent); http://selectionatlas.org/results/data (Humphrey, 59.78 percent to Ball, 39.8 percent, Wallace, 2.30 percent); Dave Lieps Atlas of Presidential Elections, http://www.ourcampaigns.com/RaceData.html?RaceID=47675. Orville Olson, running for governor on the Progressive Party slate, received 1.23 percent or 14,950 votes statewide.

66. "Youngdahl Keeps Office," *Minneapolis Tribune*, November 3, 1948.

67. Geri Hoffner, "Election Held Liberal Victory," *Minneapolis Tribune*, November 4, 1948.

10. Making History

1. Esbjornson, *Christian in Politics*, 181. On the issue of mental health, Esbjornson wrote, "There is no evidence that the Protestant churches made a concerted effort, either collectively or singly, to bring about passage of this legislation."

2. "Hospitals Plan Tours," *Minneapolis Star*, November 28, 1948. All the hospitals scheduled events except Rochester State Hospital. Superintendent Petersen likely disapproved of an open house in his institution. "Youngdahl Maps Mental Hospital Aims," *Minneapolis Star*, November 28, 1948. Youngdahl himself made the declaration of a Mental Health Week in Minnesota.

3. Mental Health Statement of Governor Luther W. Youngdahl, Sunday, November 28, 1948, 3:30 p.m., radio station WCCO Minneapolis, Luther W. Youngdahl Papers, Minnesota Historical Society.

4. *Minneapolis Tribune*, December 2, 1948.

5. *St. Paul Pioneer Press*, December 3, 1948. The Minnesota Probate Judges Association "sweepingly indorsed" the governor's mental aid program on Thursday, January 13, 1949, *St. Paul Pioneer Press*, January 14, 1949.

6. *St. Paul Dispatch*, December 2, 1948.

7. The *Winona (Minn.) Republican-Herald* ran the first installment November 30, 1948, through December 4, 1948; the *St. Paul Dispatch* and *Minneapolis Star* ran the series in the same period.

8. Editorial, "The Shame of the States," *St. Cloud (Minn.) Times*, December 3, 1948.

9. "Mental Health Unit Organized," *Minneapolis Star*, December 7, 1948. The Ramsey County Citizens Committee had fifty-five members attend their organizational meeting on December 6. Municipal Judge James C. Otis was the chairman.

10. Mental Health Statement of Governor Luther W. Youngdahl, Sunday, November 28, 1948, 3:30 p.m., radio station WCCO, Minneapolis, Luther W. Youngdahl Papers, Minnesota Historical Society.

11. "Justin Reese to Speak on State Mental Health Needs," *Winona (Minn.) Republican-Herald*, January 29, 1949. As an example of the grassroots nature of the organizing effort, in this visit the meeting was sponsored by the Mental Health Committee of the Winona College Women's Club, "the club having recently agreed to cooperate with the work of the state." The Stearns County citizens mental health committee went to Todd County to organize a citizens group

there. "Mental Health Rally Slated at Sauk Centre," *St. Cloud (Minn.) Times*, February 5, 1949.

12. A document titled *How to Mobilize Your Organization Behind the Mental Health Drive*, distributed by the Hennepin County Citizens Mental Health Committee lists 2808 West River Road (the Steefel home) as the headquarters.

13. *A Report of the Committee on State Hospitals for the Mentally Ill to the 62nd Annual Meeting of the Minnesota Unitarian Conference, June 10–12, 1949*. Unity Church-Unitarian Collection, Minnesota Historical Society. Hereafter cited as *1949 Unitarian Report*.

14. Foote, *MUC Report 1946–1949*, 13–14.

15. Jack Weinberg, "Democrat Mullin Carries Youngdahl Legislative Ball," *St. Paul Pioneer Press*, April 13, 1949. Although the Democratic and Farmer-Labor Parties had merged in April 1944, the intraparty conflict in 1948 revealed the tensions that remained. Note that Mullin is identified in the press as a Democrat, not a DFLer. Though he was, according to the legislative records, a member of the DFL, he caucused with the conservatives in the legislature that had no party designation (which meant that you ran without a party and chose to caucus with either the liberals or conservatives).

16. Richard Kleeman, "Mullin Nominated for High Senate Post," *Minneapolis Tribune*, January 4, 1949. Mullin became the president pro tempore of the Senate a few weeks later. "New Post Puts Mullin in the Spotlight," *Minneapolis Tribune*, January 5, 1949.

17. Ibid. As a great advocate for the university, Mullin also had a "warm personal friendship" with Ray Amberg, director of University Hospitals, which might have been a contributing factor in his support for mental health. The university's Medical School faculty stood to benefit from the research and training support in the reform proposals.

18. Governor's Advisory Council on Mental Health, *Recommendations for Treatment and Administrative Procedures Relating to the Care of the Mentally Ill*, submitted to Governor Luther W. Youngdahl, January 10, 1949, Luther W. Youngdahl Papers, Minnesota Historical Society.

19. Foote, *MUC Report 1946–1949*, 2.

20. Ibid., 3–17. The discussion that follows has been drawn from this report.

21. *1949 Unitarian Report*, 3. Foote wrote that the omissions occurred because the council was "pushed for time," but it was more likely that some council members had little appetite for details about ancillary personnel and didn't address them.

22. Genevieve Steefel to Luther Youngdahl, February 1, 1949. Luther W. Youngdahl Papers, Minnesota Historical Society.

23. http://www.NASWfoundation.org. Kidneigh joined the university in 1946, and became director of the School of Social Work in 1949, a post he held until 1972. "Dr. Starke R. Hathaway, 80, Invented Psychological Test," http://www.nyt.com. Hathaway created the famous Minnesota Multiphasic Personality Inventory (MMPI) in 1937, to measure psychological illness. Steefel provided the names of the participants to Governor Youngdahl "if you need to call upon them

for testimony before legislative committees or for additional memoranda which may be needed."

24. Minnesota Unitarian Conference, Committee on State Hospitals for the Mentally Ill, to Governor Luther W. Youngdahl, memorandum on the availability of teaching personnel for training schools in state mental hospitals and standards for internship training in psychiatric team training units in state mental hospitals, Luther W. Youngdahl Papers, Minnesota Historical Society. The document is undated, but the governor acknowledged receipt on January 28, 1949.

25. Foote, *MUC Report 1946–1949*, 13.

26. Luther W. Youngdahl Papers, Minnesota Historical Society. For press coverage, "Unitarians Urge Mental Aid Action," *Minneapolis Star*, February 11, 1949. See also *St. Paul Dispatch*, February 28, 1949.

27. The six guarantees included (1) adequate physical and medical care, (2) humane and courteous treatment at all times, (3) a planned activity program, (4) medical commitment procedure that protects patients from stigma of arrest and jail, and looks after property rights during illness, (5) family participation in psychiatric plans, and (6) a top-notch professional training and research program in state hospitals. Commitment reform was not included in the initial reform bill because of conflict among lawyers and doctors about the best way to proceed.

28. Foote, *MUC Report 1946–1949*, 14.

29. M. W. Halloran, "Conservatives in Control in Both Houses," *Minneapolis Star*, January 4, 1949.

30. "Roy Dunn and Donald Wright," *Minneapolis Star Tribune*, July 28, 1985. LeVander, *Call Me Pete*. See also "Legislators Past and Present," Minnesota Legislative Reference Library, http://www.leg.state.mn.us.

31. "Roy Dunn and Donald Wright," quoting an unnamed colleague when Dunn retired in 1966.

32. LeVander, interview, 55.

33. "Roy Dunn and Donald Wright," July 28, 1985.

34. Elmer L. Andersen had a long career in public service, including as governor of Minnesota from 1960 to 1962. See Elmer L. Andersen, *A Man's Reach*, ed. Lori Sturdevant (Minneapolis: University of Minnesota Press, 2000). Andersen, who became a senator in February 1949 in a special election, commented that Sullivan, a "staid orderly" man," believed seniority was everything and ignored the voices of the younger members.

35. Inaugural address of Governor Luther W. Youngdahl delivered at a joint Session of the Minnesota legislature at 12:15 p.m., Thursday, January 6, 1949, reprinted in the appendix of Esbjornson, *Christian in Politics*, 329. Reprinted in full in the *Minneapolis Tribune*, January 7, 1949.

36. Esbjornson, *Christian in Politics*, 330.

37. Ibid., 331–41. Further citations by page number are included in text in parentheses. After mental health, to which he devoted the equivalent of six pages, came education, youth conservation, human relations, housing, and law enforcement, to all of which he devoted five pages.

38. Minnesota governor, budget message of Luther W. Youngdahl, delivered to a joint session of the 56th session of the Minnesota legislature, January 19, 1949.

39. The proposed budget set aside $9 million for a new institution for the "mentally deficient," a new term to replace "feeble-minded." Other building projects included housing for staff and employees at state institutions.

40. Editorial, "It Will Take Time," *St. Paul Pioneer Press,* January 20, 1949.

41. "Winona Taxpayers Association Urges Check on Spending," *Winona (Minn.) Republican-Herald,* Feb. 8, 1949.

42. *St. Paul Dispatch,* February 8, 1949.

43. *Minneapolis Tribune,* February 8, 1949; *St Paul Dispatch,* February 8, 1949. On February 8, the *Minneapolis Tribune* reported that Youngdahl had received the Unitarian Report on staff availability and training. The *St. Paul Dispatch* published an editorial the same day, praising the report's analysis.

44. "Solons Get Youngdahl's Health Plan," *St. Paul Dispatch,* February 19, 1949.

45. Jack Weinberg, "Mental Bill Sponsorship Runs into Senate Snarl," *St. Paul Pioneer Press,* February 25, 1949.

46. "Mental Aid Compromise Proposed," *Minneapolis Star,* March 2, 1949.

47. Wallace Mitchell, "Mental Care Plan Draws Sharp Query: Lawmakers Hesitate to Grant Youngdahl Request for Funds," *Minneapolis Tribune,* March 2, 1949.

48. "Pastor Hits Move to Cut Mental Fund," *St. Paul Pioneer Press,* March 4, 1949.

49. Ibid.

50. L. D. Parlin, *St. Paul Dispatch,* March 3, 1949.

51. The Senate bill as introduced was S.F. 1217 and the House bill was H.F. 1397

52. "Welfare, Finance Bills Threatened with Defeat," *Minneapolis Star,* March 25, 1949.

53. http://www.health.state.mn.us/library/dhsjournals.chapter11.pdf. The Board of Health weighed in later believing it should handle prevention aspects of mental health.

54. *St. Paul Pioneer Press,* March 18, 1949.

55. L. D. Parlin, "Public Airing Set on Mental Aid," *St. Paul Dispatch,* March 18, 1949.

56. Ibid.

57. Ibid.

58. Steefel, memo to the Legislative Committee, March 17, 1949, Genevieve Fallon Steefel Papers, Minnesota Historical Society.

59. "Funds Urged for Early Aid in Mental Cases," *Minneapolis Star,* March 22, 1949.

60. *Minneapolis Tribune,* March 22, 1949; *St. Paul Pioneer Press,* March 22, 1949.

61. "Mental Aid Bill Passed by House," *Minneapolis Star,* April 8, 1949; "Mental Health Bill Approved, Unanimous Votes in Both Chambers," *St. Paul Pioneer Press,* April 14, 1949.

62. "Youngdahl Signs Mental Health Bill," *Minneapolis Star,* April 20, 1949.

63. "Study Shows State Mental Care History," *Minneapolis Sunday Tribune,*

March 27, 1949; "Mental Aid Cut Assailed," *Minneapolis Sunday Tribune,* April 3, 1949.

64. "What Is 'Adequate?,'" *Minneapolis Tribune,* April 1, 1949.

65. Open Forum, "Youngdahl Mental Health Program Will Cut Wasteful Extravagance," *Minneapolis Tribune,* April 7, 1949.

66. "Youngdahl 'Confident' of Victory," *Minneapolis Tribune,* April 10, 1949.

67. *St. Paul Dispatch,* April 15, 1949.

68. *St. Paul Pioneer Press,* April 17, 1949.

69. "House Votes Mental Fund," *Minneapolis Tribune,* April 21, 1949.

70. M. W. Halloran, "Youngdahl Budget Cut in Tax Jam," *Minneapolis Star,* April 23, 1949.

71. Wallace Mitchell, "Taxes, Heavy Budget Worry Legislators," *Minneapolis Tribune,* April 27, 1949.

72. LeVander, interview, 56.

73. Mitchell, "Taxes, Heavy Budget."

74. "State Starts Huge Mental Aid Program," *St. Paul Pioneer Press,* April 29, 1949.

75. *1949 Unitarian Report,* 5.

76. Records of Rochester State Hospital, Olmsted County Historical Society.

11. The First Step

1. Arlene Ora Rossen Cardozo, *Journey on the Home Front* (Bloomington, Ind.: iUniverse, 2002). Cardozo was Ralph Rossen's older daughter. Her book is a memoir documenting her childhood at Hastings.

2. See Marilyn J. Chiat, "Jewish Settlers on Minnesota's Iron Range, 1889–1924," http://www.mnhum.org.

3. Jack Weinberg, "DFLers Enjoying Republican Scrap over Sale of Bonds," *Winona (Minn.) Republican-Herald,* July 25, 1949.

4. Cardozo, *Journey on the Home Front,* 1–26.

5. Weinberg, "DFLers Enjoying Republican Scrap."

6. Ibid.

7. *Winona (Minn.) Republican-Herald,* May 2, 1949. There was inconsistency in how reporters counted the mental institutions in their stories of reform. The initial debates concerned seven mental institutions. The Faribault school was overseen by the Mental Health Unit of the DPI and specifically included in the 1949 reform legislation, making eight. Subsequently, the Cambridge School for Epileptics, which also housed individuals considered mentally ill or mentally defective, and the orphanage in Owatonna that had been converted to a training school for "retarded citizens" were added to the total.

8. "State Hospital Committees Announced," *St. Paul Pioneer Press,* June 28, 1949, 8.

9. *Winona (Minn.) Republican-Herald,* June 28, 1949.

10. "Mental Hospitals to Recruit: Nation-Wide Drive to Open," *Minneapolis Tribune,* May 20, 1949.

11. "Mental Health Official Named," *St. Paul Dispatch*, October 10, 1949.

12. "Setting the Pace," editorial, *St. Paul Pioneer Press*, May 26, 1949. "National leaders in the mental health field are already praising Minnesota's program in terms that are almost ecstatic. Directors of the American Board of Psychiatry and Neurology say, for example: 'Minnesota comes nearer than any state of the nation to meeting the recommendations of the American Psychiatric Association. Minnesota has taken the lead in mental health treatment due to your extraordinary governor and the fine mental health committee in your state.'"

13. "Extensive Mental Health Program," *St. Paul Pioneer Press*, June 19, 1949.

14. "Youngdahl Reports Big Cut in Use of Hospital Restraints," *Minneapolis Tribune*, October 5, 1949.

15. Saralena Sherman, "Youngdahl Calls for New Look at Handling of Mental Cases," *Topeka Daily Capital*, October 5, 1949.

16. "Fulfilling an Obligation," editorial, *St. Paul Dispatch*, October 6, 1949.

17. Statement by Governor Luther W. Youngdahl at the burning of restraints, Anoka State Hospital, October 31, 1949, http://www.mn.gov/mnddc.

18. Mabel Huss, former nurse at Anoka State Hospital, interview by the author, Otsego, Minn., May 10, 2015.

19. Jack Weinberg, "Dr. Rossen Appointment Hailed: Xmas Gift to State Patients," *St. Paul Pioneer Press*, December 16, 1949.

20. Jack Weinberg, "New Chief Maps Mental Health Job," *St. Paul Pioneer Press*, January 30, 1950.

21. "Dr. Rossen Named State Mental Head," *St. Paul Dispatch*, December 15, 1949; "Rossen Takes Mental Health Post," *St. Paul Pioneer Press*, February 3, 1950; "Dr. Rossen Has Best Wishes of Whole State in New Job," *Winona (Minn.) Republican-Herald*, February 7, 1950.

22. "City Unit Protests Mental Fund Move," *Minneapolis Tribune*, July 17, 1949. There was grumbling early on when state Health Department officials and the Department of Public Welfare both said mental health funds for outpatient services should be administered through their departments.

23. Rossen, *One Mentally Ill Patient: The State Hospital of Tomorrow*, preface, 2 (the manuscript is not paginated throughout, but each short topic section is separately paginated). The draft cover page indicates that it contains "excerpts" from a "soon to be published work" from "Office of the Commissioner of Mental Health" Ralph Rossen, MD, State Archives, Minnesota Historical Society.

24. Mary de Young, *Encyclopedia of Asylum Therapeutics* (Jefferson, N.C.: McFarland, 2015), 440–60, http://www.mcfarland pub.com. Doctors Kenneth Tillotson and Abraham Meyerson of McLean Hospital in Boston, a private psychiatric facility, developed the concept of total push in the late 1930s. The influence can be seen in Rossen, *One Mentally Ill Patient*, in the chapter titled "And His Total Needs," 2. The positive sociological factors included a comfortable place to live, good food, clean clothing, recreation, occupation, church services, and school services.

25. Rossen, *One Mentally Ill Patient*, chapter titled "And the Superintendent," 1; chapter titled "And His Friend the Volunteer Worker," 1.

26. Ralph Rossen, M.D., Office of the Commissioner of Mental Health and Mental Hospitals, *The Minnesota Mental Health Program: A Report to Carl Jackson,* January 1951.

27. Ibid., 44–46. The outpatient clinic at Fergus Falls and Hastings State Hospitals served as public education centers. Another center was planned for Albert Lea.

28. "U to Figure in State's Mental Health Plans," *Minneapolis Star,* August 2, 1950. Top medical school faculty, including Dean Harold S. Diehl, Dr. Owen Wangensteen, and Dr. Ancel Keys, participated in medical and psychiatric services and research.

29. https://www.nih.gov. The National Mental Health Act, passed in 1946, provided its first grant in 1947, and the National Institute of Mental Health was formally established in 1949. Grants were available for research and for training. A young psychiatric social worker, Lew Linde, received support for his graduate training on condition that he work in a mental hospital for two years thereafter. He chose to work at Hastings State Hospital from 1957 to 1959, and knew Engla Schey during that time. Lew Linde, Hastings, Minnesota, interview with the author, September 1, 2015.

30. "Sandstone Prison Sought as Annex for Mental Hospital," *St. Paul Dispatch,* April 19, 1950; "Dr. Jack Reitmann Heads New Mental Hospital at Sandstone," *St. Paul Dispatch,* July 20, 1950.

31. *St. Paul Dispatch,* February 22, 1950.

32. "Mentally Ill Fed Better, Dieticians Told," *Minneapolis Tribune,* November 14, 1949; John T. Withy, "New Program Ups Hospital Morale 'Amazingly,'" *St. Paul Dispatch,* December 20, 1949; "Anoka Mental Patient Need No Longer Wait Month for New Shoes," *St. Paul Dispatch,* December 21, 1949; "Article Praises State Mental Help," *Minneapolis Star,* April 20, 1950.

33. There are no complete Schey journals for the years 1949–51. Her diaries from 1952 through 1955 are extensive.

34. *Hospitality,* Hastings State Hospital, Hastings, Minn., January 1952, Charles W. and Eva S. Jerome and Family Papers, Minnesota Historical Society.

35. Otto, *Story of Unity Church,* 85; Edgar Crane, "How to Turn a State Upside Down: Minnesota Unitarians Lead Successful Struggle to Clean Up Mental Hospitals," *Christian Register,* June 1953, 16.

36. Report from the 63rd Minnesota Unitarian Conference on June 9–11, 1950. No copies of the 1950 report could be found. Its contents were extensively covered in news stories, however. "Group Lauds, Raps Mental Health Plan," *Minneapolis Tribune,* June 11, 1950.

37. Geri Hoffner, "Bedlam Revisited: Mental Hospitals Take on New Life," a ten-part series that ran from December 24, 1950, to January 5, 1951.

38. M. W. Halloran, "Youngdahl Files for Third Term," *Minneapolis Star,* July 12, 1950.

39. Transcript, "A Report on Mental Health Progress by Governor Luther W. Youngdahl," delivered over radio station WCCO on July 31, 1950. Luther W. Youngdahl Papers, Minnesota Historical Society.

40. Ibid., 10, 15–16

41. Youngdahl chose the term *mentally retarded* to replace the more derogatory terms *feebleminded* and *imbeciles*. He also used the term *special*. The preferred terminology now is *developmentally disabled* or *intellectually disabled*. The terms current at the time of this story, while out of favor now, are used to be historically accurate.

42. Jack Weinberg, "New Mental Asylum a Must: Youngdahl Finds Care Inadequate," *St. Paul Pioneer Press,* July 23, 1950.

43. Genevieve Fallon Steefel Papers, Minnesota Historical Society; American Unitarian Association and Unitarian Service Committee Papers, Andover-Harvard Theological Library.

44. "Sanity Review Unit Set Up," *St. Paul Pioneer Press,* March 16, 1950; "Mental Stigma Change Studied," *St. Paul Pioneer Press,* April 16, 1950. For a history of Minnesota's commitment laws, see Minnesota Department of Human Services, *Legislative Report: Mentally Ill and Dangerous Commitment Stakeholders Group,* December 2013, 7–9.

45. *Report of the Governor's Advisory Council on Mental Health, State of Minnesota, for the Period January 1, 1949, to December 31, 1950,* dated January 23, 1951. On the onionskin copy in the author's possession Arthur Foote noted, "This report was written by Frank Rarig and myself," suggesting that other members of the council showed little interest.

46. See http://www.thearc.org/who-we-are/history/segal-account for a description of the founding of the chapter in Minnesota in 1950. See also ARC Greater Twin Cities archive at Minnesota Historical Society.

47. "New Mental Group Announced," *St. Paul Dispatch,* August 22, 1950; Foote remained chairman of the Unitarian Committee and served on the board of Parents and Friends of Mentally Retarded Children.

48. Esbjornson, *Christian in Politics,* 214–15. "Constitutional Reform Group Meets in State," *Winona (Minn.) Republican-Herald,* August 28, 1950.

49. L. D. Parlin, "GOP 'Secret Rule' Called Dictatorial," *St. Paul Pioneer Press,* September 1, 1950.

50. "Youngdahl Vote 50,000 Over Ten Opponents," *Winona (Minn.) Republican-Herald,* September 26, 1950.

51. Ibid. Walter G. Olson, A. B. Gilbert, and John William Haluska in total garnered 29,000 votes to Youngdahl's 309,000 votes in the Republican primary.

52. Ibid., 12. Anderson barely squeaked by Nelsen, by 7,000 votes. Pete LeVander later recalled that many Stassen Republicans thought Anderson was weak, and preferred Ancher Nelsen. Stassen had pushed C. Elmer out in 1942 in favor of Thye. Youngdahl did not take sides between Anderson and Nelsen during this campaign, despite concerns of Peter LeVander and others. See also LeVander, *Call Me Pete,* interview, 61–62.

53. "Peterson Raps at Hospital Plan Assailed," *St. Paul Dispatch,* October 25, 1950; "State Hospital Expose Called Political Move," *St. Paul Dispatch,* October 24, 1950; "A Shameful Attack," *Minneapolis Tribune,* October 26, 1950.

54. http://www.leg.state.mn.

55. Hoffner, "Bedlam Revisited," part 10, *Minneapolis Tribune,* January 3, 1951.

56. Inaugural address of Governor Luther W. Youngdahl, delivered at a joint session of the Minnesota legislature at 12:15 p.m., January 3, 1951, reprinted in Esbjornson, *Christian in Politics,* 343–52.

57. Fred Neumeier, "Legislators Praise Youngdahl Aims but Skeptics Shy at Cost," *St. Paul Pioneer Press,* January 4, 1951.

58. Wallace Mitchell, "Legislators Praise 159 Million Budget, Hint It Can Be Cut," *Minneapolis Tribune,* January 12, 1951; "How 1951 State Budget Compares with Last Request for Funds," *Minneapolis Tribune,* January 12, 1951, 11; "Take a Seat for Press Parley with Governor," *Minneapolis Tribune,* January 12, 1951.

59. Esbjornson, *Christian in Politics,* 215; "Youngdahl Tries to 'Sell' Budget Boost," *Minneapolis Tribune,* January 12, 1951, 1.

60. *Minneapolis Tribune,* January 13, 1951; "Youngdahl Tries to 'Sell' Budget Boost."

61. Appropriation Committee minutes, 1951 Session, 1259. See also Session Laws Chapter 709, S.F. 1526, sec. 1, Division of Public Institutions, State Archives, Minnesota Historical Society.

62. Appropriations Committee minutes, 1951 session, March 27, 28, and 30, 1951, State Archives, Minnesota Historical Society. "Allen Calls Appropriations Group to First Meet Today," *St. Paul Pioneer Press,* January 13, 1951.

63. Undated Executive Council document—state in connection with its discharge of a duty prescribed by chapter 3 of Extra Sessions Laws of 1951, State Archives, Minnesota Historical Society.

64. S.F. 822, sponsored by Gordon Rosenmeier of Crow Wing County. Rosenmeier caucused as a conservative, but his district included Brainerd. House sponsors were Verner Anderson of Brainerd and Fred Schwanka of Deerwood. "Brainerd Favored as Hospital Site," *Winona (Minn.) Republican-Herald,* March 15, 1951.

65. Esbjornson, *Christian in Politics,* 216.

66. Jack B. Mackay, "Gov. Youngdahl's Program Lags in State Legislature," *Winona (Minn.) Republican-Herald,* March 9, 1951.

67. "Youngdahl Answers Critics of Fair Employment Measure," *Minneapolis Star,* February 23, 1951; "Governor Asks Voters to Back Family Courts," *Minneapolis Star,* March 14, 1951.

68. For more detail on Youngdahl's other legislative proposals, see Esbjornson, *Christian in Politics,* 214–32.

69. Wallace Mitchell, "House Snubs Youngdahl on Health Budget," *Minneapolis Tribune,* April 14, 1951; "Legislator's Talk Nearly Starts Tiff," *Minneapolis Tribune,* April 11, 1951, 13; Wallace Mitchell, "Legislature Still Split on Budget," *Minneapolis Tribune,* April 13, 1951.

70. "Youngdahl Pleads for Retarded," *Minneapolis Tribune,* April 22, 1951.

71. Ibid.

72. Wallace Mitchell, "Legislators Go Home After Repassing 4 Bills," *Minneapolis Tribune,* April 25, 1951.

73. "Record of Legislature's 57th Session," *Minneapolis Tribune,* April 25, 1951, 1, 9.

74. The convalescent home issue was important in that it began to address the limited options for elderly who could not be cared for at home. Real change did not occur until later, however, when federal Hill-Burton funds became available and state and federal regulations on safety were passed in the 1950s.

75. Session Laws, chapter 709 S.F., no. 1526 (1951).

76. The final report will be discussed in chapter 12.

77. Extra Session Laws 1951, chapter 3, sec. 7. The governor chaired the executive council, which included a small group of top leaders in the state.

78. In an undated report from the executive council discharging its duty under the law, the council acknowledged that $100,000 had been appropriated in 1951 to purchase land for the Brainerd facility. After further study, however, the council resolved to put only $50 down for an option to purchase land in Brainerd, and to return the remainder of the $100,000 appropriation to the state. The facility in Brainerd did not open until 1958; State Archives, Brainerd State Hospital, Minnesota Historical Society. "Legislators Go Home," *Minneapolis Tribune*, April 25, 1951, 9.

79. "Repassing Bills," *Minneapolis Tribune*, April 24, 1951.

80. Wallace Mitchell, "Youngdahl Calls Defeat Temporary," *Minneapolis Tribune*, April 29, 1951.

81. Wallace Mitchell, "Dunn Assails Charges by Youngdahl," *Minneapolis Tribune*, May 6, 1951.

82. "Rossen Will Return to Hastings," *Winona (Minn.) Herald-Republican*, May 29, 1951.

83. "A Fourth Term for Youngdahl," *St. Cloud Daily Times*, reprinted in the *Winona (Minn.) Republican-Herald*, May 25, 1951.

12. Lest We Forget

1. Norman Sherman, *From Nowhere to Somewhere: My Political Journey* (Minneapolis: First Avenue Editions, 2015).

2. Esbjornson, *Christian in Politics*, 231.

3. *Washington Times-Herald*, July 6, 1951.

4. Transcript of interview of C. Elmer Anderson by Lucile Kane, Russell Fridley, and Jim Bormann, Brainerd, Minnesota, April 28, 1964, C. Elmer Anderson Gubernatorial and Mayoral Papers, Minnesota Historical Society. Hereafter, Anderson interview.

5. M. W. Halloran, "Appointment of Youngdahl Applauded," *Minneapolis Star*, July 19, 1951.

6. Editorial, *Willmar Journal*, July 20, 1951.

7. LeVander, *Call Me Pete*, interview, 62.

8. Ibid.

9. "New Governor Promises Law Enforcement," *Winona (Minn.) Republican-Herald*, July 7, 1951.

10. "Youngdahl Appointed U.S. Federal Judge," *Winona (Minn.) Republican-Herald*, July 5, 1951.

11. "Dr. Rossen Wants to Leave State Mental Post," *Winona (Minn.) Republican-Herald,* August 23, 1951.

12. "R. K. Youngdahl Elected Head of New Health Group," *Minneapolis Star,* October 5, 1951; newsletter, Citizens Mental Health Committee of Minnesota, November 1951, Genevieve Fallon Steefel Papers, Minnesota Historical Society.

13. Albert Q. Maisel, "Scandal Results in Real Reforms: Hospital and Inmates Back from Bedlam," *Life,* November 12, 1951, 142–55.

14. "In Honor of C. Elmer Anderson," http://www.brainerddispatch.com/content /honor-c-elmer, posted September 29, 2001, quoting Congressman Rick Nolan on the dedication of a statue in Brainerd.

15. Anderson interview, 19–20.

16. Transcript, inaugural address of Governor C. Elmer Anderson, WCCO and network of thirty-one Minnesota radio stations, Thursday, September 27, 1951, 4–5, C. Elmer Anderson Gubernatorial and Mayoral Papers, Minnesota Historical Society.

17. *Winona (Minn.) Republican-Herald,* March 10, 1952.

18. Ibid.

19. Talk on mental health, March 15, 1952, C. Elmer Anderson Gubernatorial and Mayoral Papers, Minnesota Historical Society.

20. Jarle Lierfallom, daily journal, 1953–54, 367, Jarle Lierfallom Papers, Minnesota Historical Society. Lierfallom kept a meticulous daily log (dictated and typed) of his meetings and impressions for over twenty years; the journals are consecutively numbered by years. Page numbers from the journal for 1953–54 are hereafter given parenthetically in text.

21. "State Mental Health Director Resigns," *Winona (Minn.) Republican-Herald,* May 5, 1952.

22. "Fire Hazards to State's Mental Patients Cited," *Minneapolis Star,* August 1, 1952.

23. "Rev. Foote Says Mental Patients Diet Inadequate," *St. Cloud (Minn.) Times,* August 5, 1952.

24. "Citizens Group Disputes Claim in Hospital Diet," *Minneapolis Star,* August 8, 1952.

25. "Freeman Urges, Achieve Aims of Youngdahl's Hospital Plan," *Minneapolis Tribune,* August 13, 1952.

26. Louis C. Dorweiler had served in the House from 1919 to 1922 and again in 1939–42. He held a number of positions in the State Department of Administration, and as assistant director of the Minnesota Institute on Government Research.

27. LeVander, interview, 61. Ike won by a landslide in November. Anderson defeated Staff King in September, and then defeated Freeman in the general election, 55 percent to 44 percent. http://www.editions.lib.umn.edu/smartpolitics.

28. *Report of the Legislative Research Committee on the State Mental Institutions,* January 21, 1953.

29. Ibid.

30. Geri Hoffner, "Mental Health Progress Cited by Lierfallom," *Minneapolis Tribune,* December 6, 1952.

31. Ibid.

32. Inaugural address of Governor C. Elmer Anderson, January 7, 1953, 3, 4, C. Elmer Anderson Gubernatorial and Mayoral Papers, Minnesota Historical Society.

33. Budget message of Governor C. Elmer Anderson, delivered to a joint session of the Minnesota legislature on Wednesday, January 14, 1953, State Archives, Minnesota Historical Society.

34. Critical articles appeared in the *Minneapolis Star* and the *Minneapolis Tribune* during the week of January 12, 1953, when the Appropriations Committee was reviewing the budget requests.

35. There was extensive coverage of the Stillwater situation, e.g., "Stillwater Drug Probe Leads to Weapons," *Winona (Minn.) Republican-Herald,* December 12, 1952; "Lierfallom Takes Over at State Prison," *Winona (Minn.) Republican-Herald,* December 17, 1952.

36. "Deficit Seen, Cut Budget Drive Grows," *Minneapolis Tribune,* April 15, 1953. On April 16, 1953, Anderson accused the House of "inhumanity" and "ill-advised economy," *Minneapolis Tribune,* April 16, 1953; "Senate Hikes House Mental Health Grants," *Minneapolis Tribune,* April 16, 1953.

37. In conference, the Senate conceded $1.6 million and the House upped its recommendations by $500,000. "Governor Wins a Few Rounds in Legislature," *Minneapolis Tribune,* April 19, 1953, 1; "More than 100 new positions added," *Minneapolis Tribune,* April 19, 1953, 5; "Totals of Money Bills," *Minneapolis Tribune,* April 22, 1953, 7.

38. "Here's a Summary of Bills in Legislature," *Minneapolis Tribune,* April 22, 1953.

39. "Governor Wins a Few Rounds in Legislature," *Minneapolis Tribune,* April 19, 1953.

40. Ibid.

41. "Dr. Hastings to Head Medical Policy Group," *Winona (Minn.) Republican-Herald,* May 18, 1954.

42. "Dr. Dale Cameron Accepts Post as Medical Director," *Winona (Minn.) Republican-Herald,* March 27, 1954.

43. Judge Luther W. Youngdahl, United States District Court for the District of Columbia, speech at Hastings State Hospital, Hastings, Minnesota, April 23, 1954. Luther W. Youngdahl Papers, Minnesota Historical Society. Subsequent quotations in this chapter from this speech are from this source.

44. Youngdahl was referring to the reform legislation passed in 1949.

Epilogue

1. Minnesota Mental Health Survey, December 1956, 10, State Archives, Department of Public Welfare, Minnesota Historical Society.

2. http://www.thearc.org; www.arcgreatertwincities.org.

3. "New Mental Group Announced," *St. Paul Dispatch,* August 22, 1950.

Mental Health Association of Minnesota, *The History of MHAM: Celebrating 70 Years of Mental Health Advocacy and Education in Minnesota*, https://www.mentalhealthmn.org.

4. Ralph Rossen, *One Mentally Ill Patient: The State Hospital of Tomorrow*, State Archives, Division of Public Institutions, Minnesota Historical Society.

5. In Minnesota the mental hospital census peaked at 11,300 in 1954, dropping to 9,247 in the early 1960s. Department of Public Welfare, *Minnesota's Mental Health Program in Review, 1949–1961*, 14, Minnesota Department of Public Welfare Library, St. Paul. Most of Minnesota's mental hospitals were closed by 1978; a few converted to smaller regional treatment centers focusing on substance abuse. St. Peter is now a security hospital for the dangerous and criminally insane.

6. The Minnesota's Governor's Council on Developmental Disabilities has posted to its website numerous historical documents, including many relating to the lengthy Welsch litigation. See https://mn.gov/mnddc/past/pdf-index-html.

7. The Intermediate Care Facilities for Individuals with Intellectual Disabilities certification, an optional benefit in Medicaid (which is called Medical Assistance, or MA, in Minnesota), was added in 1971; and the Community Access for Disability Inclusion waiver provides funding for home- and community-based services for children and adults with disabilities.

8. For the history of the evolution of mental health benefits in public and private programs, see Richard G. Frank, Howard H. Goldman, and Michael Hogan, "Medicaid and Mental Health," *Health Affairs* 22, no. 1 (2003): 101–13; Center for Medicare Advocacy, "Medicare and Mental Health," http://www.medicareadvocacy.org; Colleen L. Barry, Haiden A. Huskamp, and Howard H. Goldman, "A Political History of Federal Mental Health and Addiction Insurance Parity," *Milbank Quarterly* 88, no. 3 (2010): 404–33; United States Department of Labor, Employee Benefits Security Administration fact sheet, "The Mental Health Parity and Addiction Equity Act of 2008." See Centers for Medicare and Medical Services, https://www.cms.gov/CCIIO/Programs-and-Initiatives/Other-Insurance-Protections/mhpaea_factsheet.html.

9. Virgil Dickson, "Medicaid Plans Struggle to Provide Mental Health Services," *Modern Healthcare*, July 4, 2015.

10. Minnesota Mental Health Action Group, *Road Map for Mental Health System Reform in Minnesota*, June 2005. Hereafter MMHAG, *Road Map*.

11. Sue Abderholden, interviewed on *Almanac*, Minnesota Public Radio, June 9, 2016.

12. MMHAG, *Road Map*, 5.

13. https://www.namihelps.org/publications.html.

14. NAMI, *Grading the States 2009: A Report on America's Health Care System for Adults with Serious Mental Illness*, 103–4, https://www.nami.org/grades.

15. Andy Steiner, "Mental Health Legislative Update: 2015 Achievements Acknowledged, 2016 Ambitions Outlined," MinnPost, January 6, 2016, https://www.minnpost.com/mental-health-addiction/2016/01/mental-health-legislative-update-2015-achievements-acknowledged-2016.

16. NAMI, *State Mental Health Legislation 2015: Trends, Themes, and Effective Practices,* https://www.nami.org/statereport.

17. Chris Serres, "Minn. Mental Health System Gets $48 Million in New Funding, Defying National Trend," May 20, 2016, http://www.startribune.com/chris-serres/10645926.

18. Governor Mark Dayton, Executive Order 16–02, April 27, 2006, https://mn.gov/dhs.assets.

19. *Governor's Task Force on Mental Health—Final Report,* November 15, 2016, https://mn.gov/dhs/mental-health-tf/report.

20. "In Jail, in Limbo, Untreated: Minnesota's Unraveling Mental Health System," *Minneapolis Star Tribune,* September 8, 2013; "Two More Patients Are Neglected at Security Hospital," *Minneapolis Star Tribune,* August 29, 2013.

21. Chris Serres, "Minnesota's Second-Largest Psychiatric Hospital Reaches Deal to Keep Federal Funding, Improve Care," *Minneapolis Star Tribune,* April 26, 2016, http://www.startribune.com/chris-serres/10645926.

22. Andy Mannix, "Bottleneck Traps Patients, Costs State Millions," *Minneapolis Star Tribune,* October 15, 2017.

23. Email, Geri Joseph to the author, February 2, 2017.

INDEX

Susan Bartlett Foote is a writer, historian, lawyer, and professor emerita in the Division of Health Policy and Management at the University of Minnesota. She is the author of *Managing the Medical Arms Race: Innovation and Public Policy in the Medical Device Industry* as well as articles on health and technology policy. She has served as Legislative Counsel on Health in the United States Senate and as an advisor to government agencies and health organizations. She lives in St. Paul, Minnesota.